VICTORIAN POETS AND
THE POLITICS OF CULTURE

VICTORIAN LITERATURE AND CULTURE SERIES

Karen Chase, Jerome J. McGann, *and* Herbert Tucker, *Editors*

VICTORIAN POETS AND THE POLITICS OF CULTURE

Discourse and Ideology

Antony H. Harrison

UNIVERSITY PRESS OF VIRGINIA

Charlottesville and London

The University Press of Virginia
© 1998 by the Rector and Visitors
of the University of Virginia
All rights reserved
Printed in the United States of America

First published 1998

∞ The paper used in this publication meets the
minimum requirements of the American National
Standard for Information Sciences—Permanence of
Paper for Printed Library Materials, ANSI
Z39.48-1984.

Library of Congress Cataloging-in-Publication Data

Harrison, Antony H.
  Victorian poets and the politics of culture : discourse and ideology / Antony H.
Harrison.
      p.   cm. — (Victorian literature and culture series)
    Includes bibliographical references (p.   ) and index.
    ISBN 0-8139-1818-9 (alk. paper)
    1. English poetry—19th century—History and critisim.   2. Politics and
literature—Great Britain—History—19th century.   3. Culture—Political aspects—
Great Britain—History—19th century.   4. Tennyson, Alfred Tennyson, Baron,
1809–1892—Political and social views.   5. Browning, Elizabeth Barrett, 1806–
1861—Political and social views.   6. Arnold, Matthew, 1822–1888—Political and
social views.   7. Rossetti, Christina Georgina, 1830–1894—Political and social
views.   8. Great Britain—History—Victoria, 1837–1901.   9. Medievalism—
England—History—19th century.   10. Discourse analysis, Literary.   I. Title.
II. Series.
    PR595.H5H37   1998
    821'.809358—dc21
                                                                                  98-14577
                                                                                    CIP

For Louise, Julia, and Bucky
  who make my garden teem with spices

Contents

Acknowledgments   ix

Introduction:
Discourse, Ideology, Poetry   1

I.   Medievalist Discourse and the Ideologies
of Victorian Poetry   17

II.   Merlin and Tennyson: Poetry of Power and Victorian
Self-Fashioning   44

III.   Elizabeth Barrett in 1838: "Weakness like omnipotence"   71

IV.   Matthew Arnold's Gipsies: Ideology and the Discourse
of the Other   102

V.   Christina Rossetti: Renunciation as Intervention   125

Afterword   165

Notes   169

Bibliography   175

Index   183

Acknowledgments

I AM GRATEFUL TO a number of colleagues who read and commented on earlier versions of the manuscript of this book. Herbert Tucker endured not one but two drafts of the full text, service well beyond the call of anything but friendship. Others have read portions of the book in various versions, and all of them deserve my sincere thanks: Eyal Amiran, Barbara Baines, Bob Lane, Leila May, Jerome J. McGann, Thaïs Morgan, David Riede, Jon Thompson, and Deborah Wyrick. Suggestions for improvement from two anonymous readers for the University Press of Virginia have also been helpful.

Material from chapters 3, 4, and 5 has been previously published as "Medievalist Discourse and the Ideologies of Victorian Poetry," in *Studies in Medievalism*, ed. Leslie Workman, vol. 4 (London: Boydell & Brewer, 1992), 219–34; "Matthew Arnold's Gipsies: Intertextuality and Historicism," *Victorian Poetry* 29 (1991): 365–83; "Christina Rossetti among the Romantics: Influence and Ideology," in *Romantic/Victorian: Influence and Resistance in Nineteenth-Century Poetry*, ed. Kim Blank and Margot K. Louis (London: Macmillan, 1993), 131–49; and "Christina Rossetti and the Sage Discourse of Feminist High Anglicanism," in *Victorian Sages and Cultural Discourse: Renegotiating Gender and Power*, ed. Thaïs E. Morgan (New Brunswick: Rutgers Univ. Press, 1990), 87–104.

VICTORIAN POETS AND
THE POLITICS OF CULTURE

Introduction:
Discourse, Ideology, Poetry

THIS STUDY IS the second stage of a project to explore poetry as a significant force in the construction of English culture from 1837 to about 1880. The first stage culminated with the publication of *Victorian Poets and Romantic Poems: Intertextuality and Ideology* (1990). That book examined the ways in which self-consciously intertextual uses of precursors by Victorian poets served to expose systems of sociopolitical—as well as moral and aesthetic—values embedded in their work and deployed to influence readers in specific ways. The present volume moves away from intertextual issues as such to discuss, more broadly, how the work of particular Victorian poets operated as a mode of cultural intervention. The chapters are heuristic in design, like those of the earlier volume; my goal here is to explore the constitution of cultural power as it is generated within and appropriated from the structures of meaning at work in society and, more specifically, to examine the mechanisms operating within poetic texts as they engage their culture's discursive practices and generate ideological effects.

This book thus participates in the recent movement to critique the formalist analysis of artworks, specifically poetic texts, as exclusively aesthetic objects. I consider poems as social and cultural artifacts of historical importance in part because they display subtle if not covert attempts to seize describable categories of cultural power by transmitting ideology. They do so under the guise of eliciting pleasure. "A thing of Beauty" may be a "joy forever," but literary texts also act as material forces in the world and mold readers' values, expectations, and behavior in reality; they thus advance not only the fame of their authors but also their power in society. Such a broad formulation of the political operations of artistic works hardly does justice to the subtlety of their activities in the arena of cultural conflict. The particular analyses of such phenomena in the chapters that follow refine upon this formulation, focusing on a specialized set of artistic texts generated by middle-class writers during a historical period when the hegemony of the middle classes was clearly established but nonetheless threatened, both from below and from above.

One assumption underlying much of my analysis has been usefully explained by Terry Eagleton: "The construction of the modern notion of the aesthetic artefact is . . . inseparable from the construction of the dominant ideological forms of modern class-society, and indeed from a whole new form of human subjectivity appropriate to that social order" (*Aesthetic*, 3). Artworks and, more specifically, poetic texts as highly self-conscious, socially produced art forms to varying extents thus collaborate in "the dominant ideological forms of modern class-society," intervening in the discourses that constitute them and appropriating the power they wield. Works of art nonetheless sometimes also powerfully challenge those dominant ideological forms and present themselves as alternatives to them. They thus operate as "eminently contradictory" phenomena (3). For Eagleton, art appears most often to reflect what Raymond Williams describes as "emergent" values and structures of feeling in the social world, and it is powerful precisely because of its "contradictory" constitution. Eagleton observes that "power is at its best" when it is "neither centralizing nor hegemonic [but rather] rescued at once from despotism and interiority and applauded as self-causing and self-sustaining," that is, when it is "non-instrumental, non-teleological, autonomous and self-referential" (389). In this view power "at its best" inheres in works of art and literature that grounds itself "in the living sensibilities of its subjects" (27). But those subjects are always in part constructed by the frameworks of value—both reflected in and perpetually reconstituted by artistic discourse—that dominate the societies in which they live. The qualities and demonstrable operations of the power literary works have over people, nonetheless, easily elude discussion. This book suggests that such matters can be best understood when poetic texts are positioned within the particular discursive and ideological contexts of their production and reception.

A second and equally important theoretical position at work throughout this study has been recently developed in an important article by Trevor Purvis and Alan Hunt. These two sociologists argue that the positive concept of ideology derived from the Marxist tradition as it has evolved through the work of Althusser, Gramsci, and Raymond Williams is compatible with discourse theory as it emerges from the work of Saussure and Foucault. This argument suggests both that discursive activity can have clear ideological effects and that "culture" is largely constituted by discursive practices and the discursive formations these practices generate (whether legal, political, amatory, religious, or feminist, for example). Whereas thinkers in the Marxist tradition attempt to understand the function of *ideology* in observing social relations of domination and subordination, *discourse* has been developed as a term through which we can "grasp the way in which language and other forms of social semiotics not merely convey social experience, but play some major part in constituting social subjects (the subjectivities and their associated identities), their relations, and the field in which they exist" (Purvis and Hunt, 474). Discourse not only provides a medium for thought and communication but can also thus be viewed as the basis for action in the social world. As discourse analysts building on the work of Bahktin and V. N. Volosinov have persuasively argued in recent years, language and ideology are mutually constitutive. That is, ideology is inseparable from the signs in which it is represented, and these signs always operate within concrete forms of social intercourse. The belief that "the sign and its social situation are inextricably fused together," determining "from within the form and structure of an utterance," thus becomes the basis of "a materialist theory of ideology" that "grants the materiality of the word, and the discursive contexts in which it is caught up, their proper due" (Eagleton, *Ideology*, 195). As I argue in the following chapters, the cultural power of literary works normally depends precisely upon the operations of the discourses in which they participate.

As Purvis and Hunt explain, discourses operate as economies "with their own intrinsic technology, tactics, [and] effects of power, which in turn they transmit" (488). This is to say, ultimately, that power is inherent in discourse and that it accrues to those who successfully shape and disseminate discourse. Because a given discourse has relatively permeable borders between itself and other discourses, it can appropriate and be appropriated; it is therefore necessarily the site of perennial struggle and contestation. Yet changes in many social discourses, especially those associated with dominant belief systems, professions, and institutions, are slow to appear. Such discourses seem stable even though they are always already being transformed through the very processes of social activity that constitute them. Any attempt at historical analysis of discourse must proceed with full awareness of this dynamic and yet begin its project by entering a moment in the past at which, according to the record in texts, discourses appear fixed and continue to do so for some time. I therefore find it useful to adapt and expand Foucault's notion of *discursive formations* to suggest unified groups of "more or less stable aggregated discourses" (Purvis and Hunt, 486) that are visibly active in a culture during a given period of time and that contribute to mutually reinforcing *ideological effects.*

Ideology is admittedly a vexed term with a long and difficult history. Throughout this study I employ it not in the negative or critical sense concerned with ways in which subordinate social groups unwittingly work to reproduce existing social relations through the assimilation of illusions or false consciousness. Instead, I accept the sociological conception of ideologies as multiple. According to this view, "competing ideologies are . . . linked to some conception of social position and objective interests," and "ideology is 'real,' or material, rather than fictional or delusory." It is thus "unavoidable in that it simply describes the framework of meanings and values within which people exist and conduct their social lives" (Purvis and Hunt, 478–79). James Kavanaugh has usefully described ideology "as a system of representations, perceptions, and images that . . . encourages men and women to 'see' their specific place in a historically peculiar social formation as inevitable, natural, a necessary function of the 'real' itself." I accept his conclusion that "ideological analysis in literary or cultural study" must concern itself with "the institutional and/or textual apparatuses that work on the reader's or spectator's imaginary conceptions of self and social order in order to call or *solicit* . . . him/her into a specific form of social 'reality' and social subjectivity" (Kavanaugh, 311).

Since at any historical moment ideologies, like discourses, are multiple and heterogeneous, they conflict and compete with one another and are dynamic in the arena of social (including political) activity. Identifiably separate but usually complementary frameworks of value and meaning thus often dominate various areas of an individual's activity in the world. I therefore often speak of discrete and internally consistent *aesthetic, domestic, religious,* or *patriarchal* ideologies, for instance, that interact, overlap, and compete with one another both within the social subject and within the field of his or her activities. Social and political events in Victorian England, as today, were in part determined by the collusions and collisions of such ideologies, some of which were dominant and widely accepted, indeed virtually monolithic and inescapable, whereas others were largely subcultural or countercultural. Although, as Karl Mannheim has insisted, "a society is possible in the last analysis because the individuals in it carry around in their heads some sort of picture of that society" (xxiii), that picture is neither static nor consensual. Raymond Williams and many commentators after him have shown that although we may speak of a *dominant* ideology in a particular sphere of human social activity, *residual* and *emergent* elements are always at work within it. Similarly, the social subject who makes visible through speech, writings, or behavior the activities of ideology is, in a sense, always under construction.

Althusser's crucial concept of *interpellation* allows us to understand how discourse exists as the medium through which ideology is both internalized and transmitted; taking a lead from the work of Stuart Hall, Purvis and Hunt explain that "it is through discourse that individuals are interpellated as subjects; ideology represents those specific forms of discourse whose contents are inadequate to articulate the interests of those social categories (classes, groups, etc.) who are constituted through those discourses." Accordingly, discursive practices can have ideological effects because they perpetually constitute and reposition the subjects engaged in them. They also therefore "exist as potential arenas of contestation," in part because it is always possible to open up "'new discursive spaces' that aim to unite disparate and dispersed discursive elements" cohesively (Purvis and Hunt, 483–84). This can be accomplished in radical fashion, as in Gramsci's project of counterhegemony, or in more subtle, revisionist ways so as to redirect the ideological effects of a given discursive formation. In the first chapter I consider both orders of attempt: in Swinburne's manipulations of mid-Victorian medievalist discourse to challenge its "traditional" ideological effects and in Dante Rossetti's appropriations of medievalist discourse for ostensibly apolitical, aestheticist purposes. In other chapters I describe the ideological effects of poetic interventions in a variety of popular Victorian discourses or "sets of ready-made and preconstituted 'experiencings' displayed and arranged through language" (Purvis and Hunt, 485). This is to say that certain familiar linguistic sign sets evoke specific networks of intellectual and emotional responses from individuals when used in particular patterns and particular social contexts at a given historical moment within a given culture. Such responses often have significance for the operations of ideology within that culture. What Gramsci claimed of philosophy is equally true of poetic activity (that poetry is often a source or reflection of philosophy reminds us how easily these disciplinary borders break down): such activity may be conceived as "a cultural battle to transform the popular 'mentality' and to diffuse . . . innovations that will demonstrate themselves to be 'historically true' to the extent that they become concretely—i.e., historically and socially— universal" (348).

It has been nearly forty years since Raymond Williams, in *Culture and Society*, brought to our attention the significant fact that a group of related terms, many of them integral to an inquiry like the present one, either came into existence or took on altered meanings early in the nineteenth century with the emergence of *Industrialism* (first so called in the 1830s), a word describing the collective institutions and activities of manufacturing and production (13). Among the terms listed by Williams that then acquired their current meanings are not only *ideology, capitalism, class* (in the sense of social class), and *art* but also *culture*. These terms have been much discussed in recent years by sociologists, anthropologists, historians, and literary theorists, so that the history of their use and meanings has become enormously complex, although most readers (correctly) assume a fundamental understanding of them. *Ideology* and *culture* are certainly two of the most multivalent among them, and some additional elaboration of the meaning I ascribe to the latter term is essential to understanding my argument in this book.

The constellation of interacting discursive formations (competitive or complementary) within a society constitutes *culture* as I employ the term. The broad and various areas of human activity covered by *culture* and "the vertiginous indeterminacy to which one is . . . almost inescapably led by the . . . culture concept" (Herbert, 11) might at first glance appear to limit the usefulness of the term, but in fact just the opposite is the case. Recent studies such as John Brenkman's *Culture and Domination*,

Giles Gunn's *The Culture of Criticism and the Criticism of Culture*, Steven Connor's *Theory and Cultural Value*, and Christopher Herbert's *Culture and Anomie* have made this point forcefully. But such works could not have emerged on the current critical scene without Raymond Williams's initial explorations of the complex operations of art, and specifically of literature, within culture. The term itself enables particularized discussion of the relations among discursive formations that on the surface appear as discrete as religion, sexuality, politics, industry, law, and art. Herbert makes the crucial point that

> *what gives [the term* culture*] significance . . . is the presumption that [the] array of disparate-seeming elements of social life composes a significant whole, each factor of which is in some sense a corollary of, consubstantial with, implied by, immanent in, all the others. Culture as such is not, therefore, a society's beliefs, customs, moral values, and so forth, added together: it is the wholeness that their coexistence somehow creates or makes manifest. . . . For theorists of all persuasions, a cultural formation takes its meaning from its involvement in what Darwin, speaking not of culture but of nature, called an "inextricable web of affinities" . . . and it is this presumption that renders [its] various elements systematically* readable. (5)

With this project I attempt to read through "various elements" in Victorian poems in order to discuss the cultural work they accomplish. Such work involves, for instance, the deployment of particular discursive formations (such as those surrounding love or medievalism) to particular ends or the appropriation and transvaluation of culturally prominent mythologies, such as the exaltation of motherhood as a domestic ideal, the Romantic idealization of transcendent art, or the idealization of the gipsy as a culturally alien, exotic Other. It may employ a retreat into the sphere of rigid Christian values, from which protected vantage point a wholesale attack on other Victorian cultural values can be launched (Christina Rossetti's tactic); or it may, through a variety of intertextual maneuvers, challenge, revise, and correct precursory literary texts. Such cultural work may even attempt a usurpation of power traditionally invested in the monarchy (work initiated in poems from 1837 by both Elizabeth Barrett and Alfred Tennyson, as I shall show). Through analysis that brings such textual activities and their ideological consequences to light, we come to see, at an unusually high level of specificity, how literary works "are structures for the accumulation, transformation, representation, and communication of social energies and practices" (Greenblatt, "Culture," 230).

We learn that successful works of literature are powerful as soon as we begin to read. But their effects exceed the emotional and intellectual responses that we are conscious they generate. The almost unfathomably complex sign systems we call works of art speak to us, as well, at myriad visceral and subconscious levels, and the composite responses they elicit operate subjectively to reconstruct us. As Stephen Greenblatt has observed, "Something happens to objects, beliefs, and practices when they are represented, reimagined, and performed in literary texts, something often unpredictable and disturbing. That 'something' is the sign both of the power of art and of the embeddedness of culture in the contingencies of history" ("Culture," 230−31).

A particular argument implicit in my analyses of the ways poems intervene in cultural discourses is that the highly developed formulaic and conventional aspects of poetry as a linguistic medium—its specialized verse forms, traditions of figuration, metrical structures, and so on, which carry with them certain experiential expectations—establish it as a remarkably useful example for understanding the ideological effects of discourse generally. This view emerges, for instance, in my discussion of the subversive ideological effects accomplished by William Morris's appropriation of the dramatic monologue form (chapter 1) and in my commentary on Tennyson's use (in *Idylls of the King*) of what Benjamin described as *indeterminate allegory* in compelling readers to recognize that poets possess prophetic authority, a unique access to mysterious truths, and consequently genuine power in the world (chapter 2).

As I have suggested, by eliciting particular, heightened sensations of pleasure poetic texts, as social "organisms" that "mutate" according to the circumstances of their production and reception, intervene in discourse and accrue power. The pleasurable emotional and intellectual experiences they generate both within and by means of certain formal and conventional constraints uniquely catalyze their ideological effects. Although it is possible for this process to occur soon after a work's initial publication (the case, for instance, with Tennyson's *Idylls* or Dante

Rossetti's *Poems*, 1870), the success of a poetic text in this regard most often grows over time as its audience enlarges and as it reconstitutes the discourse in which it initially intervened. Frequently, of course, the influence of an immediately popular poem will die out quickly (as happened, for instance, with Alexander Smith's *A Life-Drama*), leaving it ideologically ineffectual despite its initial cultural significance.

The power generated and accrued by poets and their poems can be variously measured in historical terms: sales, income, readership, reviews, and testimonials. Such measures of contemporary reception and influence are helpful, yet they only partially explain how a literary text operates as cultural intervention. As Eagleton has argued, power is "individually authenticated" when there is "constructed within the subject a new form of inwardness" whereby power shifts its location "from centralized institutions to the silent, invisible depths of the subject itself" (*Aesthetic*, 27). Effective literary works change not only what a reader feels but the basis for feelings; not only what a reader thinks but the process of thinking; not only what a reader believes but the practical effects of those beliefs. Such works also achieve durability and longevity. The cultural power of writers, whether canonized or recuperated, may discover itself in the reconstitution of subjectivities generation after generation.

Any argument that poets, as compared with writers of prose, shared significantly in such power in postindustrial England is likely to be received with some skepticism. Utilitarian attacks upon the value of poetry were commonplace in the early Victorian period, and the market for new poetic texts was, by all accounts, minuscule (Armstrong, *Scrutinies*, 15–16; Altick, 134–35). June Steffensen Hagen has usefully summarized the circumstances that faced new poets just before Victoria came to the throne: "Taking everything into consideration, the prognosis for poetry in 1830 was dismal indeed. The audience was restless and increasing the pace towards fiction; the nature of poetry itself—and its worthiness as a serious pursuit in an enlightened age—was under attack both by secular Utilitarians and religious evangelicals; once-prestigious publishing firms were going bankrupt; and the idea of a poet's being able to secure a livelihood from poetry alone was becoming more remote" (4). Not surprisingly, the market for poetry in early Victorian England was slow to expand. Yet expand it did, as the fortune Tennyson made from his works demonstrates: in August 1864, for example, *Enoch Arden* sold seventeen

thousand copies on the day of publication, and within five months the
entire first edition of sixty thousand copies was exhausted (Hagen, 112).
And five years later, when the new books of *Idylls of the King* appeared, prepublication orders for forty thousand copies were in hand (Altick, 387).

Yet even such figures for best-selling Victorian poems cannot compete with sales of the novel, both in serialized and volume format. The
first number of Dickens's *Nicholas Nickleby* (1838–39) sold fifty thousand
copies, a figure that was sustained throughout the issue; and *Uncle Tom's
Cabin* sold a stunning one and one-half million copies during its first year
in print (Altick, 383–84). But numbers only partially reflect the significance of poetry as a form of public discourse with unique modes of circulation in Victorian England. Especially after the work of Byron, Wordsworth, and Shelley had become widely known, encounters with poetic
texts were unusually complex psychological and emotional events for
nineteenth-century readers. This was true not only because of the anticipated formal difficulties of such texts but also because of widespread expectations that poetic words on a page *meant* a good deal more than other
writing: they embodied the voice of a being possessed of extraordinary
epistemological capacities. In "The Poet" (1830), for instance, Tennyson
anatomizes an artist who

> . . . saw thro' life and death, thro' good and ill,
> He saw thro' his own soul.
> The marvel of the everlasting will,
>   An open scroll,
> Before him lay; with echoing feet he threaded
>   The secretest walks of fame:
> The viewless arrows of his thoughts were headed
>   And winged with flame.

Claims of this sort were continually made by poets as well as by the critics
who reviewed them during the nineteenth century. A commentator in
the *Scottish Review*, for example, quotes the spasmodic poet Philip James
Bailey's view of the poetic vocation only to agree with it as a commonplace: "He says, 'Poets henceforth are the world's teachers.' But so they
have ever been. It is no new office this" (Armstrong, *Scrutinies*, 11).
Readers of Victorian poetry stood ready to be instructed by public figures
whom they (like Thomas Carlyle) very often accepted as bards and vi-

sionaries, beings of a different order from that to which they belonged. That the writings of such individuals had an influence more intense and enduring than that of novelists is made clear throughout the period not only in reviews and in an enormous number of testimonials[1] but also in the fact that the cultural progress of transcendent poetic ideals often demonstrates their ability to overtake realities they challenge.

The power of Victorian poetry by midcentury was enhanced by the institutionalization of particular channels through which it circulated. Poetry was "consumed" in more varied forms than was other literature. Not only was it published in volumes but it appeared in periodicals, it was material for public recitation, it was set to music, it was copied into commonplace books, it was memorized and rehearsed at parties and family gatherings, it was anthologized and taught in the schools. In short, a typical Victorian might very well be repeatedly exposed to the same poem in various settings, both solitary and social, and in each of those settings different aesthetic, moral, intellectual, or spiritual effects of the work might be privileged. The same poem cited authoritatively by a politician, recorded lovingly in a diary, quoted by a priest at a funeral, memorized as a touchstone of love or belief, declaimed at a party, or read to family and servants on a domestic evening may opportunely intervene in a variety of discursive formations that dominate the culture in which it circulates.

Two very different initial illustrations, one public, one private, begin to suggest the ideological efficacy of poetry as a literary medium in Victorian England. The first derives from Alexander Macmillan's prepublication reading of Christina Rossetti's poem *Goblin Market* in October 1861, the second from a well-known section of John Stuart Mill's *Autobiography* describing, from the high Victorian perspective of 1873, events that took place in 1826–27.

By the fall of 1861 Alexander Macmillan, whose Cambridge publishing house was not yet a decade old, had decided to risk bringing out a volume of poetry by Christina Rossetti, a writer nearly unknown except for three works published that year in *Macmillan's Magazine* and a handful of poems printed in other periodicals. Macmillan's decision appears to have rested in part on his own test of the market: a reading of the title poem of Rossetti's volume to a small workingmen's society. After its initial publication in late March 1862, *Goblin Market* became (and remains today) Rossetti's most famous poem, a fairy tale narrative of two virtually twin sisters living a pastoral idyll, one of whom succumbs, however, to the temptation posed by the "succous pasture" of fruits hawked by demonic Goblin men. The "feast" is nearly fatal, but Laura is in the end saved by the actions of her heroic sister, Lizzie, who braves the Goblin men and is brutalized by them but returns dripping with juices from their fruits, which prove the "fiery antidote" to the poisons destroying Laura.

In a letter to Dante Rossetti of 28 October 1861 Macmillan describes the response elicited by his reading of this poem to the Cambridge "working-men": "They seemed at first to wonder whether I was making fun of them; by degrees they got as still as death, and when I finished there was a tremendous burst of applause" (95). The ideological dynamic of these lower-class men's response to this poem is instructive. Their initial feelings of affront, as assumed by Macmillan, are understandable: typically such men would have taken their evenings' intellectual endeavors seriously. Being read to in the first instance effectually reduced them to children, and having a fairy tale about girls read to them would appear to reinforce that insult. That this text takes the form of a poem of the sort normally aimed at a leisured middle- or upper-class audience would have increased their distrust by underscoring the difference between the men's social position and those of the poem's author as well as its reader. Yet the socially constructed pleasure this particular text elicits triumphs over apparent obstacles to its ideological efficacy. Presumably, such pleasure would have derived not only from the (now famous) sensuousness and musicality of Rossetti's verse, the familiarity of the narrative form, and the intensity of familial relationships and events presented in the poem but also from an intuition by the men that this literary work had social value. (Why else applaud?)

Yet *Goblin Market* intervenes in a variety of discursive formations that would normally conflict with the frameworks of value dominating such Englishmen's lives in 1861. The particular formations at issue surround sibling relationships, courtship and marriage, relationships between men and women, and Christian religion broadly defined (Lizzie is clearly represented as a Christ figure in the poem). The potential ideological effects of the poem are therefore profound since in regard to all of these discursive fields the narrative is revisionist and potentially subver-

sive. Through its use of transparent allegorical devices the poem unabash-
edly privileges the value of women over men, espouses "sisterhood" as a
social dynamic, reviles men, and denounces the sexual pleasures of marriage (in its repeated allusions to the dead Jeanie, "Who should have been
a bride" but instead became a victim of the goblin fruits, here equated
with "joys brides hope to have"). If Macmillan's description of the workingmen's enthusiastic response to his reading is authentic, then his narrative clarifies the mechanism through which a poetic text simultaneously
elicits complex forms of pleasure and refocuses discursive fields, gaining
power over the feelings and thoughts of an audience and thereby holding
the prospect of accomplishing notable ideological effects.

My second example of the process through which poetic texts ex-
ercise power over their readers is perhaps more familiar to students of the
Victorian period. It is based in a private experience presented as a highly
public testimonial nearly fifty years after the events described occurred.
When Mill's *Autobiography* was published posthumously in 1873, he was
the most famous (and in some circles notorious) philosopher in Victorian
England, and his work was likely to attract an enormous audience.
Therefore his description of the healing power of poetry in the chapter
entitled "A Crisis in My Mental History: One Stage Onward" must be
seen as blatantly ideological; that is, it publicly describes a transformation
in one of the most significant frameworks of value and meaning through
which Mill conducted his life in society, and it does so in order to disseminate his fervent belief in the power and uses of poetry, a belief that
flies in the face of the doctrinaire utilitarian values in which he had been
thoroughly educated by his father and which he fully accepted. Moreover, in constructing this segment of his memoir Mill borrows from
varied bodies of religious discourse a familiar and, for great numbers of
Victorian readers, normally seductive genre, the conversion narrative. "A
Crisis in My Mental History" demonstrates how poetry can be viewed
as a privileged discourse that mediates the transformation of *structures of
feeling*, as defined by Raymond Williams,[2] into ideology.

Most readers will recall John Stuart Mill's explanation that late in
1826 he found himself "in a dull state of nerves. . . . the state, I should
think, in which converts to Methodism usually are, when smitten by
their first 'conviction of sin.'" His depressed condition was precipitated
by his realization that the utilitarian goal of his life's work, helping to

generate a society that would allow the greatest happiness for the greatest number of people, had lost its attractiveness. He became aware simultaneously that his analytical habits of mind had "dried up" his emotional capacities. As a result, "the cultivation of the feelings became one of the cardinal points in my ethical and philosophical creed"; he undertook a program of immersion in the arts in order to achieve a "due balance among the faculties" (86). The only effective stimuli for his dormant emotions, however, turned out to be the poems of Wordsworth, which "addressed themselves powerfully to one of the strongest of my pleasurable susceptibilities, the love of rural objects and natural scenery" (88). Mill makes extraordinary claims for the power of this verse:

> *What made Wordsworth's poems a medicine for my state of mind was that they expressed, not mere outward beauty, but states of feeling, and of thought coloured by feeling, under the excitement of beauty. They seemed to be the very culture of the feelings, which I was in quest of.*
> (89) *In them I seemed to draw from a source of inward joy, of sympathetic and imaginative pleasure, which could be shared in by all human beings; which had no connexion with struggle or imperfection, but would be made richer by every improvement in the physical or social condition of mankind. From them I seemed to learn what would be the perennial sources of happiness, when all the greater evils of life shall have been removed.*

The extent of Wordsworth's ideological power over Mill, at least by the time of this writing, can be measured by his adoption of key words, phrases, and concepts (immediately recognizable to readers of Wordsworth) that constitute the discursive basis of what Jerome McGann first delineated as "the Romantic Ideology." "Thought colored by feeling," "excitement of beauty," "inward joy," "sympathetic and imaginative pleasure," and "perennial sources of happiness" all echo passages from Wordsworth's famous preface to the *Lyrical Ballads* (1802) and find various adaptations in his poetry, especially the "Ode: Intimations of Immortality," which Mill acknowledges as a favorite work.

For McGann and for critics who follow him, a central strategy of Romantic poems, especially those by Wordsworth, Coleridge, and Keats, is that they "develop different sorts of artistic means with which to occlude and disguise their own involvement in a certain nexus of historical relations. This act of evasion . . . operates most powerfully whenever the poem is most deeply immersed in its cognitive (i.e., its ideological) materials and commitments" (McGann, *Ideology*, 82). Mill is quite literally overpowered by the success of such elisions in Wordsworth: he sees the poetry's "evasions" as linguistic embodiments of universal human experience and of transcendent truth. One effect is his conviction that "sympathetic and imaginative pleasure" can be "shared in by all human beings" and has "no connexion with struggle or imperfection." Just as Wordsworth suppresses the particular historical (and biographical) circumstances out of which his poems emerged and from which they constitute a deliberate strategy of escape,[3] Mill embraces the opportunity to forget the dreadful historical particulars of industrial England before the first Reform Bill: conditions of poverty, exploitation, and despair among the working classes that his father's and Bentham's utilitarian philosophy had addressed and to the amelioration of which Mill himself had been devoted. The result of Mill's baptism in Wordsworth, he tells us, "was that I gradually, but completely, emerged from my habitual depression, and was never again subject to it" (90).

But his psychological regeneration had more far-reaching effects, one of which—a divorce from "his habitual companions who had not undergone a similar change"—is typical among religious converts. The most radical of these effects, however, is more complex. Mill explains that he now made strenuous public arguments for what amounts to a profound transcendentalist reconceptualization of utilitarian materialism: "I urged . . . that the imaginative emotion which an idea, when vividly conceived, excites in us, is not an illusion but a fact, as real as any of the other qualities of objects" (91). Coming from a philosopher, this is a highly significant statement, especially since Mill claims to have acted thereafter upon this belief. Such views entered into his public debates and published works, not least of all the *Autobiography*. Not only did Wordsworth's poetry thus accomplish radical ideological changes in Mill but those changes found new discursive spaces in which to be played out.

Private testimonials to the cultural power of poetry such as Mill's, especially commentaries that demonstrate a sophisticated consciousness of how personal psychology operates in connection with particular social discourses, are rare indeed. Anecdotes like Macmillan's are similarly hard to come by. Yet the examples of Mill and Rossetti suggest how poems can and do acquire power as they operate within various cultural forums, whether that power is acknowledged or not. My main concern in the following chapters is, therefore, not to trace reception (an issue I nonetheless do periodically discuss) but rather to investigate the ideological investments and strategies of Victorian poems as these confronted, challenged, extended, opposed, rejected, or embraced relevant social discourses current when they were produced and disseminated. Discussion of the discursive formations in which poetic texts under analysis intervene is prominent in this study, as is the examination of (frequently elided) political events and social circumstances surrounding the writing and publication of particular works. But since ideological effects in poetry very often involve revisionist evocations of texts by precursor poets who are seen to possess established cultural power, I also regularly attend to the intertextual operations of featured works. By means of such critical strategies I hope, as my chapters proceed, to demonstrate how not only "social energies and practices" associated with literature but also power, accrued through the ideological interventions that poetry constitutes, circulated within Victorian culture.

I

Medievalist Discourse and the Ideologies of Victorian Poetry

IN *THE ARCHAEOLOGY OF KNOWLEDGE* Michel Foucault began a project, extended in his later works, to describe how bodies of knowledge and understanding are always historically heterogeneous and interactive and how activity in the human sciences can best be understood in terms of the discursive formations operating synchronically within societies. At a given historical moment within a culture discrete and codified linguistic sign systems—terminologies and frames of reference that derive from and speak to particular widespread values and behaviors—are often used to communicate across diverse fields of social activity. Such formations can be specified and analyzed to see how they operated upon horizons of expectations within cultures or subcultures. If a discursive formation "constitutes a 'matrix of meaning' or system of linguistic relations within which actual discursive processes are generated" (Eagleton, *Ideology*, 195), we must understand that even when such a formation appears unified, it is subject to a continuous process of fracture and irruption. This process presents openings for ideological analysis of cultural values in flux. Foucault argues that "the systematic erasure of all given unities enables us first of all to restore to [a] statement the specificity of its occurrence, and to show that discontinuity is one of those great accidents that create cracks not only in the geology of history, but also in the simple fact of the statement; it emerges in its historical irruption" (28). Fruitful cultural critique therefore comes about when we examine "the incision" a statement or text—literary or nonliterary—makes, both within a culture at large and within the discursive formation it engages.

The phenomenon of Victorian medievalism offers a case study for this form of analysis and a useful introduction to the cultural critique of Victorian poetry generally. Studies over the last two decades—by Alice Chandler, Mark Girouard, Kevin Morris, Raymond Chapman, R. J. Smith, Jerome Mitchell, and others—have demonstrated that the term *Victorian medievalism* describes more than a widespread cultural phenomenon. From the late eighteenth century forward a strong interest in medieval history and all things medieval in fact generated an interdependent group of cultural discourses that had permeated the conceptual life and practical behavior of English men and women well before the debacle of the Eglinton Tournament in 1838 and continued to do so at least until the end of the First World War. By the early Victorian period a reified language of medievalism had become current and visible in politics, literature, art, architecture, theology, love-making, and popular entertainments. It was characterized by a specialized vocabulary, a distinctive iconography, the use of particular literary genres (historical novels, ballads, narrative romances, love lyrics), and it involved a network of value-laden associations. This coded discourse was especially attractive to many writers, and their adaptations or appropriations of it can be seen to have generated particular ideological effects. Well before midcentury medievalist discourse was universally understood and commonly employed by educated individuals, comparable, perhaps, to the discourse of political economy or evangelical Protestantism. Medievalist discourse employed an array of conceptual terms that denoted particular belief systems and modes of conduct wholly integrated into middle- and upper-class culture. These included such patriarchal ideals as chivalry, manliness, selflessness, gallantry, nobility, honor, duty, and fidelity (to the crown as well as to a beloved). It also promulgated a belief in the spiritual power of love and in the positive moral influence of women. Such ideals were either formulated explicitly or understood implicitly in terms of medieval literature, mythology, and iconography. As Mark Girouard has demonstrated, they are everywhere embedded in Victorian literature, painting, architecture, and religious documents, all of which frequently employ the language of chivalry, courtly love, and gothicism.[1]

We may attempt to enter the field of social relations in which this discursive formation participated by analyzing the ideological effects of a highly popular text published during the period. The first version of Tennyson's *Idylls of the King*, consisting of "Enid," "Vivien," "Elaine," and "Guinevere," was published by Moxon & Co. in July 1859. The first edition consisted of forty thousand copies. Ten thousand copies sold within six weeks, and the demand was so great that a second edition was needed within six months. By the time the second series of *Idylls* was issued in 1869, six more editions had been produced (Hagen, 109–10). The extraordinarily wide dissemination of this poem may be explained by the convergence of author and subject matter in a cultural project that benefited from the public's engagement with both. As a notable specimen of medievalist discourse in mid-Victorian England, the *Idylls* thus provides a profoundly ideological text against which to investigate the instabilities of a discursive formation and examine selected "irruptions" within it over a period of not quite two decades, from the publication of Matthew Arnold's *Tristram and Iseult* (1852) to the (first truly public) appearance of Dante Rossetti's "The Blessed Damozel" in his *Poems*, 1870. Tennyson's first four *Idylls* stand more or less at the center of this period.

Tennyson's work best illustrates what might be described as a traditionalist and conservative engagement with medievalist discourse in mid-Victorian England. Like so many of his contemporaries, including Arnold, Browning, Swinburne, Morris, and the Rossettis—among Victorian poets—Tennyson discovered the usefulness of medievalist topoi early in his career, by 1833 producing important poems like the "Morte d'Arthur" (published in 1842) and "The Lady of Shalott" (published in 1832). (In this respect he resembles earlier writers as diverse as Sir Walter Scott, Richard Hurd, and Kenelm Digby.) For the next forty years Tennyson continued to deploy the discourse of medievalism. From 1833 to 1885 he wrote Arthurian poems, most of them finally assembled into rhis Arthurian epic, *Idylls of the King*, which appeared in its "completed" form in 1888. Setting this long and immensely popular work by the poet laureate against other poetic manipulations of medievalist vocabulary and iconography in mid-Victorian England affirms Foucault's assertion that any ostensibly unified discursive formation is actually a colloquy of "irruptive" voices. Analysis of medievalist works by William Morris, Matthew Arnold, Dante Rossetti, and A. C. Swinburne further demonstrates how these poets, like Tennyson, employ a culturally pervasive discourse so as to achieve varied ideological effects through which their work acquires cultural power.

In 1862 Tennyson dedicated the newest edition of his first four *Idylls*

to the memory of Victoria's beloved Prince Albert, setting up specific
political and ideological contexts for the poem as a whole. The laureate
resurrects Albert as an incarnation of Arthurian perfection: "He seems to
me / Scarce other than my [Arthur's] ideal knight":

> . . . modest, kindly, all-accomplish'd, wise,
> With what sublime repression of himself,
> And in what limits, and how tenderly;
> Not swaying to this faction or to that;
> Not making his high place the lawless perch
> Of wing'd ambitions, nor a vantage-ground
> For pleasure; but thro' all this tract of years
> Wearing the white flower of a blameless life,
> Before a thousand peering littlenesses.

(Ricks,
Poems,
3 : 264)

This description, with its emphasis on Albert's selflessness, presents Victoria's influential consort as a politically neutral ideality. "A lovelier life,
more unstained than his," the narrator claims, is unimaginable. Albert,
father of England's future kings, is harbinger of an "ampler day" in
Tennyson's perfectibilian system of beliefs. "Laborious for [the land's]
people and her poor," he is seen as the "Far-sighted summoner of War
and Waste / To fruitful strifes and rivalries of peace," possessing a "Sweet
nature gilded by the gracious gleam / Of letters." He is therefore

> . . . dear to Science, dear to Art,
> Dear to thy land and ours, a Prince indeed,
> Beyond all titles

(3 : 265)

In this dedication and throughout *Idylls* Tennyson presents an array
of positive values he associates with Arthur's Camelot as natural, inevitable, unquestionable, and absolute—as nonideological, in fact. Nonetheless, the sentimental and romantic image of Albert he foregrounds
here and the idealizations of Arthur deployed throughout the body of his
poem operate as ideology usually does: the systems of value and belief
they support are assumed to be valid, generally accepted, and, in the case
of this poem, divinely sanctioned. Tennyson could succeed with such an
assumption because the ideological formulas that operated as subtexts for
medievalist discourse in Victorian England were fundamental to the process of middle- and upper-class socialization (Girouard). Tennyson directly articulates these formulas in "Guinevere."

In this stridently antifeminist idyll Arthur travels to the nunnery at Glastonbury, to which Guinevere retreated after her infidelity was exposed. War (between the king and Lancelot, as well as between the king and Modred's forces) is destroying Camelot. Arthur ostensibly makes this journey to affirm his love for Guinevere despite events, but he first upbraids her mercilessly, reminding her that she has ravaged "that fair Order of my Table Round, / A glorious company . . . To serve as model for the mighty world" (Ricks, *Poems*, 3 : 541–42). Rehearsing the oaths his knights swore, Tennyson through Arthur ventriloquizes a system of values and a code of conduct so prevalent in Victorian England that varied forms of medievalist discourse automatically elicited them. These values and behaviors constituted an essential horizon of expectations for educated readers, and Arthur reinscribes them in a litany of infinitive constructions that point toward the ideal of a perfected, albeit amorphous, sociality. Arthur's knights promised—as all true, strong, and good Englishmen presumably should—

> To reverence the King, as if he were
> Their conscience, and their conscience as their King,
> To break the heathen and uphold the Christ,
> To ride abroad redressing human wrongs.
> To speak no slander, no, nor listen to it,
> To honour his own word as if his God's,
> To lead sweet lives in purest chastity,
> To love one maiden only, cleave to her,
> And worship her by years of noble deeds,   (542)
> Until they won her; for indeed I knew
> Of no more subtle master under heaven
> Than is the maiden passion for a maid,
> Not only to keep down the base in man,
> But teach high thought, and amiable words
> And courtliness, and the desire of fame,
> And love of truth, and all that makes a man.

This passage adapts the discourse of medievalism to advocate a historically particular, that is, mid-Victorian, network of values widely accepted by the middle and upper classes. Quite obviously it valorizes Christianity as, implicitly, the exclusive domain of truth and honor. In the political arena it promulgates an alliance between monarchy and religion (conscience) that sanctions imperialism ("to break the heathen"). By association with Christianity and by means of authoritative testimonial (Arthur's), it asserts the ultimate value of desexualized love in the service of self-reformation (keeping down "the base in man") and summons a host of abstract, politically manipulable ideals: "high thought," "amiable words," "love of truth," and, most strikingly, "all that makes a man." Here women exist as chaste ciphers to subserve the patriarchy in its pursuit of goals ("courtliness" and "the desire of fame") that will sustain and reaffirm an elitist power structure in society. In short, Tennyson adopts medievalist discourse in the service of Tory social, political, and religious values.[2]

Tennyson's early medievalist work provides a pattern for such later ideological leanings; for example, the "Morte d'Arthur" (1833), as Herbert Tucker has shown, employs the disparaged form of the epic, albeit fragmentarily, in the service of ultimately conservative cultural values. Tucker persuasively argues that "the subject of 'Morte D'Arthur' is cultural transmission, the handing on or handing over of a communal ideal whose . . . essence is communication" (318). Thus, "the traditional epic ideal of transmitting a culture yields at last . . . to an ideal of culture *as* transmission" (321). This ideal is not only represented by the sword Excalibur (in obvious fashion) and thematically embedded in Tennyson's tale, it is also symbolized in the very effort of generating an epic narrative.

Arthur's final command (around which the narrative of this poem is built), that Bedivere hurl Excalibur into the mere, tries his remaining knight's loyalty, his sense of duty, and his wisdom, here specifically defined by the articulate values of the once and future king. In microcosm, Arthur's imperial imperative allows for an examination of some of the roles human agency, in all its unpredictability, plays in the maintenance, transmission, and securing of ideology. When Bedivere fails twice to remit Excalibur to its source (the Lady of the Lake) and thus to enable transmission of the values it represents, Arthur views Bedivere's inaction serially as self-betrayal (l. 71), as a betrayal of the laws of "fealty" (l. 73), as disobedience to "the bond of rule" (l. 92), and finally as resistance to "duty" (l. 126). What each of these judgments, grounded in an absolutist and authoritarian ethos, makes clear is that " 'Mort D'Arthur,' like *Idylls of the King*, is a profoundly conservative poem" (Tucker, 344), one that demonstrates Tennyson's "ambition to legislate for [his public] and join them to the authoritative past that he believes to be modern culture's longest-term need" (343−44). Tucker properly views the poem's "victories" as "gained on thoroughly elitest grounds." Inspecting "the social and ideological content of the poet's Arthurian fable," he concludes that it is

> *bounded by fairly insular poles: at one pole a moribund aristocratic*
> *ideal of ordered fealty, at the other, a parvenu (and to Tennyson's*
> *imagination a diminished) bourgeois ideal of expansive change and*
> *communication. These poles also represent the chief constituents of*
> *his readership, as of the mixed, but far from open, ruling class in*
> *which his birth and education had installed him. Tennyson's public*   (344−45)
> *wager in 'Morte d'Arthur' succeeded . . . because in transmitting the*
> *mythology he had received from an antique culture he found means*
> *of pitching it right to the class he knew contained the majority of his*
> *readers.*

In all of these respects this poem foreshadows *Idylls of the King* (to be discussed at length in chapter 2).

William Morris's "The Defence of Guenevere," from *The Defence of Guenevere and Other Poems*, published in 1858, provides an apposite ideological contrast to the laureate's highly popular poem built upon his fragmentary epic of 1833. Published at Morris's own expense by Bell and Daldy a year before the first four of Tennyson's *Idylls*, *The Defence* sold few copies. In part because the texts in the volume were seen as ideologically estranged, it was largely ignored by Victorian reviewers and readers alike.[3] A second edition was not called for until 1875, when Ellis and White took it over, long after Morris had become famous for other work. The title poem is fraught with ideologically *emergent* elements.[4] "Guenevere" manipulates the dramatic monologue form and plays upon typical Victorian expectations of medievalist discourse, including those Tennyson's poem sanctions, in order to challenge them. The poem is both formally and, by the dominant mid-Victorian standards, morally "impure." Its dramatic monologue form is sullied by the insertion, at strategic moments during Guenevere's speech, of a narrator who serves to clarify and enforce the explosive ideological effects of both her self-presentation and the poet's presentation of her as a physically, emotionally, and intellectually seductive icon. The elements of Morris's poem thus constitute a series of irruptions in the dominant values attached to medievalist discourse by mid-Victorian audiences as these might be measured by the ideological effects of Tennyson's "Morte D'Arthur" and his first four *Idylls of the King*.

"The Defence of Guenevere" is an epiphanic poem that draws readers in through the use of a culturally familiar discourse, only to awaken them to the illusory idealizations purveyed in that discourse. The poem counters Victorian ideals of manliness (derived from medieval codes of chivalry) by making Guenevere a genuine heroine. About to be burned at the stake, she delivers a monologue that sanctions sexual passion rather than chastity. She distracts her audience of knights with blatant sexual displays, denies the authority of kingship, interrogates divine justice, and exposes the self-interested hypocrisy of "chivalrous" behavior and "respectable" public morality.

Unlike Tennyson's Arthur, Morris's narrator sees Guenevere as both heroic and victimized. Her monologue displays her bravery, admired at every turn: "Though still she stood right up, and never shrunk, / But spoke on bravely, glorious lady fair!" (Lang, *Pre-Raphaelites*, 163). Guenevere also perceives her own performance in chivalric terms: "So, ever must I dress me to the fight," she murmurs at one turning point in the poem. Guenevere is uniquely a female combatant, however, and her best weapon is her beauty, which she flaunts, playing upon the traditional medievalist equation of beauty with virtue. Standing at the stake, wet and apparently naked, she repeatedly taunts her audience (both the knights and Victorian male readers) with the irony of that equation, "passionately twisting . . . her body there" (163). Recalling the day of her first meeting with Lancelot, she confides seductively, "I dared not think, as I was wont to do, / Sometimes, upon my beauty," which she invites her audience to enjoy. "[I]f I had / Held out my long hand up against the blue," she gestures,

> And, looking on the tenderly darken'd fingers,
> Thought that by rights one ought to see quite through,
> There, see you, where the soft still light yet lingers,
> Round the edges; what should I have done,
> If this had joined with yellow spotted singers,
> And startling green drawn upward by the sun?
> But shouting, loosed out, see now! all my hair.

(165, ll. 122–28)

She continues the seduction relentlessly, often interrupting her own argument that she is "better than innocent." Near the conclusion of the poem, she performs onanistically:

> See my breast rise,
> Like waves of purple sea, as here I stand;
> And how my arms are moved in wonderful wise. . . .
> See through my long throat how the words go up   (168)
> In ripples to my mouth. . . .
> And wonder how the light is falling so
> Within my moving tresses.

The poem's explicit challenge to the Victorian equation between virtue and medievalist discourse appears at this crux in her monologue: "will you dare . . . / To say this thing is vile?" she rhetorically asks the mesmerized knights.

Not once does Morris's Guenevere deny her infidelity. Rather she portrays all sexual passion as natural and irresistible, comparing its effect to slipping "slowly down some path worn smooth and even, / Down to a cool sea on a summer day." Reaching that haven, one feels "strange new joy" and a sense of purgation. The "worn head" lay

> Back, with the hair like sea-weed; yea all past
> Sweat of the forehead, dryness of the lips,   (164)
> Washed utterly out by the dear waves o'ercast.

Through her seductive performance Guenevere compels her auditors' awareness of their own irrepressible sexual urges. She makes a special example of her accuser, Gauwaine, whose "dear pity" for her, she observes, "creeps / All through [his] frame, and trembles in [his] mouth." Moreover, he is guilty, too, of moral and sexual hypocrisy, she insists, through association with his mother, whose infidelity elicited "Agravaine's fell blow"—"her head sever'd in that awful drouth / of pity" called revenge. Guenevere further deflates the self-righteous behavior of her accusers and the chivalric code they follow with the example of Mellyagraunce, the "stripper of ladies" who discovered blood from Lancelot's tourney wounds on Guenevere's sheets and publicly announced the adultery. This timid knight, however, would accept Lancelot's challenge of a trial by arms only when he agreed to fight "half-arm'd" and with his "left side all uncovered." Divine justice reduced Mellyagruance to "a spout of blood on the hot sand" (167). Guenevere has, nonetheless, already challenged and perplexed accepted notions of such justice. At the beginning of her monologue she compares her choice between Arthur and Lancelot to an arbitrary but forced decision between two deceptively symbolic cloths: trying to be dutiful—choosing the blue cloth of "heaven's colour" rather than the red one—leads to her damnation. This is in part because of Arthur's inadequacy as a husband. Unlike Tennyson's would-be savior of the world, Morris's Arthur is a philistine, out of touch with animating and salving natural passions, who "bought" Guenevere with "his great name and his little love" (163).

"The Defence of Guenevere" thus appropriates the dramatic monologue form and transposes standard materials of medievalist discourse in a manner that operates to undercut the conservative, patriarchal ideology typically identified with it. Here Christian values are supplanted by erotic ones, chivalry is a fraud, and Christian ideals of virtue are displaced by ideals of amoral beauty, sexual indulgence, and political subversiveness as these are displayed in the heroic person of Guenevere and in her adulterous relationship with Lancelot, who, predictably, comes to the rescue in the poem's final lines.

"The Defence of Guenevere" failed as cultural intervention at the time of its publication. Most of those who read the poem and the volume in which it appeared in 1858 found it so radical, both ideologically and formally, that they simply did not know what to make of it. The *Saturday Review* spoke for such readers in describing Morris's work as "not like anything we ever saw." Only the reviewer for the *Tablet* found in it what later readers did: "power everywhere" (Lindsay, 97). For subsequent generations the first poem of Morris's first volume became his best known and most influential work, and eventually the collective efficacy of his writings led to his canonization among the saints of poetry.

As I have observed, the ideological strategies of work by such poets becomes institutionalized in the apparatuses that perpetually reinforce and reconstruct cultural values: it is memorized in classrooms, anthologized in textbooks and display books, discussed in periodical literature, and strategically positioned in political speeches, for example. Effective poets *are* seen, as Thomas Carlyle insisted on seeing them, as heroes and visionaries. Great claims are made for their value in the social world, as

W. B. Yeats demonstrates in the case of Morris, and such claims are largely based, I would argue, on the ideological effects of their poetry. In his essay "The Happiest of the Poets" Yeats insists that Morris's "mind was illuminated from within and lifted into prophecy in the full right sense of the word, and he saw the natural things he was alone gifted to see in their perfect form" (Yeats, 62). In Yeats's commentary on Morris we also come to understand how the ideological effects on the intellects and spirits of social subjects exposed to successful poets (through the embeddedness of their work in a variety of media) are practical and immense: in ways rarely applicable to writers of fiction the ideals poets promulgate are seen to transcend but also to *overtake* the realities those ideals challenge. As Yeats asserts, Morris "knew as Shelley knew . . . that the economists should take their measurements not from life as it is, but from the vision of men like him" (63).

In the Arthurian poetry of Morris and Tennyson amatory and religious, or erotic and spiritual, impulses are reconcilable. In Tennyson's work the suppression of lust facilitates Christian virtue and "civilized" behavior. In Morris's poem passionate self-expression enables psychological health, "joy," and personal fulfillment. A number of other important Victorian poets, however, employ medievalist discourse in a manner that argues for the opposition between love and religion. Among them are Matthew Arnold, Christina and Dante Rossetti, A. C. Swinburne, and Thomas Hardy, for example, whose works' various manipulations of the topoi, iconography, and terminology of medievalism result in special ideological effects when they appropriate this traditional dialectic.

Poems by three of these writers, all published between 1852 and 1870, demonstrate how medievalist discourse appears to have set the terms for a midcentury dialogue among Victorian poets concerning the vexed relations, and difficult choices to be made, between love and faith. Significantly, the poems I discuss by Arnold (*Tristram and Iseult* and "Dover Beach") and Dante Rossetti ("The Blessed Damozel") were conceived and initially composed during or soon after a period in Europe characterized by near political chaos, and in England by great social turmoil reflected in the highly public debates surrounding the franchise and the cause of improved conditions for the working classes. Such debates were often focused on the Chartist movement (1828–48). In poems by Arnold and Rossetti that exploited the language and iconography of Victorian medievalism, however, the political discourse surrounding events in England and the conflicts in Europe became either refocused (in Arnold's work) or altogether elided (in Rossetti's) so as to privilege a concern with spiritual and aesthetic matters (love, faith, art). The ideological effect of such strategies was to devalue activity in the socio-political world and open up discursive spaces through which readers might achieve the illusion of transcending that world (as was the case with Yeats's response to Morris).

In a letter to Herbert Hill written on 5 November 1852 Arnold acknowledged that his plan for *Tristram and Iseult*, published in 1852, had been conceived during one of his two trips to Thun in September 1848 and September 1849: "I read the story . . . some years ago at Thun in an article in a French Review on the romance literature: I had never met with it before, and it fastened upon me: when I got back to England I looked at the Morte d'Arthur and took what I could, but the poem was in the main formed, and I could not well disturb it" (Arnold, *Letters*, 247). This episode from "romance literature" clearly provided a distraction for Arnold from the explosive political events going on around him.

In the months prior to his first visit Europe was politically chaotic: revolutionary activity had broken out in Sicily in January, in Paris on 24 February, and in Germany and Italy in March. With the fall of Metternich, Austria was in the throes of political disintegration, and the Russians were preparing for war. In April war broke out between Germany and Poland. By the spring of the following year matters had not improved. In March 1849 Sardinia renewed its war against Austria. By 30 April French forces had clashed with Garibaldi's republican troops. (Although Louis Napoleon's true intentions remain uncertain, on 31 May the Roman republic accepted French protection.) Also in April, Austrian and Hungarian forces became embattled, and in July Russian troops moved to occupy Moldavia and Wallachia to quash the stirrings of a revolutionary movement there. Russia's actions precipitated the reopening of the Eastern question and resulted in negotiations for an alliance between England and France that were concluded in October 1849. On 6 October Britain ordered its Mediterranean fleet to proceed to the neighborhood of the Dardanelles (Taylor, 4–34).

For Matthew Arnold, at the time secretary to Lord Lansdowne, who, as a Whig elder statesmen, was in the thick of English political activity, these events would have been of great moment. From Thun on 23 September he wrote a letter to Arthur Hugh Clough expressing a fear that on his return to England he would be unable to maintain any distance from the chaotic swirl of political activity surrounding him: "When I come to town," he lamented, "I tell you beforehand I will have a real effort at managing myself as to newspapers and the talk of the day" (Arnold, *Letters*, 156). Arnold's poetry composed during this period in fact became a vehicle for the repudiation of "the talk of the day" and the sociopolitical issues privileged by such discourse.

Typically Arnold's verse is elegiac, a poetry of lost love or lost faith. But uniquely for his personae love and faith often appear to be interchangeable spiritual impulses: in Arnold's work love is drained of its eroticism, and faith of its asceticism. Much of his poetry laments the permanent loss of both, as does the plaintive narrative voice in an ideologically central passage from *Tristram and Iseult*:

> . . . 'tis the gradual furnace of the world,
> In whose hot air our spirits are upcurl'd
> Until they crumble, or else grow like steel—
> Which kills in us the bloom of youth, the spring—
> Which leaves the fierce necessity to feel,
> But takes away the power—this can avail,
> By drying up our joy in everything,
> To make our former pleasures all seem stale.
> This, or some tyrannous single thought, some fit
> Of passion, which subdues our souls to it,
> Till for its sake alone we live and move—
> Call it ambition, or remorse, or love—
> This too can change us wholly, and make seem
> All which we did before, shadow and dream.

(Arnold, *Matthew Arnold*, 128)

As is common in Arnold's poetry of this period, this passage employs generalized metaphors that at once suggest and disguise an array of urgent public issues and refocus the discourse that would normally attach to them. These lines employ a notably industrial metaphor—"the gradual furnace of the world" that either chars spirits or refines them as "steel"— to condemn involvement in the external world of economic competition and labor that metaphor suggests. But the ideological strategy behind his narrator's acknowledgment that a single (internal) obsession—ambition, love, remorse—can equally destroy us implies through an ironic reversal that the prepossession with escape from social (and implicitly political and economic) reality may have the power to reduce that reality to illusion—"shadow and dream"—and thereby restore the spirit's access to "joy."

Arnold's *Tristram* is a formally hybrid medievalist poem about the fatality of love, but the crucial term in the ostensibly generalized critique of human nature this passage articulates is, ultimately, "joy," whose reference is ambiguously spiritual *and* erotic. Although Arnold's description of "some fit of passion, which subdues our souls to it," especially in the context of the Tristram myth, ostensibly refers to sexual passion, we cannot read these lines without acknowledging the allusion to Wordsworth. His "Strange Fits of Passion" is, of course, echoed here, but by 1852— only two years after the laureate's death—no Victorian could think of Wordsworth and hear the word *joy* without recalling the Intimations ode, whose urgent concern—in the face of "all that is at enmity with joy"— is with the recovery of joy in our spiritual lives. *Tristram and Iseult* is ultimately about spiritual unfulfillment. As we have seen, Arnold's central metaphor—the "furnace of the world"—locates his critique historically. The experience of spiritual debility he deplores, like "this strange disease of modern life" lamented in "The Scholar-Gipsy," is uniquely the effect of the industrial revolution.

Tristram and Iseult, like Morris's "Defence of Guenevere," is ideologically oppositional, and in a variety of ways. From its opening, where we find Tristram already on his death bed, the poem formally undercuts traditional versions of the Tristram myth. He is fading in and out of consciousness, taunted by memories and yearning for the irrecoverable past while tenuously hoping for the arrival of Irish Iseult. This "peerless hunter, harper, knight" (109) is no longer heroic but pathetic. The story Arnold narrates is Iseult of Brittany's tragedy, not Tristram's, and it is one that altogether challenges the value of romantic love. The "spring-time" of Tristram's fatal passion

(113)   Is already gone and past,
               And instead thereof is seen
               Its winter, which endureth still.

He is tormented by "a secret in his breast / Which will never let him rest"—unable even in his dreams of the past "to get free / From the clog of misery" (115–16). And in the present, when Irish Iseult arrives no joy resurges. We find only that "both have suffer'd / Both have pass'd a youth consumed and sad," and "both have brought their anxious day to evening, / And have now short space for being glad!" (121). Like Tristram, Irish Iseult has been tortured rather than fulfilled by her love, described as a "longing" that "dogg'd by fear and fought by shame / Shook her weak bosom day and night," devouring "her beauty like a flame" (123).

Arnold's medieval story of victimized lovers nonetheless does not serve to illustrate the evils of erotic indulgence or to advocate self-suppression and chastity, as Tennyson's *Idylls* do. Iseult of Brittany, for all her wholesomeness, fares no better than the lovers united by the fatal draught: "Joy has not found her yet, nor ever will" (126). Her noble and selfless devotion to Tristram has produced a "fatigued" woman "dying in a mask of youth" (127). Love, variously idealized in medievalist discourse, is here denounced and repudiated altogether, presumably in favor of emotional detachment from experience, a philosophical approach to life that Arnold promotes everywhere in his major poems and prose works. His narrator is vitriolic in attacking amatory ideals because they exemplify "tyrannous single thoughts" that ruin human lives:

> And yet, I swear, it angers me to see
> How this fool passion gulls men potently;
> Being, in truth, but a diseased unrest,
> How they are full of languor and distress   (128)
> Not having it; which when they do possess,
> They straightway are burnt up with fume and care,
> And spend their lives in posting here and there
> Where this plague drives them.

Thus, Arnold's *Tristram* exploits a medieval topos and setting to disparage in generalized but absolute terms the "furnace" of a world in which fulfillment is unattainable through the usual channels. The pursuit of love (like Tristram's) is as fruitless as the pursuit of fame (illustrated by the examples of "bald Caesar" and "Alexander, Philip's peerless son"). Religious faith is similarly not available as a source of fulfillment. Although described as "The sweetest Christian soul alive" (110), Britannic

Iseult remains unrewarded for her devotion. This poem implicitly adopts a stance of secular nihilism, and that stance is patently ideological. Its deep pessimism requires a repudiation not only of the materialist, utilitarian, perfectibilian, amatory, and Christian values embraced by many middle- and upper-class Victorians of the period (including Tennyson) but also of the spiritual illusions proffered by the Romantics, especially Wordsworth, as alternatives to those values. This poem in fact propounds a transvalued Byronic ideology of defiant martyrdom, a self-assertive "ideology against ideology" that is also central to Arnold's other major compositions of the late 1840s and early 1850s, including "Dover Beach," a work seldom thought of as medievalist.

Probably composed about the same time as *Tristram and Iseult* (529), this dramatic monologue more directly acknowledges its political sub-texts, suggested by the famous concluding image of its speaker hearing "confused alarms of struggle and flight, / Where ignorant armies clash by night" across the English channel. But this image signals a retreat from the political world rather than engagement with it, and Arnold appro-priates the dramatic monologue form here to assault other frameworks of value dominant in mid-Victorian England than those challenged in Morris's "Defence of Guenevere." A lament for lost spiritual certainties, "Dover Beach" presents as its central metaphor the medieval "Sea of Faith," which was once "at the full, and round earth's shore / Lay like the folds of a bright girdle furl'd," a reference to the widespread Victorian belief that spiritual life in pre-Reformation Europe was harmonious. (By 1867, when "Dover Beach" was first published, Victorian audiences would have recalled two familiar touchstones for such a belief in Carlyle's *Past and Present* and Ruskin's "The Nature of Gothic.") The speaker in "Dover Beach," whose voice is more forceful than that of the narrator of *Tristram and Iseult*, employs this metaphor to decry the intellectual, moral, and spiritual chaos of the modern world mirrored in political conflicts also rendered metaphorically. He does so—cleverly—by means of the feint to idealize the religious harmony of medieval Europe ("a land of dreams"). However, this move serves primarily to explode ideals—"joy," "love," "light," "certitude," "peace"—that Victorians like Carlyle and Ruskin ascribed to medieval culture and then attempted to transpose onto their own.

According to this poem, whatever spiritually unifying and redemptive effects the medieval church may have had are long gone, existing in idealized histories only to highlight the modern world's pervasive insufficiencies. The withdrawal of the Sea of Faith, reenacted here as the poem exposes illusions among its Victorian audience that medievalist idealities can recur, horribly reveals "the vast edges drear / And naked shingles of the world" (136). The only ideal that remains for Arnold's persona turns out to be intellectual commitment: to a realistic view of the world mutually held as a bond between himself and his auditor (and, implicitly, between Arnold and his reader). The monologue's dramatic situation, with its manipulation of the props of traditional romantic liaisons, is employed strictly in the service of such a world-view:

> Ah, love, let us be true
> To one another! for the world, which seems
> To lie before us like a land of dreams,
> So various, so beautiful, so new,
> Hath really neither joy, nor love, nor light,   (136)
> Nor certitude, nor peace, nor help for pain;
> And we are here as on a darkling plain
> Swept with confused alarms of struggle and flight,
> Where ignorant armies clash by night.

"Dover Beach" here brings two prominent Victorian discursive formations—medievalist and amatory—into collision so as ultimately to oppose both and to affirm one variety of antisocial solipsism. As in Arnold's *Tristram*, self-affirmation in defiance of the illusory optimisms propagated by "the world" (whether under the sign of love or under the sign of faith) is an ideological stance, specifically a reversion to the iconoclastic impetus behind Romanticism, but one that disallows the ultimately compensatory ideologies formulated by all the major English Romantic poets except Byron.[5]

The success of such oppositional strategies in Arnold's poems of this period is not best measured by the sales of his 1852 volume or his 1853 volume (in which *Tristram* first appeared) or by the reviews, which in 1852 were unsettling enough to prompt his writing of the famous preface to the 1853 volume. Rather, the movement toward the ideological ascendancy of the initially marginal aesthetic and social values normally embedded in Arnold's poems is truly realized in their author's acceptance and promotion within institutional apparatuses for the dissemination of (high) culture during his era. In 1857 Arnold was elected professor of poetry at Oxford. In 1870 he became senior inspector of English schools (and was promoted to chief inspector in 1884). And in 1883 he was given a Civil List pension.

Like Arnold, Dante Rossetti, in his most famous poem, "The Blessed Damozel," is concerned with the relations between love and faith. Originally drafted in 1847, when Rossetti was nineteen, the poem was not widely read until its publication in *Poems*, 1870. Unlike Arnold's work of the late 1840s and early 1850s, "The Blessed Damozel" (like the other medievalist poems of the 1870 volume) fully elides the historical contexts of its composition, focusing its action, image patterns, and emotional field in the discourses of medievalism and romantic love. (This is, more specifically, the framework of values associated with what since the end of the nineteenth century has been called courtly love, a system of amatory values seen to originate in late-twelfth-century France.) These discourses in the poem engage, subsume, and usurp Christianity, implicit as an alternate discursive formation, and they generate Rossetti's well-known, literal conceptualization of a Heaven of Love. The poem thus creates an imaginative space that challenges the sociopolitical space in which he (and Arnold and every other European of the era) actually lived.

It was impossible to be in the Rossetti household during this period and not be immersed in European politics. The family patriarch, Gabriele Rossetti, had been forced to flee Italy in 1821 because of his revolutionary activities as a member of the Carbonari. Political visitors passed regularly through the Rossettis' parlor, where evening after evening, while Dante Rossetti was growing up, they called to exchange political news and verbally eviscerate the kings of Naples and of France, the pope, Metternich, and the Austrians. By 1847, when Rossetti composed the first version of "The Blessed Damozel," he was himself inevitably engaged in discussions of European politics. In the summer of 1847, for instance, he wrote to his mother:

(Rossetti, letter no. 24)

> *I suppose you have not heard that the Austrians have been forced by a general rising to retreat from Ferrara. The papers also affirm, as a certain fact, that the Pope has said that, if [their] unjustifiable interference [in Italy] is continued, he shall first make a protest to all the Sovereigns of Europe against Austria; that, in case this should fail, he will excom-*

*municate both the Emperor and people; and that, when driven to the
last extremity, he will himself ride in the van of his own army with
the sword and the Cross, and that then five millions of Christians
shall rise and follow him.*

During the course of Rossetti's early career such concerns with international politics give way to an obsession with art in which struggles for power are nonetheless implicated. The formation of the Pre-Raphaelite Brotherhood, with its own aesthetic manifesto (espoused in the poems and prose of *The Germ*, in which Rossetti first published "The Blessed Damozel"), for instance, self-consciously challenged the dominant, official schools of art in England, especially the Royal Academy. But increasingly for Rossetti art became the site of the only variety of power worth having in the world because it allowed access to and provided mirrors of human psychological and emotional realities that he believed were of ultimate interest to all people, whether fully engaged in the sociopolitical world or not. That is, Rossetti as an eminently modern artist appears to have understood the necessity of estrangement from industrial society to meaningfully survive life in it. The ideological effects of his work demonstrate that a kind of social power can be accrued through an art of defamiliarization, and he was able to produce such art by developing highly complex strategies of parody.

In "The Blessed Damozel" of 1870, for instance, Rossetti appropriates medievalizing language and iconography parodically. The poem interrogates the relations between erotic and religious impulses using a tone that fluctuates between the serious and the ludicrous (as I have argued elsewhere).[6] In appropriating specific semiotic features of medievalist discourse the poem destabilizes the language, image patterns, and conceptual frameworks of both conventional courtly love literature and traditional Christianity, especially orthodox concepts of the afterlife. Such features include numerological symbolism (the "three lilies" in the Damozel's hand, the "seven stars" in her hair, the "lady" Mary's "five handmaidens"); linguistic archaisms ("damozel" and "aureole"); emblematic image patterns (the "white rose of Mary's gift"; the "Dove" whose "plumes" touch "every leaf" of "That living mystic tree"); direct references to medieval musical instruments ("citherns and citholes"); and mention of "God's choristers," which recalls medieval concepts of the music of the spheres. But as these elements of the poem become focused exclusively on its erotic drama rather than on the spiritual values implicit in the language employed to "decorate" that drama they are drained of traditional Christian meaning.

In effect the poem presents a Heaven that exists only in the language of physical desire. But even the credibility of amatory impulses that dominate the poem is undercut because their value is so exaggerated that they overtake the religious system of beliefs they normally subserve in familiar medieval literature, from the *Romance of the Rose* to Dante's *Vita Nuova*. The parodic procedures in this poem are not primarily iconoclastic, however; they do not serve to subvert serious Christian and Petrarchan values that might be held by Rossetti's audience. Rather, they draw attention to the conceptual silliness of the poem itself, which must be viewed, ultimately, as a hyperartificial construct, a seductive and ornate bricolage and conflation of preexisting ideologies. In the final analysis, "The Blessed Damozel," like Rossetti's painting on the subject, presents itself as an aesthetic object that refuses any ideological commitment—to courtly love values or to medievalizing religious belief—that a reader might normally expect of such a work. Appropriation of these traditions in the poem instead projects a virtual ideology of aestheticism, in whose service other value systems and varied modes of discourse might be exploited.

The success of *Poems*, 1870, which "The Blessed Damozel" introduced, was sensational for a first volume of poetry. It represents a particularly remarkable instance of cultural intervention, accomplished in part because (as Walter Pater observed) the volume was widely anticipated. By 1870 Rossetti was already a cult figure, reputed as the originator of the Pre-Raphaelites, as a painter whose work was immensely intriguing because it fetched huge sums (though it was never exhibited), and as a bohemian artist who had "something about him of mystic isolation" (Pater, *Appreciations*, 213). In his retrospective essay on Rossetti, first published in 1883, Pater explains that "some of his poems had won a kind of exquisite fame before they were in the full sense published. *The Blessed Damozel*, although actually printed twice before the year 1870, was eagerly circulated in manuscript; and the volume which it . . . opens came at last to satisfy a long-standing curiosity as to the poet, whose pictures also had become an object of the same peculiar interest" (213). Indeed, two months before Rossetti's death John Addington Symonds argued that even without his having published any major poetic works, the "inspiration which in [Rossetti] and in his eminent associates was original and sincerely felt, has [already] been simulated at second and third hand by imitators, who have attracted the curiosity of the fashionable world, furnishing material for good-natured satire to our comic journals, and figuring in their most salient humours on the comic stage" (313). Reviewers reacted variously to this "inspiration" as an exciting novelty or a deplorable quality of self-conscious artificiality, in either case recognizing the inherent aestheticism of the work. Pater recognized how Rossetti altered horizons of expectations for readers, noting in his productions "a poetic sense which recognised no conventional standard of what poetry was called upon to be" and "a vocabulary, an accent, unmistakably novel" (Pater, *Appreciations*, 214). By contrast, an anonymous reviewer of Rossetti's *Poems*, writing in the *Spectator* in 1870, was disturbed by "too much art in proportion to the intensity of feeling" and too much by way of "elaborate expression," a style "apparently strained, manneristic, elaborated beyond nature" (724).

Clearly, the fecundity of Rossetti's aestheticism, his stylistic excesses—"a definiteness of sensible imagery, which seemed almost grotesque to some," according to Pater—played a significant role in transforming aesthetic expectations among a substantial group of poetry readers. His work, "simulated at second and third hand," unquestionably helped to inaugurate the decadent artistic values of the 1880s and 1890s, and the medievalist discourse that his poetry often engages (through the exploitation of its iconography and other semiotic features, its poetic forms, especially the ballad and sonnet, and its linguistic archaisms) contributed significantly to this accomplishment. If we accept the view widely held among literary historians that a general movement toward aestheticism and away from a concern with social, political, and moral issues took place in Victorian literature between about 1860 and about 1885, the ideological interventions of Rossetti's poetry (and painting) in forwarding that movement are clear.

Its ideological effects introduced a large audience of readers to a novel kind of textual pleasure, if we are to believe Pater, and that audience was expanded immeasurably, as Symonds notes, through imitations, parodies, and theatrical productions. But impressive sales figures also support such an assertion. *Poems*, 1870, was issued at the end of April at a price of twelve shillings. On 3 May Rossetti wrote to his friend and mentor Ford Madox Brown to announce that F. S. Ellis, his publisher, had "sold out my first [edition of] 1000 [copies] all but 200, and is going to press again at once; so the two editions . . . will bring me £300 in a few weeks—not so bad for poetry after all, even if the public find themselves glutted after the second thousand" (Rossetti, letter no. 1009). They did not: "By the first of June, *Poems* had entered its third edition of five hundred copies each; in September its fourth, to be followed by a fifth and sixth before the end of the year" (Doughty, 450).

One measure of the success of Rossetti's work as cultural intervention is the bitterness of negative responses to it. The most famous of these is, of course, Robert Buchanan's article, "The Fleshly School of Poetry," first published pseudonymously in the *Contemporary Review* for October 1871 and republished as a much expanded pamphlet the following year. That this review, unlike the angry attacks upon Swinburne's *Poems and Ballads* of 1866, which appeared in the press immediately, required well over a year's deliberation suggests how strong an ideological challenge Rossetti's "fleshly" aestheticism represented to dominant social, moral, and literary values of the day. As Rossetti's biographer, Oswald Doughty, insists,

(486)
> In describing the poetry of Rossetti as "fleshly," [Buchanan] had maliciously seized upon a word calculated to rouse all the prejudice and irrational emotion which the violation of a dominant taboo . . . inevitably excites. "Fleshly," for the mid-Victorian had all the mystic power of a word that embodies a contemporary complex, a word energized by all the repressions of the taboo . . . upon any unnecessary exposure of the body in actuality, and upon its counterpart in the world of art; the ban upon realism, upon nudity, upon passion.

That Buchanan indicts Rossetti as the leader of a school of writers whose work is already insidiously invading the sacred precinct of the Victorian parlor and corrupting its angelic inhabitants suggests the cultural power the poet had rapidly achieved. "A strange phenomenon," Buchanan claims, "has converted [London] into a Sodom or a Gomorrah. [Sensualism] lies on the drawing room table, shamelessly naked and dangerously fair. It is part of the pretty poem which the belle of the season reads, and it breathes away the pureness of her soul" (349). Thus, very soon after its publication Rossetti's work was already seen to have grounded itself "in the living sensibilities" and "invisible depths" of the social subject (Eagleton, *Aesthetic*, 27).

If Rossetti's poetry aestheticizes medievalist discourse, Swinburne's, by contrast, manipulates it iconoclastically, both to counter what he perceived as false idealizations of the Middle Ages and to attack the "respectable"—that is, Christian, politically conservative, and materialist—values he saw as dominant in Victorian society. Typically in Swinburne's poetry, relations between faith and love break down. In familiar works from his *Poems and Ballads, First Series* (1866) that privilege medieval contexts or motifs, such as "The Triumph of Time," "Hymn to Proserpine," "Laus Veneris," and "The Leper," an elegiac faith in the supreme power and value of erotic love in human lives supplants all varieties of traditional Christian religious faith, whose hostility to eros Swinburne consistently reviles. In many of these poems (which I have discussed at length elsewhere)[7] the only indications that devotees of eros live in a world dominated by Christianity are profane and even sexually suggestive uses of God's or the Virgin Mary's name.

"In the Orchard," for example, imitates the Provençal alba or aubade, a medieval lyric form in which two illicit lovers lament the approach of dawn and their imminent parting. But the poem is also a dramatic monologue, a form comfortingly familiar to Victorian audiences by 1866. Swinburne's strategy of formal hybridization is deceptive, however; the poem employs both the form and the topos to ideologically oppositional ends, extolling the power of erotic love as a challenge to love of God while appropriating and transvaluing the imagery of Romantic naturalism in the service of that exaltation. The poem further compels Victorian readers viscerally to confront the power of sexuality in human lives, and it does so both explicitly and through the use of puns. All this is accomplished in the space of fifty lines.

The poem's initial strategy is to overturn traditional gender roles: the entire lyric is spoken by a woman who commands her "fair lord" to "take . . . my flower, my first in June, / My rose, so like a tender mouth." In her refrain this woman—clearly a medieval chatelaine, rather than a Victorian Angel in the House—not only invokes God's name blasphemously but also suggests a belief that God is a force opposed to her passion, like the implacable dawn: "Ah God, ah God, that day should be so soon." Otherwise in the work the operations of nature are analogous to the operations of human passion, and its elements appear to exist solely to serve lovers' needs:

(Swinburne, *Poems*, 1 : 102)

The grass is thick and cool, it lets us lie.
Kissed upon either cheek and either eye,
    I turn to thee as some green afternoon
Turns toward sunset, and is loth to die.

At the heart of the poem, and at its structural center, is an apotheosis of erotic love's inescapable power: passion is ultimately insatiable and can be quelled only in death. "Ah," the speaker sighs,

(1 : 103)

. . . my heart fails, my blood draws back; I know,
When life runs over, life is near to go;
    And with the slain of love love's ways are strewn,
And with their blood, if love will have it so.

"Do thy will now; slay me if thou wilt," she concludes, but not without a punningly explicit thrust at a prudish audience, designed to raise their sexual consciousness: "Yea, with thy sweet lips, with thy sweet sword; yea, / Take life and all, for I will die, I say." Despite such playfulness, the poem's framework of values is clear and serious: "Love, I gave love, is life a better boon?" the chatelaine rhetorically asks.

    Swinburne's use of medievalist discourse is usually more complex, more scholarly, and more sophisticated than that of his contemporaries. In addition to writing many medievalist lyrics and composing two long medievalist narratives in the epic tradition (*Tristram of Lyonesse* and *The Tale of Balen*), Swinburne produced ideologically skewed translations of works by the single medieval poet he acclaims the equal of Sappho and the preeminent balladist of the period, François Villon.[8] In these translations, as well as in his elegiac celebration of Villon's genius in "The Ballad of François Villon" (1878), common mid-Victorian uses of medievalist discourse are turned against themselves, everywhere undercutting the moral values and ideological expectations of his audience. Just as in the infamous "Dolores" he parodies the Victorian revival of medieval hymns (in translations and editions generated by High Anglican churchmen such as R. W. Trench, J. M. Neale, and Richard Chenevix), so in his canonization of Villon, Swinburne affronts respectable bourgeois values and sensibilities that Victorian medievalist discourse most often served to reaffirm.[9]

In 1863 Swinburne began an essay on Villon that he never finished. Like so much of his private and published writing designed to undermine conventional middle-class values, the commentary is simultaneously serious and self-parodic in tone. But from these five manuscript pages, as from his "Villoneries," it is clear that Swinburne's exaltation of this poet's "beautiful life" as an "unfledged gallows-nightingale" is sincere (Swinburne, *New Writings*, 185–86). He begins the essay sarcastically, as a general commentary on "gallows-birds" of "various kinds and classes," but immediately turns his attention to Villon as preeminent among members of this tribe of anti-idealist, humanitarian poets. Villon's work demonstrates that "his sponsors were Priapus and Laverna" and that "he was dipped in the font of Venus Cloacina." He thence "emerged in full bud of promise, and broke into full blossom of performance, a thief, pimp, and poet of incomparable excellence" (185). In every sensationalized detail of his biography and poetry—equally relished by Swinburne—Villon embodies the antithesis of widespread Victorian human and poetic ideals. His avoidance of the destined gallows is, for Swinburne, both miraculous and an ironic manifestation of divine justice:

> *Over every page in the metrical biography of François Villon, poet, pimp, and pickpurse, the extended arm of his native gibbet casts the significant shadow of its fond beckoning hand. In the simultaneous exercise of these three fine arts, relieved by an occasional murder, gilded by many loves and embroidered with many excesses in the* (184) *way of furtive meat and dishonest drink, he stole and sang his melodious and infamous way through life. . . . Again and once again and yet again did the laureate of all the villainies alive break the faith plighted at his birth to the gibbet.*

Swinburne acknowledges but disclaims "the hideous rumour that Villon died decently," an inappropriate end indeed for this great singer who took "his degree in klepto-dipso-porno-poetics" and who ultimately must be canonized not only for his ballads and lyrics but also for "the freshness and freedom of his repentances . . . clear of all hypocrisy or whimpering—his tenderness and kindness and gratitude" and "his faith and goodwill to his friends" (186). Swinburne's portrait of Villon constitutes a radical extreme among "irruptions" to be discerned in Victorian medievalist discourse. And although it remained unpublished during his lifetime, its rhetorical design and ideological strategies are clearly parallel to those that operate in the medievalist poems of 1866 that so shocked the reading public.

As with Rossetti's work, the success of Swinburne's appropriations of medievalist and amatory discourse is evident in the reactions elicited by his poems of 1866. The reception history of *Poems and Ballads* is well known: reviewers widely condemned the book as "unclean for the sake of uncleanness," "depressing and misbegotten," "utterly revolting," and "publicly obscene" (Hyder, xix–xx). Mudie's Library withdrew it from circulation, and Edward Moxon, the volume's publisher, decided to do the same. (After some difficulties, Swinburne was able to transfer the imprint to the less reputable firm of John Camden Hotten.) Unlike Rossetti's poems of 1870, Swinburne's were reviled or admired less for their unfamiliar (i.e., aestheticist) manipulations of familiar discourses than for their blatant assault upon the dominant religious and amatory ideologies of mid-Victorian England. One reviewer's castigation of the work as "a mere deification of incontinence" (Hyder, xix) is telling in this respect. Yet, as cultural intervention the poems failed because of their extremism. Swinburne's work of this period stands in perfect opposition to what Hans Robert Jauss designates as undemanding literature, popular because audiences exposed to it experience no "horizontal change": it speaks to familiar values and expectations. Nor was Swinburne's poetry gradually assimilated into the culture, as was that of Rossetti, whose readers at first experienced in it an "alienating new perspective" that disappeared for later readers "to the extent that the original negativity of the work" became "self-evident" and "itself entered into the horizon of future aesthetic experience, as a henceforth familiar expectation" (Jauss, 25). The radicalism of Swinburne's attacks upon widely accepted concepts of and attitudes toward love and religion ultimately prevented its "original negativity" from dissipating. Still, like Arnold's and Rossetti's poems, Swinburne's often deployed Victorian medievalist discourse to definable ends. Whereas in Arnold's poetry medieval allusions and settings enabled defiant self-assertion in a chaotic and meaningless world, and Rossetti's poems exploited medievalist props to draw attention to the power and beauty of artistic surfaces, Swinburne's appropriated medieval literary genres and settings to extol erotic love—rather than a repressive Christian God—as the ultimate power in the human world.

Analysis of Victorian medievalist poems, whether by Tennyson, Morris, Arnold, Rossetti, or Swinburne, supports Foucault's claim that a text "constructs itself only on the basis of a complex field of discourse." That is, "the frontiers of a book are never clear-cut: beyond the title, the first lines, and the last full stop, beyond its internal configuration and its autonomous form, it is caught up in a system of references . . . it is a node within a network" (23). Like so many of his contemporaries, from Gerard Genette to Julia Kristeva, Foucault understood how the intertextual operations of discursive formations—such as Victorian medievalism—serve to communicate subtle ideological positions. Such discourses are often employed in ways that influence or alter the field of social relations in which ideologies invariably compete for dominance. On the battlefield of Victorian poetry conservative and elitist values—Christian, materialist, and imperialist like those of the laureate—were often under siege by emergent systems of belief. These might be aestheticist, intellectual, egalitarian, or amatory. With this scenario in mind, we may now begin more fully to understand, for example, how the poetry of Morris, Arnold, Rossetti, and Swinburne marshaled medievalist discourse in the immediate service of cultural criticism.

The chapters that follow further demonstrate how the work of particular Victorian poets—Alfred Tennyson, Elizabeth Barrett, Matthew Arnold, and Christina Rossetti—appropriated for ideological purposes various cultural mythologies and discursive formations. In the process significant cultural power accrued to their authors; that accomplishment is demonstrated not only in the reception and influence of their works in literary circles but more subtly in their success at generating new "forms of inwardness" whose assimilation by readers eventually enabled altered or alternate cultural values to emerge in Victorian England.

II

Merlin and Tennyson: Poetry of Power and Victorian Self-Fashioning

The Age of Tennyson

A slow-developed strength awaits
Completion in a painful school;
Phantoms of other forms of rule,
New Majesties of mighty States—

The warders of the growing hour,
But vague in vapour, hard to mark;
And round them sea and air are dark
With great contrivances of Power.
"Love thou thy land, with love far-brought" (1833–34)

Popularity is not what I am particularly anxious for.
Alfred Tennyson to Edward Moxon, 20 November 1832

FROM HIS EARLY DAYS AS A POET trying with little success to establish his work in the literary marketplace, Alfred Tennyson understood that a writer's popularity might have little to do with his attainment of enduring influence, given the flux of politics and the tempest of cultural developments across Europe during his uncertain era. An eccentric and reclusive giant whose life was by some measures uneventful, Tennyson was nonetheless deeply interested in the host of issues surrounding "contrivances of power," that is, the attainment of all varieties of social, political, and cultural power (Ricks, 79). In one view these constitute the obsessive themes of his poetry. In another his work itself, including his career as a poet, which from its earliest stages fashioned itself as a Romantic narra-

tive, operates to appropriate varieties of power "diffused in [the] ideological structures of meaning" at work in his culture (Tucker; Greenblatt,
Self-Fashioning, 6).

Throughout his career Tennyson navigated controversial waters and
explored unsettled territories marked by ideological tensions, conflicts,
and struggles—between social classes, between nations, between men
and women, rulers and their subjects, artists and society, beauty and truth,
old ideas and new orders of inquiry. In the course of his odyssey his bear-
ings sometimes shifted according to the social, philosophical, religious, or
political concerns of his work and the genres in which he chose to inscribe them. One thing is certain, however. From his earliest to his latest
verses Tennyson manipulated a variety of cultural discourses in order to
fashion not only poems but also a poetic self, sometimes with seductive
explosions of beauty, often with ringing declamations of prophetic authority, but most characteristically with bursts of strategic ambivalence.[1]

In 1837 Tennyson, like his contemporary Elizabeth Barrett and
many less well known figures, celebrated in verse the accession of a new
queen to the throne, and he surely did so without any prophetic inkling
that he would, in the future, write again and again to the queen. By the
time of his death no previous English laureate had established such a relationship with such a monarch, and Tennyson's public representations of
that relationship over the course of his career help us begin to understand
the discursive strategies and ideological effects of various attempts at cultural intervention fashioned in his work for a new kind of reading public
in the first truly industrial age. In 1892 Victoria declared Tennyson's
death "a great national loss." Her admiration exposes how culturally and
ideologically embedded his work had by then become: "*his ideas,*" she
confessed in her diary, "were ever grand, noble, elevating." She extended
these comments in a letter to Gladstone (one of Tennyson's several politically eminent friends): "a Tennyson we may not see again for a century,
or—*in all his originality*—ever again" (Charles Tennyson, 211, my emphasis). By this time Victoria had appropriated his "ideas" (and accepted
the cloak of originality in which they were garbed), just as Tennyson, in
his self-appointed role as poet-prophet and literary mage, had appropriated her sovereignty. Their relationship constitutes a remarkable example
of cultural symbiosis, poet and monarch alike accruing enhanced symbolic capital from it.

From 1837 to 1892 Tennyson's growing dedication to Queen Victoria and the aristocratic milieu over which she presided bears directly upon the process of poetic self-creation that enabled a poet's unprecedented attainment of cultural power in an era subsequently often called "the age of Tennyson." In recent years even Sir Charles Tennyson has acknowledged that "Tennyson owed his success as Laureate to the circumstances of the time and the character of the Sovereign no less than to his own character and abilities" (204). Indeed, although the queen was unaware of the fact, their relationship began with her coronation.

Although by 1837 Tennyson had published three volumes of poetry, he could claim only a tiny coterie following, had made no money from his work, and was struggling with reviewers. When he dashed off "The Queen of the Isles" in June, he was eager for public recognition: he sent the poem to his close friend James Spedding, asking that it be forwarded to the *Times* "or some paper with a circulation" (*Poems*, 2:95). In many respects a formulaic toasting song ("A health to the Queen of the Isles"), the poem nevertheless establishes political ideals and generates discursive strategies enabling the assumption of cultural power that Tennyson refines upon in his subsequent works of importance dedicated to the queen or to Prince Albert (including the "Dedication" to *Idylls of the King* and its epilogue, "To the Queen").

A striking feature of the political discourse deployed in "Queen of the Isles" is its combination of populist nationalism and intellectual elitism. These ideals remain in tension throughout Tennyson's later sociopolitical poetry (a very large segment of his work), which, as we shall see, is normally marked by abstract and ambivalent prophetic utterances (Sinfield, *Tennyson*, 154–85). In "The Queen of the Isles" they emerge in the third stanza when, designedly or not, the speaker positions himself as an insider, one stationed to advise the queen. Quickly refocusing attention from the "reigns of her fathers," Tennyson looks to "those of [the queen's] council that have the chief voice" (Tennyson, *Poems*, 2:95), hoping they will "Be true hearts of oak," presumably like the hearty toastmaster of this poem. This speaker is politic. He echoes the *Westminster Review*'s counsel to eighteen-year-old Victoria that she "take the advice of [her] ministers . . . allowing her youthful will and judgment to make their influence on public affairs as little perceptible as possible" (Stein, 62). But he is also canny.

Through a sleight of rhetoric in the next stanza the speaker fully identifies with "those of her council" and thus authorizes his own (present and future) bold and forthright speech, a mode of political discourse that he associates (positively) with the patriarchy and with constitutional democracy:

> No slaves of a party, straightforward and clear,   (Tennyson,
> Let them speak out like men without bias or fear   *Poems,*
> That the voice of her people may reach to her ear.   2:96)

By the eighth stanza, however, the poet-speaker has risen above the historical moment and adopted the voice of prophecy, familiar from popular religious discourse, to herald the secular millennium—"a thousand years hence"—when people will look back on an age

> . . . so fruitful in genius, in worth and in sense
> That a man's eye shall glisten . . .   (2:96)
> When he reads of the Queen of the Isles!

That is, when he reads Tennyson, a fruitful genius indeed, who has begun, with this simple song that intervenes directly in contemporary political discourse, to fashion himself as an insider/outsider, poet of genius and prophet, demagogue and democrat, who is destined to "keep a sound in [the queen's] ear like the sound of the deep" (2:95).

Tennyson's claims of sovereignty over the sovereign are blatant in stanzas he suppressed in the dedicatory poem to Victoria from his first volume as laureate, *Poems,* 7th ed., 1851. There, like a Romantic working in the tradition of secular apocalypse familiar from the early Wordsworth (the "Prospectus" to *The Recluse*) and from Shelley ("The Masque of Anarchy," "Ode to the West Wind," etc.), he describes poets—"that often seem / So wretched"—as "a kind of kings." Nor, he insists, "is their empire all a dream" (Tennyson, *Poems,* 3:599). Not only do "Their words fly over land and main," but "Their voices heard hereafter add / A glory to a glorious reign." (Appropriately, as Wordsworth's heir, Tennyson echoes his Intimations ode: "Where is it now, the glory and the dream?") The poet's power in the hereafter, that is, the social as well as the spiritual future, extends but also exceeds the monarch's, whose immortality depends upon the poet's work:

(3:600)

> Not less the king in time to come
> Will seem the greater under whom
> The sacred poets have prevailed.

This is unequivocally the language of conquest spoken by a "kingly poet," whose self-suppression in revising this work for publication served merely to confirm and assure the power he was still, in 1851, hesitant to acknowledge publicly. By the time of his death that power was widely accepted (despite his disparagers) beyond royal circles, and it took a variety of visible forms, including his enormous popularity, the acquisition of a baronetcy and very great wealth, and a level of critical acclaim hardly known by previous English poets during their lifetimes.[2]

The eulogies in 1892 are easily forgotten and bear rehearsing, at least briefly. The *Pall Mall Gazette* (6 October) proclaimed Tennyson "the greatest of England's poets." The *Academy* (15 October) goes further: Tennyson is "the greatest poetic artist of the English speaking race." One notice accurately described him as "a popular hero . . . one of our recognized glories, hardly less than if he had been a politician or a soldier" (Baum, 7). The *Open Court* (17 November) acknowledged Tennyson's attainment of sovereign and imperial status: "He was borne to his grave with more homage than any King could hope for, from all classes and all parties." Two other descriptions suggest the sources of Tennyson's extraordinary cultural influence: the mysterious aura surrounding the prophetic persona fashioned in his poetry and his appropriation of the dominant middle-class discourses in which ideals of the English gentleman and of chivalry were inscribed. In the *New Review* (November 1892) Edmund Gosse properly insisted that "Tennyson had grown to be by far the most mysterious, august, and singular figure in English society. He represented poetry." Ten years later, in the Poetry and Life series, Brimley Johnson reminded readers of an obvious but highly significant sociohistorical fact about Tennyson's poetry of power: it "is permeated with idealism of the English gentleman, the Victorian Knight-errant," a fact that Tennyson himself had drawn attention to in the "Dedication" of his masterwork, *Idylls of the King*. Johnson's conclusion recalls Victoria's own sense of her laureate's embeddedness as both mirror and shaping ideological power in his culture: "He lives as a complete, consistent force: with a meaning and value for all time. He sings the messsage of Victorianism" (Baum, 23).

This chapter explores how Tennyson's poetry deployed particular Victorian discursive formations in ways that allowed his work not merely to intervene in the culture of his era but, as Victoria's remarks on the occasion of his death indicate, to create the illusion of engineering the construction of that culture. Because the historical particulars in which Tennyson's poetry is grounded have been so effectively discussed by others (Armstrong, Sinfield, McGann, and Ricks), my analysis here focuses largely on the operations of discourse and ideology in his work.

Victorian Self-Fashioning

I sit . . .
Half fearful that, with self at strife,
I take myself to task;
Lest of the fulness of my life
I leave an empty flask:
For I had hope, by something rare,
To prove myself a poet.

"Will Waterproof's Monologue" (ca. 1837)

Tennyson achieved great fame in part because his poetry successfully negotiated a number of conflicting Victorian discourses: historicist and transcendentalist; populist and elitist; nationalist and imperialist; positivist and spiritualist; feminist and antifeminist. Like his close friend Carlyle, his speakers repeatedly rail against Midas-eared mammonism or antiwar and antinationalist sentiment, as is the case in "Locksley Hall" and *Maud.* *In Memoriam* adapts new scientific developments and Hegelian modes of historical inquiry to (Broad Church) theology. *The Princess* treats issues surrounding "the woman question," but with typical ambivalence. *Idylls of the King* and later lyrics adopt vaguely allegorical formal strategies to extend Tennyson's explorations of these and a host of other ideologically controversial topics being debated in mid-Victorian England.

Yet Tennyson's poetry appears, at least in the eyes of Victorian readers, to have succeeded best at ideological negotiation when its speakers adopt the metapolitical stance of the sage prophet, presenting its author as the Merlin of Victorian England and deploying abstract and idealized poetic discourse to inscribe a predominantly cosmic—rather than particularized—historical awareness. His epic masterpiece, *Idylls of the King* employs such a narrative stance as it interweaves spiritual, social, and sexual issues with rare complexity (as we shall see). The apparent conflict in Tennyson's work throughout his career between gestures of specific sociohistorical commentary on the one hand and visionary activity on the other reflects two impulses fundamental to his writing, the one frequently presented as petty when the other is perceived as sublime. The speaker adopts the prophetic role in his late poem "Vastness" (1885), for instance, where topical issues that often dominate other poems by Tennyson are derided as trivial:

Raving politics, never at rest—as this poor
    earth's pale history runs,—
What is it all but a trouble of ants in the gleam
    of a million million of suns?

(*Poems*,
3 : 134)

By contrast, in familiar passages from *Maud*, the Locksley Hall poems, "The Charge of the Light Brigade," and dozens of less well known works (especially those of 1832–34) Tennyson participated enthusiastically, albeit often with deliberate equivocation, in the "raving" political debates of his era. His poems engaged the political discourse of the day by entering into the controversies surrounding the first Reform Bill just as eagerly as he later denounced—in a Carlylian, apocalyptic voice—the demise of conservative social and political values.

    In a lyric from the early thirties unpublished during his lifetime, for example, Tennyson's speaker presents himself as a libertarian, but in typically metaphorical or abstract and highly generalized language. Speaking "before the storm" of a feared revolution, he claims to be above politics—"Wed to no faction in the state"—and to love "Freedom for herself, / And much of that which is her form," that is, to love the threatened institutions of British government. Typically, however, Tennyson's poems are reluctant to endorse an ideal of wholly democratic government. Beyond the fray but disturbed by the possibilities of political upheaval, they proclaim an organicist concept of a free state that is self-fulfilling and thus independent of human action:

The state within herself concludes
The power to change, as in the seed,
    The model of her future form,
And liberty indeed.

(2 : 44)

Some fifty years later, after passage of the third Reform Bill, Tennyson's speaker in "Locksley Hall Sixty Years After" decries Demos, "working its own doom, / . . . Freedom, free to slay herself, and dying while [the people] shout her name" (3 : 153 – 54). As in these works, in most of Tennyson's later political poems he remains strategically ambivalent, speaking in abstractions characteristic of Victorian sage discourse. "Politics," one of three poems addressed to Gladstone in the 1880s (the other two are "Compromise" and "Captain, Guide"), illustrates the point:

> We move, the wheel must always move,
>   Nor always on the plain,
> And if we move to such a goal
>   As Wisdom hopes to gain,
> Then you that drive, and know your Craft,
>   Will firmly hold the rein,   (3 : 131)
> Nor lend an ear to random cries,
>   Or you may drive in vain,
> For some cry "Quick" and some cry "Slow,"
>   But, while the hills remain,
> Up hill "Too-slow" will need the whip,
>   Down hill "Too-quick," the chain.

This poem appears to present a politics of moderation, formally reflected in the straightforwardness of alternating iambic tetrameter and trimeter lines and in the use of a simple rhyme scheme. But the poem's voice can be seen to accrue special authority and to betray a deeply conservative bias by focusing its counsel in the metaphor of a pseudomythic journey guided by "Wisdom" to a transcendent goal and by employing topo-graphical images familiar especially from traditional religious discourse. Moreover, in the age of steam, using the antiquated image of travel by horse-drawn coach is particularly telling. The hyper self-conscious, sage voice in such overtly political poems from the second half of Tennyson's career appears portentously evasive, establishing no precise "political" principles or direction. Although that voice appears to assume an elite class that "drives" the craft of state along and exhorts it to ignore advice from without, these works ultimately are fashioned as prophetic and mysterious voices of "the deep."

The apparent stance and purpose of Tennyson's designedly metapolitical poetry produced over the course of his career qualify Hallam Tennyson's simplistic statement in the *Memoir* that his father "took a lively interest in politics." The poems do something other, and in fact a good deal more, than formulate the particular political views Hallam attributes to his father when he explains that Tennyson was "among the young supporters of the Anti-slavery Convention, and advocated the Measure for abolishing subscription to the Thirty-nine Articles, while admiring as statesmen Canning, Peel, and the Duke of Wellington" (Tennyson, *Memoir*, 1:41). More accurate precisely because of its vagueness is Tennyson's own statement of his politics (attributed to him by his son): "I am of the same politics as Shakespeare, Bacon, and every sane man" (1:42). This assertion conforms to the strategies of mystification central to Tennyson's sage poetry. It also responds to the new and often internally contradictory middle-class ideologies of postindustrial England (Christianity and capitalism, for instance) and helps us to understand the tensions among various ostensibly conflicting self-presentations in Tennyson's work that can be considered broadly political. The explanation of Tennyson's remarkably successful process of self-fashioning as a sage poet who attained enormous popularity, prestige, and cultural power is to be sought in the fact that his speakers are both insiders and outsiders, populists and elitists, politicos and prophets, jingoists and stately poets.[3]

My emerging argument here is that by means of the multiple voices of his poetry, including that of the mage often projected as his metapoetic self, Tennyson's art intervenes in the cultural politics of his era more effectively than has been admitted even by the two strongest recent commentators on his work's political energies: Alan Sinfield and Isobel Armstrong. Both critics simultaneously address and circumvent the crucial problematic of "intentionality" that inevitably arises in such discussions, Sinfield by viewing Tennyson's poems largely as products of and responses to cultural and pathological forces that constructed him as a social subject and that were often beyond his control, Armstrong by insisting (in the tradition of deconstructive approaches to Tennyson) on a very high degree of autonomy for Tennyson's texts.

Armstrong acknowledges the importance but also astutely diagnoses the limitations of Sinfield's Marxist approach to Tennyson; she argues that for Sinfield, who reads him as a cultural materialist and a fundamentally conservative poet, "Tennyson's aesthetic solutions to political problems were either timid or straightforwardly reactionary. The poet's evasiveness

leads to a perpetual emptying out of signification in which language re-
sorts to a fetishistic preoccupation with its own surfaces" (*Poetry*, 9).
Armstrong sees two difficulties with Sinfield's commentary: that he must
"eliminate the possibility of ambiguity in poetic language" and that
"Tennyson's 'real' interests as a sympathizer with the landed gentry and
as a supporter of nationalism and imperialistic interests must give a poem
a particular historical meaning even when it appears to be struggling
against it" (9). Armstrong's critique of Sinfield is suggestive: he does not
attempt to confront the multivocality and ideological multivalence, that
is, the interactive qualities (or what Armstrong designates as Bahktinian
dialogism) typical of many poems by Tennyson, both those that are frequent subjects of critical discussion and those (like "The Queen of the
Isles") that commentators ignore.

Armstrong's own sophisticated project takes fuller account of formal, linguistic, deconstructive, *and* ideological elements deployed "inten-
tionally" but also operating autonomously in Tennyson's poems: "The
problem of deciding what is 'really' a poet's interest politically or what is
'really' intentional as against unconscious can be circumvented by a more
generous understanding of the text as struggle . . . struggle with a chang-
ing project, struggle with the play of ambiguity and contradiction. This
is a way of reading which gives equal weight to a text's stated project and
the polysemic and possibly wayward meanings it generates." Thus, "to
see the text as a complex entity defining and participating in an area of
struggle and contention is to make intentionality a much wider and more
complex affair and to include the contradictions and uncontrolled nature
of language within the text's project. For the escape of language from
univocal order becomes one of the text's areas of contention" (10).

I would argue further that the multivocality and the ludic energies
of Tennyson's verse, including various forms of ideological "play," such
as parody, self-parody, linguistic ambiguity, and irony, are essential components of his ongoing project of self-fashioning, which most insistently
reveals itself *as a project* (a course deliberately attempted) in his political
and metapolitical poems. These frequently indeterminate texts, whose
ideological effects could not have been predicted with certainty by their
author, adopt a variety of Victorian sage discourse that positions him
at once within a profound but historically localized tradition (that of
Carlyle, Ruskin, and George Eliot, for instance) and within a far more
expansive Christian prophetic tradition whose cosmic resonances help

authorize the mysterious identity of the sage poet and generate his cultural power.

Since occasions arise throughout this and later chapters to employ the concept of sage discourse, it will be useful here briefly to explain at the theoretical level the operations of a rhetorical genre with which all students of the Victorian period are familiar at the level of practice. Thaïs Morgan has laid the groundwork for such an explanation:

> *Victorian sage writing is "discourse" in the sense of being a dialogue*
> *between a speaker—the sage—and a contemporaneous audience whose*
> *expectations about and reactions to the sage's words constitute what*
> *Mikhail Bahktin has called "the verbal-ideological world." As "a social*
> *phenomenon," sage discourse of any genre is constantly "dialogized" by*
> *the "multiplicity of social voices" and ideological interests that comprise*
> (Morgan, 3) *Victorian culture. Although engaged in a dialectical process of persua-*
> *sion, rebuttal, and promising, the sage always aims to establish her or*
> *his worldview as the right, true, and authoritative one. From a Bahktin-*
> *ian perspective, then, Victorian sage writing, characterized by a mixture*
> *of genres, epitomizes the way in which "heteroglossia"—or competing*
> *affectional voices and ideological interests—enters written language,*
> *where differences are entertained but never completely resolved.*

Sage discourse was, of course, itself the product of historical and ideological forces, unimaginable as a successful rhetorical strategy, for instance, early in the eighteenth century. A historically fortuitous coincidence of claims made and accepted for literature by Romantic writers with intellectual, psychological, and emotional insecurities spawned in Victorian readers by the first industrial age, however, had opened up a social space for this discourse by the 1830s, when it began to proliferate. But precisely because it was recognized as a vehicle of ideology, sage discourse was decidedly more contestatory in Victorian England than, say, the discourses of romantic love or motherhood or even medievalism, all of which appeared to retain relative stability over long periods of time in popular usage despite their sometimes radical manipulation by some writers. Sage discourse was thus an unusually "dynamic and heterogeneous kind of discourse" (2). That is to say, the "irruptions" to which it was susceptible from its employment in the service of various social and political ideologies and from its operations in a variety of genres caused it to be perpetually reconstituted while nonetheless remaining recognizable as a discursive formation. It was also a uniquely appropriable and self-fulfilling mode of discourse: one measure of triumph in manipulating sage discourse was simply the recognition of an author's prophetic or visionary status by the reading public.

In 1889 Frederick Meyers, attempting to sum up Tennyson's accomplishment during his lifetime, insisted that the laureate be viewed as "a *prophet*, meaning by that term much more than a self-inspired mystic, an eloquent visionary." He is one, according to Meyers, who speaks "to us of those greatest, those undiscoverable things which can never be wholly known but must still less be wholly ignored or forgotten . . . a sage whose wisdom is kindled with emotion, and whose message comes to us with the authority of a great personality, winged at once and weighted by words of power" (Jump, 396). Meyers's commentary demonstrates how Tennyson had by the end of his career fashioned a body of poetry that struck satisfied readers as the fulfillment of a biblical paradigm, as well as a bardic ideal derived largely from Romanticism, but one that could, unlike much ideologically marginal or subversive Romantic poetry, be wholly embraced by the propertied as well as the aspiring middle and upper classes. If, especially in the modern age, the bourgeois self is fashioned at the intersection between the individual will and the cultural pressures everywhere exerted by an ideological superstructure (heterogeneous as its constituent discourses might be), then Tennyson can be seen as a model of success in negotiating the two, so as at once to enhance the Romantic cult of individualism and to achieve the outer limits of cultural power available to artists or intellectuals within their own lifetimes. He may be understood, in short, as a master of self-commodification whose poetry effectively engaged emergent structures of feeling in Victorian society through the appropriations of sage discourse.

Allegories of Power

> . . . *men, in power*
> *Only, are likest Gods, who have attained*
> *Rest in a happy place and quiet seats*
> *Above the thunder, with undying bliss*
> *In knowledge of their own supremacy.*
>
> "Oenone" (1842)

Especially among the high Victorians sage discourse was most effective when deployed in the ambiguous linguistic space we call allegory. That *Idylls of the King*, the capstone of Tennyson's prophetic poetry, operates in this space is apparent from his response to contemporary commentators' interpretations of the work: "They have taken my hobby, and ridden it too hard, and have explained some things too allegorically, although there is an allegorical or perhaps rather a parabolic drift in the poem" (*Memoir*, 2:126–27). As these remarks suggest, the much discussed typological habits of the Victorian mind enabled success in discursive arenas—from sermons to scientific inquires to work in painting and poetry—that elicited hermeneutic approaches like those demanded by allegory, where images and characters are normally seen to have historically local and topical referents along with universal and metaphysical ones.[4] As W. D. Shaw has shown, however, in some very important ways Victorian uses of the allegorical tended to differ from those of medieval writers the Victorians so admired. For Keble, Ruskin, and Pater (exemplary Victorians in this regard), Shaw asserts, "the mystery of life and its arts does not allow the poet to fix or assign one meaning only to each visible type of the spiritual world." In fact true allegorical symbols (at least according to Ruskin) are untranslatable. They "lack an assigned connotation" and "imply far more than they say." In fact they are ciphers that primarily assert their creators' sense of authority to signify that which cannot be delimited in language. Ambiguity is thus symptomatic of this mode of discourse, and ultimately "the symbols of a great visionary poet are unconsummated" (Shaw, *Veil*, 176). For writers (such as Ruskin) who defined Victorian concepts and uses of allegory, its value as a signifying practice lay not in tracing imaginatively suggestive correlations between symbol and ideological referent but in bodying forth "with remarkable precision experiences that are generally thought to be indefinite, ungraspable, and therefore unsayable" (177).[5] That is, concrete imagery is used not to point to particular beliefs, values, morals, or dogmas but to distill mystery in such a way, ultimately, as to enhance its power rather than diminish it. Victorian allegory is often, in Walter Benjamin's phrase, "empty-handed" allegory. It is thus a distinctive variety of discursive activity that can even include, at its most teasingly self-parodic, the impulse to subvert allegory. As Shaw remarks, "Ruskin's theory"—widely accepted in Victorian high culture—"is less applicable to a genuine allegory like *The Faerie Queene* than to a curiously

indeterminate poem like *Idylls of the King*" (177). In such allegories tele-
ology and the logos remain always veiled; only the sage poet has access
to either *and* to the final "meaning" of his own aesthetic efforts that
point in the direction of the logos. In Carlyle's phrasing, the poet has
"penetrated . . . into the sacred mystery of the Universe; what Goethe
calls 'the open secret.' . . . that divine mystery, which lies everywhere in
all Beings, 'the Divine Idea of the World, that which lies at the bottom
of Appearance'" but which in fact is not accessible to "all Beings"
(Carlyle, 80).

That Tennyson from his earliest works embraced this idealized Romantic, specifically Shelleyan view of the poet is by now a critical commonplace and is illustrated in early lyrics such as "The Poet's Mind"
(1830):[6]

> Vex not thou the poet's mind
> With thy shallow wit: (*Poems*,
> Vex not thou the poet's mind;   1:245)
> For thou canst not fathom it.

This poem appears to resolve the anxious equivocations informing works
of the same period that treat matters of artistic vocation, poems such as
"The Palace of Art" and "The Lady of Shalott": readers of poetry are
instructed to embrace the indeterminate as a fundamental source of textual pleasure.

Tennyson's adaptation of Shelleyan allegorical practices in his early
years (which he developed with increasing sophistication in later works)
is apparent from metapolitical poems written during that period. Eventually titled "Freedom of Old" in 1865, the following verses, for example,
were originally composed about 1833:

> Of old sat Freedom on the heights,
> The thunders breaking at her feet:
> Above her shook the starry lights:
> She heard the torrents meet.
>
> · · · · ·   (2:42)
>
> Then stept she down through town and field
> To mingle with the human race,
>
> And part by part to men revealed
> The fullness of her face.

Here, as in "Politics," Tennyson suggests the people's need for external guidance in political matters, their incapacity to discover freedom within themselves. The poet participates in the continuing process of its revelation as a privileged and mysterious being, employing a highly simplistic allegorical device embedded in prosodically simple verses to evince his participation.

The layered and equivocal allegoricity of many passages in Tennyson's later poetry, by contrast, generates both mesmeric power and intellectual complexity. (Such use of allegory features prominently in the most sophisticated examples of Victorian sage discourse, from Carlyle's *Past and Present* to Christina Rossetti's "Goblin Market.") The authority of the "indeterminate" allegory in *Idylls of the King*, for instance, must either be acceded to or condemned as authorial contrivance, that is, failed parable. But the latter reaction confesses the reader's insusceptibility to narrative magic (a positivist refusal to suspend disbelief) as well as his ideological marginality (if we accept the assertion that the *Idylls* embodies, among other matter, unsystematized elements of particular Victorian discursive formations that supported dominant ideologies, including antifeminism, imperialism, hero worship, the idealization of chivalry, medievalism, and, of course, Christianity). That Tennyson's impulse to allegorize takes its most visible form in *Idylls* is a critical commonplace, but discussion of his frequent practice of "speaking otherwise" (Miller, 356) as his characteristic mode of cultural intervention has hardly begun.

Tennyson himself suggested the particular operations of this rhetorical strategy in his poem when he warned readers not to "press too hardly on details whether for history or for allegory" (Tennyson, *Poems*, 3:266). *Idylls of the King* in fact tempts us to read allegorically while it frustrates that attempt. If allegories are, as Benjamin claims, "in the realm of thoughts, what ruins are in the realm of things" (177–78), then *Idylls* constitutes an allegory that is preemptively ruined in such a way as to refocus attention from the matter of the poem (broadly, the failure of ideals) to its own mysterious designs and those, presumably, of its prophetic creator, who is figured in the poem by Merlin, mage and allegorist. This is why Merlin, who is throughout *Idylls* portrayed as the power behind Arthur's monarchy, figures so prominently in the work, why his demise at the hands of Vivien is the pivotal event (book 6 of the twelve-book sequence) in the fall of Camelot, and why the power of his "book" is the central issue in the contest between the forces of goodness and evil represented, respectively, by him and Vivien.

Before I discuss Merlin as a failed allegorist, and thus a figurative projection of the allegorist of moral and imperial decay who fashioned him, some generalized discussion of how truncated allegory operates in the *Idylls* will be helpful. One quality that distinguishes Tennysonian "indeterminate" allegory from traditional (i.e., medieval and early Renaissance) allegory is the impossibility of right reading: in such allegory the truth the text points to is beyond articulation, secret and mysterious, as my earlier remarks suggest. If Edmund Spenser's Arthur, as ventriloquized through his Red Crosse Knight, lamented how

> Full hard it is . . . to read aright
> The course of heavenly cause, or understand
> The secret meaning of th' eternal might
> That rules men's ways and rules the thoughts of wight,

(The Faerie Queene 1.9.6, 6–9)

then Tennyson's poem argues that such understanding is available exclusively to the poet. Tennysonian allegoresis accords with J. Hillis Miller's description of the entire genre's paradoxical operations: "The word *allegory* always implies not only the use of figures, but a making public, available to profane ears, of something which otherwise would remain secret," while in publicizing that which is normally inaccessible and mysterious, allegory "involves the expectation of mimetic verisimilitude, which seems to be its own opposite." But because allegory is characterized by "a larger degree of manifest incompatibility between the tenor and the vehicle" than we expect with symbolism, "oddly enough . . . the more exoteric . . . the more down to earth, homely, and realistic it is on the one hand, the more esoteric and in need of commentary it is on the other." Ultimately, to speak allegorically "is a sure way to keep [the most important thing we have to say] secret" (Miller, 356–57).

The opening and closing books of Tennyson's epic especially demand typological and allegorical interpretive strategies of any reader who wishes to achieve intellectual control of the text (in part by breaking its allegorical codes), but they also frustrate those strategies. In "The Coming of Arthur," for instance, we are provided with alternative accounts of Arthur's origins, each of equal mythic status. Leodogran finally agrees to wed his daughter Guinevere to Arthur only because he is convinced in a dream vision of the king's legitimacy. The portentous images that emerge in the dream typify the self-conscious allegoricity that dominates the narrative: Leodogran sees a "haze-hidden" mountain peak "and thereon a phantom king" who is shortly revealed as "the King" standing "out in heaven, / Crowned" after the

(Tennyson,
Poems,
3:278–79)

> . . . haze
> Descended and the solid earth became
> As nothing.

Similarly, in "The Passing of Arthur" (as we saw in chapter 1) Bedivere's three attempts to cast away the sword invite allegorical reading. In the event itself he beholds an arm

(3:557)

> Clothed in white samite, mystic, wonderful,
> That caught [Excalibur] by the hilt, and brandished him
> Three times, and drew him under in the mere.

Despite the Trinitarian resonances of this passage, for instance, or the openly Christological analogies evoked by Leodogran's dream narrative, in the allegorically loaded descriptions that pervade the *Idylls* we still miss the detailed and consistent correspondences between descriptions or characters and their referents (ideas, values, dogmas, and institutions on the one hand or historical personages and events on the other) that we expect of allegory. In the end, that is, we are left mystified, "empty handed." Exaggerated, even self-parodic instances of truncated allegory also appear throughout the text, most often in association with Merlin, its premier allegorist.

Bellicent's narrative in "The Coming of Arthur," for example, concludes with the myth of Arthur's origin in "the great deep" on an apocalyptic night when "the bounds of heaven and earth were lost":

> It seemed in heaven, a ship [appeared], the shape thereof
> A dragon winged, and all from stem to stern
> Bright with a shining people on the decks,
> And gone as soon as seen.

Bleys and Merlin "watched the great sea fall"

(3:277)

> Wave after wave, each mightier than the last,
> Till last, a ninth one, gathering half the deep
> And full of voices, slowly rose and plunged

> Roaring, and all the wave was in a flame:
> And down the wave and in the flame was borne
> A naked babe, and rode to Merlin's feet,
> Who stoopt and caught the babe and cried "The King!"

This passage invites an allegorical reading that seeks clear understanding of the relations between its dominant symbols: the ship, its "shining people," the ninth wave "full of voices," and finally the flaming wave. But such a reading is hard to come by.

When Bellicent asks Merlin to verify this narrative, she is understandably baffled by his response in "riddling triplets of old time," mirrors of the mystifying allegories with which Tennyson, the poet of the new time, presents us.

These triplets are at once playful and self-parodic, loaded with ambiguous symbols—signifiers without clear signifieds—that leave Bellicent, Leodogran (her auditor), and readers of the *Idylls* unenlightened:

> Rain, rain, and sun! a rainbow in the sky!
> A young man will be wiser by and by;
> An old man's wit may wander ere he die.
> Rain, rain, and sun! a rainbow on the lea!
> And truth is this to me, and that to thee; (3:277–78)
> And truth or clothed or naked let it be.
> Rain, sun, and the free blossom blows:
> Sun, rain, and sun! and where is he who knows?
> From the great deep to the great deep he goes.

These lines invite multiple responses. One may dismiss them as nonsense, for instance, on grounds they themselves provide: "An old man's wit may wander." It might be misguided to do so, however, in the context of Leodogran's momentous quest for true knowledge of Arthur's origins. If, unlike Bellicent, who is merely "angered" by these riddles, we attempt to read them parabolically, we are frustrated by an exaggerated uncertainty about the relations among signifiers: if the rainbow (taken as a traditional Christian symbol) indicates a covenant, who exactly are the parties to it and what might be its substance? Is the emphasis on uninformed youth and doddering age anything more than a commonplace here? Does the statement of truth's relativity preemptively undercut Leodogran's, the reader's, and the text's presumed pursuit of it? If so, does the experience of narrative (and by extension the narrative of experience) yield only intellectual frustration? Is the pleasure of this text, then, the perverse pleasure of mystification? Does the principle of that "pleasure" lie in the knowledge that we are subject to the control of unknown forces (some "he who knows" and comes and goes from and to "the great deep")?

Responses to all such questions generated by Merlin's riddle redirect us to the central question in "The Coming of Arthur": where do power and authority originate? Merlin, the poet in this passage, not only controls the questions we are led to ask and the frustration pursuit of them yields but also, as this opening idyll reminds us at every turn, is responsible for the creation of Camelot as a feudal utopia and for Arthur's success as king, upon which civilization and the array of Christian values associated with it depend for survival: "Merlin through his craft . . . / Had Arthur crowned" (3:273).

As Percivale unwittingly suggests in "The Holy Grail," Merlin represents the poet who has created him, whereas Camelot, the city built to music by Merlin, is analogous to the poetic work in which it figures. Camelot is an allegorical construct nested within the broader moral, spiritual, and political allegory of the *Idylls*. Its "architecture," Percivale explains to Ambrosius, culminates in "the mighty hall that Merlin built," girded by "four great zones of sculpture / . . . with many a mystic symbol."

> And in the lowest beasts are slaying men,
> And in the second men are slaying beasts,
> And on the third are warriors, perfect men,
> And on the fourth are men with growing wings,
> And over all one statue in the mould
> Of Arthur, made by Merlin, with a crown,
> And peaked wings pointed to the Northern Star.
> . . . . .

(3:471–72)

> [Within] twelve great windows blazon Arthur's wars,
> And all the light that falls upon the board
> Streams through the twelve great battles of our King.
> Nay, one there is, and at the eastern end,
> Wealthy with wandering lines of mount and mere,
> Where Arthur finds the brand Excalibur.
> And also one to the west, and counter to it,
> And blank: and who shall blazon it? when and how?—

Unlike the more common and "indeterminate" patterns of allegory that give mysterious substance to the *Idylls* as a whole, the allegory of this passage is determinate: that is, various correlations between the represented images and a Christianized perfectibilian mythology are immediately "visible and audible . . . to ordinary eyes and ears" and "accommodated to limited vision" like Percivale's (Miller, 358). Similarly visible is the answer to the concluding query, such that it becomes a mere rhetorical question. Merlin's successor, Tennyson, "blazons" the blank window with his allegorical epic.

But Tennyson's book, like Merlin's, constitutes a deliberation on failure, both thematically and formally. In "Merlin and Vivien" the ancient mage, before succumbing to his own inevitable failure, describes for Vivien the "book" from which he gleans his powers. Reading the text itself is an impossibility:

> Thou read the book, my pretty Vivien!
> O ay, it is but twenty pages long,
> But every page having an ample marge,
> And every marge enclosing in the midst
> A square of text that looks a little blot,
> The text no larger than the limbs of fleas;
> And every square of text an awful charm,
> Writ in a language that has long gone by.
> . . . . .
>
> And every margin scribbled, crost, and crammed
> With comment, densest condensation, hard
> To mind and eye; but the long sleepless nights
> Of my long life have made it easy to me.
> And none can read the text, not even I;
> And none can read the comment but myself;
> And in the comment did I find the charm.

(Tennyson, *Poems*, 3:413–14)

The "book" is an exclusive domain, and its power is sustained precisely because readers cannot decipher it or even narratives of previous attempts to do so. (It is, from a Marxist viewpoint, pure ideology.) In effect, the text as a signifying entity vanishes, while power and authority accrue only to one who can decipher "the comment." Similarly, the allegorical feints of Tennyson's poem simultaneously invite and frustrate interpretation while they reinforce the poet's mesmeric power as aesthetic *display* sanctioned by the cultural authority of mysterious legend. (The poetic voice is deciphering commentaries on Arthurian myth.)

According to Benjamin (as J. Hillis Miller reads him), allegory inevitably fails because it depends largely upon personification (*prosopopoeia*) to convey meaning. But the attempt to use *personae* as signifiers always "exposes itself as . . . unsuccessful projection" because of the "disjunction between the inscribed sign and its material embodiment." The *Idylls* makes an art of exposing the incapacity of symbolic language to contain the meaning it would at first appear to convey.[7] This process is exaggerated when the poem deploys prospectively allegorical figures whose relations, as well as their symbolic capacities, fail readers' attempts to make systematic sense of them. But the excess signification of the textual figures, to which such failure draws our attention, ultimately becomes *our* failure to assert power over the text and thus reinforces our awareness of the poem's ability to captivate us and compel our acceptance of its mysterious authority.

Magic and Ideology

> *Grant me some slight power upon your fate.*
>
> "Merlin and Vivien" (1857)

Alan Sinfied has, at the most general level, effectively explained this linguistic strategy in Tennyson's poetry as fundamentally ideological:

> *The magic of Tennyson's poems is not separable from their political stance: it informs totally their claim to lyric-prophetic authority. Magic is what prophets have, and it enables them to assert "truths" that violate credibility from a purportedly outsider position. The magic of Tennyson's poetry—its verbal power and its strategic use of story—facilitates a claim of sagacity. The prophets' mystical powers are the direct analogue of Tennyson's verbal magic. . . . The idea of the writer as beleaguered prophet . . . is attractive metaphysically because it imagines a source of wisdom somewhere beyond the customary interactive processes through which meaning is produced in society. And it is attractive politically because it claims to mark out a superior discourse, one that can justifiably override other people's needs and preoccupations.*

("Prophecy," 187)

My developing argument provides evidence (not introduced by Sinfield) to support these claims, which can be validated not only from within the text of poems such as *Idylls of the King* but also in more subtle and revealing ways by analyzing the impact of textual strategies deployed in Tennyson's poems on readers' ideological horizons. That is, a body of widespread cultural mythologies is invoked in them in a stylistically and formally novel but otherwise *antisubversive* fashion. This is not to say that the values embedded in his laureate poems—antifeminist, imperialist, conventionally Christian—are merely conservative, as has often been argued. Rather, such values are deployed in ways that refresh and reinvigorate dominant cultural frameworks of value and belief.

Narratives of failure, from "Mariana" to *Maud* and the *Idylls*, became one of Tennyson's poetic specialties. It is no paradox, however, that from the cultural interventions of such texts he derives prophetic authority. This is so in part because these works engage pervasive cultural myths that transpose failure into success or defeat into victory, myths as various but interdependent as those of Christ's life and "death," or, from pre-Christian tradition, King Arthur's coming and passing, or, from classical tradition, the legend of Oenone. As Tennyson understood, the Romantics replicated the thematics of stories like these in revisionist works such as Byron's *Manfred*, Shelley's *Prometheus Unbound*, and Wordsworth's *The Prelude*. Such myths insist that success will be seized *ultimately* from failure, but it is their essential quality that success be indefinitely postponed. The assertion of achieved success or a perfected social and political order, as *Idylls of the King* demonstrates, is of course always open to critique. The potential for success is permanently retained, however, when "something" prospectively ideal is only "evermore about to be." The poet, represented as mage and prophet in touch with telos and the logos, whether in allegorical or open treatments of his flawed culture (e.g., in the *Idylls* or *Maud*), presents a pessimism that is nonetheless reassuring: it is undergirded with hope for the future veiled in mysteries to which only he is privy. Such is Tennyson's transposition, especially in his major works as laureate, of mainstream Victorian perfectibilian discourse.

Tennyson's second dedication of the *Idylls*, "To the Queen," positioned as the work's epilogue, reveals with some precision how that transposition is effected through the embrace of imperialist discourse. By the time this poem was appended in 1873 all of the idylls but "Balin and

Balan" were in print.[8] Responses to the work evidenced its acceptance as a new (and comfortingly Victorian) national epic of heroism rooted— despite their eventual collapse—in ideals of social order and spiritual purity (all the more powerful precisely *because* of their failure). The epilogue, appropriately, takes as its topic a crisis of confidence in the empire and in the fabric of Victorian cultural values, and it is an undisguised effort to recolonize English hearts and minds. This effort constitutes a response not only to a general mood in some quarters but also, more specifically, to the position of William Gladstone, for whom Tennyson "had a high personal regard" but whose foreign policy he "*loathed* and *detested*" (Tennyson, *Letters*, 3 : 358).[9] Gladstone, on the evidence of "To the Queen," would have categorized Tennyson as one of "the materialists of politics" whose "faith is in acres and in leagues, in sounding titles and long lists of territories." In warning that unrestrained "ambition and cupidity" had *over*extended the empire, Gladstone insisted that such individuals "forget that [its] entire fabric . . . was reared and consolidated by the energies of a people . . . and that if by some vast convulsion our transmarine possessions could be all submerged, the very same energies of that very same people would either discover other inhabited or inhabitable spaces of the globe on which to repeat its work, or would without them in other modes assert its undiminished greatness" (269).

True to the discursive strategies at work in the *Idylls* itself, the tone of Tennyson's epilogue is portentous and apocalyptic, its convoluted syntax is often mystifying, and its mode is quasi-allegorical. Recalling the reception of Victoria and Edward, the Prince of Wales, at a public appearance made upon his recovery from typhoid fever (the disease that killed his father), the poem equates their popularity among the "trebled millions," through whom "roll'd one tide of joy," with the legitimacy of empire:

> . . . The loyal to their crown
> Are loyal to their own far sons, who love
> Our ocean-empire with her boundless homes
> For ever-broadening England, and her throne
> In our vast Orient, and one isle, one isle,
> That knows not her own greatness.

(*Poems,* 3 : 562)

To those who view the empire as "too costly" or "a burthen," he responds, "Is this . . . the faith / That made us rulers?" Is this the "voice of

Britain, or a sinking land, / Some third-rate isle half-lost among her seas?" And he dismisses those deceived "by morning shadows," those who fear

> . . . wordy trucklings to the transient hour,
> And fierce or careless looseners of the faith,
> And Softness breeding scorn of simple life,
> Or Cowardice, the child of lust for gold,
> Or Labor, with a groan and not a voice,
> Or Art with poisonous honey stolen from France.

(3 : 563)

Despite his claim that "The goal of this great world / Lies beyond sight," the poet's concluding optimism suggests an intuition of the telos. Tennyson stridently rebukes anti-imperialists because, as an ideological imperialist *within* his culture, he has an enormous investment in the process of "ever-broadening" power he defends.[10]

The success of Tennyson's poetry as ideologically imperialistic work is demonstrated in both the sales and the reception history of the *Idylls*. Some well-known statistics are worth recalling. Although the first volume of *Idylls* (1859) was expensive at seven shillings, ten thousand copies sold in the first six weeks (out of an edition of forty thousand). A second edition was called for within six months, and six more editions were issued before the second series of *Idylls* appeared in 1869. During their first five years in print the first four of the *Idylls* brought Tennyson £11,500, a fortune in mid-Victorian England, where fewer than 10 percent of households had an income of more than £150 a year (Hagen, 110). Though such sales figures may not quite compare with those of *Enoch Arden* (which sold seventeen thousand copies on the day of publication), they are by any standards huge for a volume of poetry (112).

One reason for the enormous and immediate success of the 1859 *Idylls* with both readers and reviewers (a contrast with the reception of *Maud* four years earlier) is, as I have suggested, that its ideological values were perceived by readers as uncontroversial (except among the most precise). Its strategy, Sinfield notes, is to "absolut[ize] local values" ("Prophecy," 160), but this strategy depends upon the reader's acceptance of the mysterious authority accrued by the poet through his deployment of sage discourse throughout the work. This is exactly the effect repeatedly manifest in written responses (reviews, letters, recorded conversations) to the *Idylls*.

The full emergence of the Tennysonian persona Frederick Meyers defined as "prophetic" comes in fact with the first four *Idylls of the King*, as a letter to the laureate from his friend, the duke of Argyl, makes clear: "The applause of the 'Idylls,' goes on crescendo, and so far as I can hear without exception. Detractors are silenced" (Tennyson, *Memoir*, 1:450). Walter Bagehot, in his 1859 review of the first four books, echoes the assertion exactly. Although "everybody admires Tennyson now," he explains, fifteen years earlier he had only a coterie of followers: but he has finally "vanquished" his detractors (Jump, 216). His success in this project is notably dependent for Bagehot on Tennyson's *lack* of originality, that is, the ideological compatibility of his major work with mainstream values. Although "the amount of thought held in solution . . . in Mr. Tennyson's poetry, is very great," we are told, "his reflections are often not new." Indeed that "thought" is precisely cultural *reflection*, and this is its greatest virtue. Even Tennyson's strongest admirers "would not claim for him, the fame of an absolutely original thinker." Instead, he possesses "a kind of faculty which in an age of intellect and cultivation . . . possibly is even more important than the power of first-hand discovery. He is a first-rate *realiser*" of dominant cultural values (235). Such a view is also suggested in Gladstone's review when he remarks on the "deep ethical insight" of Tennyson's "metaphysical analysis," even such that "many of his verses form sayings of so high a class that we trust they are destined to form a permanent part of the household-words of England" (Jump, 261). The ideological implications of this paradoxical statement are evident: Tennyson expresses transcendent but culturally embedded values with such felicity that "his sayings" will be reduced to commonplaces. Gladstone, who himself moved among the highest classes, who was among the power elite of Victorian England, and who understood the subtle workings of cultural power in all its forms, presents one of the most intriguing perspectives on the ideological effects of Tennysonian verbal magic (in employing prominent social and political discourses) when he admires "the quantity of power that Mr. Tennyson can make available." That "he is not given to a wanton or tyrannous use of it" is "great proof of self-discipline" (261). Tennyson, in short, is a master of ideology who through its dispensation has accrued a level of influence and authority, in Gladstone's view, comparable to that normally exercised in openly political arenas. But, of course, the power of ideology operates more subtly, durably, and pervasively than this: *Idylls of the King*

became a favorite text for schoolboys, for instance, who were deeply influenced by the (conservative) cultural values it promulgated. Herbert
Warren, a Clifton boy, responded typically. The *Idylls*, he insists, "had an
immense influence upon us. . . . The contrasted knightly types, Galahad,
Percivale, Lancelot, Bors, the sage Merlin, above all King Arthur himself,
were very much to us. Side by side with Homer and Greek history, they
gave us our standards. We saw them in our Head, in our Masters, and in
our comrades" (Girouard, 18−19).[11]

That admiration for Tennyson and his cultural influence had largely
evaporated within a decade after his death and remained irrecoverable for
much of the twentieth century derives precisely from the fact of his
Victorian representativeness. This is not to say merely that the decline
of Tennyson's reputation inevitably accompanied the reactionary anti-
Victorianism of the modern era. It is instead to imply that despite Tennyson's appropriation of particular Romantic moods (Byron's brooding
melancholy) and values (the idealization of the alienated poet), he dis-
carded the goal of *ideological* subversiveness or marginalism self-advertised
in the work of Wordsworth, Blake, and Shelley, for instance. That Tennyson labored intermittently for half of his career on a poem (*Idylls of the
King*) that he himself understood as archaic is symptomatic of his ultimately rejecting poetic materials that might threaten to be novel or non-
conformist. At the close of 1858 Tennyson had written to "disabuse" the
minds of his American publisher, Ticknor and Fields, "of the fancy that
I am about an Epic of King Arthur," insisting that "I should be crazed
to attempt such a thing in the heart of the 19th Century" (Tennyson,
Letters, 2:212). Yet he was inevitably driven to attempt it in part, it would
seem, because the conservative matter of the myth could be appropriated
to the prophetic demands of his developing persona as well as the demands of ideological ambiguity that could enhance the sage aura of a high
Victorian laureate. As Mark Girouard and others have demonstrated, Arthurian and medievalist topics were, by this moment in the nineteenth
century, pervasively woven into the fabric of English culture, having
emerged in part as a reaction against increasingly dominant positivist and
materialist social values.[12]

Reception theory here again helps to explain in these terms the operations of the *Idylls* and, it might be argued, most of Tennyson's important poems: the greater the distance between previous aesthetic experience and that introduced by a new literary work, the more it provides a

"pleasing or alienating new perspective" and alters the reader's horizon of expectations for future aesthetic experience. *Maud*, it could be argued, is Tennyson's last major work to present an *aesthetic* challenge of this kind, although it is ideologically conventional, both when the speaker attacks the materialism of his age and when he chooses to sacrifice himself for the nationalist ideals of his fundamentally materialist culture at the poem's conclusion.[13] By contrast, a work that does not demand any "horizonal change," whether formal, stylistic, or ideological, merely fulfills "the expectations prescribed by a ruling standard of taste" and "confirms familiar sentiments" or "sanctions wishful notions" and "raises moral problems, but only to 'solve' them in an edifying manner as predecided questions" (Jauss, 25). This description, the reviews demonstrate, clearly fits *Idylls of the King*.

As Jerome McGann has convincingly argued, Tennyson's poetry "believes itself able to anticipate . . . multifarious readings and readers, believes itself ready to accommodate not so much all *levels* of reading as all the interests and ideologies of its readers" (*Inflections*, 180). As a result, his poetry is valuable today as much for the cultural revelations it offers us as for its aesthetic qualities that enhance these revelations. More than one hundred years after Tennyson's death the power of his poetry—no matter its emotional effects upon particular readers—is reconstituted. In complex and beautiful, mesmeric language it most often told Victorian readers what they already knew and believed. It tells us, by contrast, what we can only with difficulty understand about them.

III

Elizabeth Barrett
in 1838: "Weakness
like Omnipotence"

I assume no power of art, except that power of love towards it,
which has remained with me from my childhood until now.
Preface to *The Seraphim and Other Poems*

IN 1838 thirty-two-year-old Elizabeth Barrett published *The Seraphim and Other Poems*, her third and most significant book of poetry and the first printed under her own name.[1] With this volume she proved herself to be a poet of great promise—learned, versatile, and accomplished in many poetic forms. Temperamentally Barrett was witty, strong willed, ambitious, and self-confident. But just before her new book appeared she felt unprecedented anxiety about its reception. On 26 March she wrote to her close friend Hugh Stuart Boyd: "I feel very nervous about it—far more than I did when my [translation of] Prometheus [1833] crept out of the Greek, or I myself out of the shell, in the first Essay on Mind [1826]. Perhaps this is owing to . . . a consciousness that my present attempt *is* actually, and will be considered by others, more a trial of strength than either of my preceding ones" (Browning and Browning, 4:21). The "trial of strength" evinced in the reception of this volume involved issues that were not only aesthetic but also ideological and, not surprisingly, gender marked. In conspicuous as well as subtle ways Barrett's book constituted a new stage in the pursuit of success and influence as a female poet that had driven her since childhood. Here and in the two-volume collection of *Poems* that followed in 1844 she engaged important cultural discourses and deployed adventurous poetic strategies that clearly demonstrated her impressive intellectual abilities and virtuosity as a poet. The effect of this effort in her work was to transvalue literary authority: by the 1850s a variety of cultural power had accrued to Elizabeth Barrett Browning that not only exceeded the traditional province of the woman poet but also challenged that of the most acclaimed male poet of her day, Alfred Tennyson. Tricia Lootens has reminded us that "by the time she was suggested for Poet Laureate in 1850, Barrett Browning often emerged in periodical literature not only as a major poet but as a form of national heroine—as what the *English Review* celebrated as England's 'Queen of Song'" (126).

This chapter discusses the complex discursive strategies operating in Elizabeth Barrett's poetry of 1838 and their ideological significance. In order to fully understand the operations of these poems, as well as the quality and extent of the influence they earned their author, however, a twentieth-century reader must recuperate the backgrounds and contexts of her larger poetic project. At issue here are not only her lifelong quest for success as a poet but also her "naive" transcendentalist ideals of poetry during this period and the theoretical implications of such apolitical ideals as they are embodied but also undercut in her poetic performances of 1838. These works variously engage Victorian discourses of aesthetic value, love and romance, motherhood, and religion in accomplishing ideological effects of which their author was, at least in some cases, apparently unaware.

Poetics and Politics

Despite living in an "age . . . forlorn as to its poetry," as Elizabeth Barrett described early Victorian England (Browning and Browning, 3:218), she had decided upon the poetic vocation by the age of ten or eleven. As Dorothy Mermin has explained, Barrett "was always entirely serious about the supreme value of poetry" and she "never in fact succeeded in eradicating her poetic ambition, [although] she usually described it as an aberration from which she had safely recovered" (11). The truth of both these assertions is clear from Barrett's early letters and from the prefaces to her volumes of poetry published in 1838 and 1844. On 14 December 1836, for instance, she wrote to her intimate friend Mary Russell Mitford that "poetry is more to me than I often dare say, for fear of the Cain-brand of affectation" (Browning and Browning, 3:208). In her preface to *The Seraphim* Barrett went public with her infatuation, explaining, "I never can feel more intensely than at this moment . . . the sublime uses of poetry, and the solemn responsibilities of the poet" (*Works*, 1:171). The conclusion of her preface to *A Drama of Exile* (1844) is even more personal and more earnest in tone, and it was widely quoted by reviewers at the time as proof that a formidable new variety of the species "poetess" had emerged on the Victorian literary scene:

> *While my poems are full of faults . . . they are not empty shells. If it must be said of me that I have contributed immemorable verses to the many rejected by the age, it cannot at least be said that I have done so in a light and irresponsible spirit. Poetry has been as serious a thing to me as life itself . . . there has been no playing at skittles for me in either. I never mistook pleasure for the final cause of poetry; nor leisure, for the hour of the poet. I have done my work, so far, as work . . . as the completest expression of that being to which I could attain . . . [and I feel] its shortcomings more deeply than any of my readers, because measured from the height of my aspiration.*
>
> (2:148–49)

Barrett's modesty in this passage is not disingenuous, but neither is the earnest statement of her high "aspiration," which reviewers of 1844, in their litany of praise, often thought fulfilled. Even Barrett herself was finally compelled to acknowledge, when the *Blackwoods* review belatedly appeared, that her work had elicited "such praise, as . . . has not [been] given I think, to any poetical work, for years" (Browning and Browning, 9:233). The addition of this collection of poems to her achievement in *The Seraphim* made her a power in the mid–Victorian literary world.

In that earlier volume, nonetheless, as in *A Drama of Exile and Other Poems*, Elizabeth Barrett assailed and renounced "Ambition, idol of the intellect," even as she pursued the fulfillment of her own poetic ambitions. She does so in "The Student," for instance, a poem that ironically bears a self-consciously pedantic epigraph from the original Greek of Marcus Antoninus. This work portrays the seduction and destruction of a scholar by the allure of "*fame, / . . . its divineness and beatitude.*" In a homiletic afterword the narrator decries ambition as a power

That art a very feebleness!—before
Thy clayey feet we bend our knees of clay,
And round thy senseless brow bind diadems
With paralytic hands, and shout "a god,"
With voices mortal hoarse! Who can discern
Th' infirmities they share in? Being blind,
We cannot see thy blindness: being weak,
We cannot feel thy weakness: being low,
We cannot mete thy baseness: being unwise,
We cannot understand thy idiocy!

(Works, 2:101)

Although the strained use of anaphora hardly redeems the poem's concluding lapse into hollow castigation, the point is clear, as is Barrett's transparent attempt to appropriate a Christian discourse of humility (with its emphasis on weakness, unworthiness, and ignorance) in denying the desire for fame and influence that, throughout her adult life, motivated her attacks on all desires for fame and influence. Just two months before *The Seraphim and Other Poems* was published, she wrote to John Kenyon, "Altho' ambition is a grand angelic sin, I fell a good way from the sphere of it, soon after I left the nursery" (Browning and Browning, 4:16). Rejecting the quest for fame, Barrett was, of course, responding to a ubiquitous social dictate perhaps best expressed in Robert Southey's famous letter to Elizabeth Gaskell written the year before Barrett published *The Seraphim*: "Write poetry for its own sake; not . . . with a view to celebrity. . . . So written, it is wholesome both for the heart and soul; it may be made the surest means, next to religion, of soothing the mind and elevating it."[2]

As early as *An Essay on Mind*, Barrett's first book of verse, published anonymously in 1826, she had repudiated visibly self-interested writing and embraced idealized intellectual and moral aims as those of true poetry:

Leave to the dross they seek, the grovelling throng,
And swell with nobler aim th' Aonian song!
Enough for thee uninfluenc'd and unhir'd,
If Truth reward the strain herself inspir'd!
Enough for thee, if grateful Man commend,
If Genius love, and Virtue call thee friend!

(Works, 1:95)

> Enough for thee, to wake th' exalted mood,
> Reprove the erring, and confirm the good;
> Excite the tender smile, the generous tear,
> Or rouse the thought to loftiest Nature dear.

Such moral and intellectual goals, nonetheless, hardly exist in a vacuum. In her polished neoclassical couplets "reproving" those who write self-interested poems young Elizabeth Barrett appears insensitive to the bald desire for power expressed in these lines, as well as the late-eighteenth-century sentimental (Christian and liberal) framework of values embedded in them. Clearly, acquiring the gratitude, commendation, and admiration of her audience both demonstrates and enhances the poet's capacity to move, inspire, and influence readers. Indeed, to "Reprove the erring, and confirm the good" is a patently ideological project, but the absolutist language in which it is expressed elides the obvious question it raises: according to what particular system of socialized values will virtue and desirable behavior be determined?

As this passage from *An Essay on Mind* suggests, Barrett's work, at least through 1844, always presents itself as "high poetry"; it aligns itself with "noble aims." All consciousness of the ideological designs on readers that arise from sociopolitical conditions and events surrounding the production of poetry is repressed (whereas it is foregrounded in her work of the 1850s). The subjects of these earlier poems and their treatment make them appear to transcend merely worldly matters. Yet they nonetheless expose a continuing "high aspiration" to write "memorable verses," that is, substantial and aesthetically polished poetry of the sort traditionally rewarded with lasting fame and influence. The major characteristics of such poetry Barrett defined early in her career as "profundity, vivacity, descriptiveness, sentiment, boldness of conception, and variety of expression" (Browning and Browning, 2:195).

The ideality of her concept of "true" poetry, reminiscent of the Romantic theories of it available to her from Wordsworth and Coleridge, is visible in a letter of May 1828 to Boyd, in which she insists:

> *With the poet . . . matter is not an* object *but a* medium. *He looks thro' nature that he may look beyond nature! He binds together the moral & the natural with golden bands,—rendering what is beautiful in nature, more hallowed, by associating it with what is*   (2:138)

*elevated in intellect,—& rendering intellectual conceptions more dis-
tinct & definite by a reference to material objects. How the artist parti-
cularizes! . . . How the Poet generalizes! How he delights in abstractions—in depth & height & silence & space!!*

Barrett here instinctively positions herself within the idealizing discourse
of transcendental—especially Wordsworthian and Coleridgean—aesthetics. (This passage echoes both the preface to the *Lyrical Ballads* and
the *Biographia Literaria*.) By this time she appears unselfconsciously to have
assimilated particular concepts of art and the artist widely diffused in her
culture. Yet the "boldness of conception" that she also idealizes and, more
significantly, practices as an ambitious *woman* poet drew her inevitably
outside of those ideals and established in her work a perspective from
which to critique them. Within a decade she had revised and challenged
some, but certainly not all, of the Romantic mythologies she earlier
embraced. "The Poet's Vow," from her 1838 volume, exemplifies this
process.

Extremely popular with the reviewers, this poem is an antiromantic
narrative (in five formal parts) that embraces ideals of romantic love,
brotherhood, and poetry itself. It features a poet disaffected from mankind who "vow[s] his blood of brotherhood / To a stagnant place apart"
(*Works*, 1:208). "Forswear[ing] man's sympathies" he determines, in an
at once Byronic and Wordsworthian gesture, to reclude himself in Cour-
land Hall, a gothic, anti-Palace of Art, where

(1:217)
> The bats along the ceilings cling,
> The lizards in the floors do run,
> And storms and years have worn and reft
> The stain by human builders left.

Like the soul who luxuriates in the "pleasure place" of Tennyson's precursory Palace of Art and eventually turns sated hedonist and psychotic,
this arrogant poet, who refuses to acknowledge his contagion by Original
Sin and rejects his humanness, also "did grow / Of his own soul afraid"
(1:217). He nonetheless remains oblivious to the prospective redeemers
who pass by his window: "Three Christians wend[ing] to prayers," "A
bridegroom and his dame" happy and blushing, and "A child with inward
song" (1:218).

Eventually he is taught his undeniable humanity and kinship with fallen mankind by Rosalind, who had been his fiancée before the misguided epiphany that led him to abandon the human world and to reject his identity as a fallen man. At the moment of that revelation, he asked,

> *We*! and *our* curse! do *I* partake
> The desiccating sin?
> Have *I* the apple at my lips?   (1:209)
> The money-lust within?

Rosalind, according to the sentimental and melodramatic conventions of the ballad form that Barrett appropriates here, pines and dies after ordering the eventual delivery of her corpse to the poet's door, along with a scroll in her own hand charging him now to acknowledge his humanity by expressing the pain and remorse he feels at the suffering he has caused her. He spontaneously does so in a fatal "lion-cry" that "rent its tenement / In a mortal agony."

As is clear even from this brief summary of the poem's events, "The Poet's Vow" appropriates and transvalues, rather than imitates, characteristic traits of the Byronic hero, the Wordsworthian recluse, and the Tennysonian aesthete. As with much of Barrett's poetry, the veiled power of this work emerges from its mix of convention and originality, which speaks, in a feat of cultural close reading, directly to Victorian tastes for sensation, melodrama, and the gothic but also for the sort of authority in writers that accrues from their manipulation of visible literary traditions and from their responses to authors who work within them. This reactionary poem ultimately deploys its formal, allusive, and iconic elements not to challenge its readers' values but to reinforce a number of orthodoxies reemerging in Victorian England—beliefs in the supreme importance of romantic love, in the ubiquitousness of human sin, and in the need for the work of the poet to help redeem man from sin and self-indulgence. It functions to reassert evangelical values in the face of Romanticism's secularization of them. The self-effacing poet behind this narrative operates openly in the public sphere. She records an arrogant and insensitive, misguided male poet's vow and implicitly asserts her differences from him: her kinship with her fellows in love and sin, as well as her commitment to help them endure in a fallen world, to prophetically correct irreligious and antisocial impulses, and, not insignificantly, to satisfy their literary tastes. This poem functions to appropriate and re-direct the cultural authority of male poets highly regarded by 1838 who did not subscribe to the social and religious beliefs embedded in her poem at the level of ideology. These poets include Byron, Wordsworth, Shelley, and (among a few, select readers) Tennyson, poets who had cultivated a paradoxical form of social power based, despite their frequent claims to the contrary, largely in representations of their own sage (and often ec-centric) individuality and hence in an implied moral and spiritual distance between themselves and common humanity. What this poem does not disavow, however, is a belief in the reformist power and transcendent value of poetry itself.

Despite such performances that challenge her precursors by embrac-ing mainstream religious, social, and amatory values during this crucial early period of her career, Barrett nonetheless appears oblivious to the ideological content of her work and to the reasons readers perceived it as original. (Previous "poetesses" had rarely presented serious ideological critiques of their culturally influential male counterparts; nor had any done so at such a high level of technical accomplishment.) Her friend Harriet Martineau finally commented at length upon these features of her poetry in 1844, but her observations apply equally to many of Barrett's poems of 1838:

> *The predominant impression is . . . of your originality. Of this I am perfectly certain. Your mind is to me a new one: & its utterances are fresh as if no one had spoken poetry before you. This, taken together with the depth of the ideas & feelings,—the wide spiritual experi-ence—I take to be the reason why (as seems to me) you are yet so far*
(Browning and Browning, 9:142)
> *from being appreciated. The few notices & reviews I have seen are re-spectful & admiring: but they are, I think, unspeakably inadequate. The reviewers have no conception of what they have in hand: & I see indeed that reviews cannot ever do you justice. Your fame will not be brought into houses & chambers by periodicals. It will be carried out into critical literature hereafter, from chambers & nooks of meditation & tête à tête. I know nothing like this poetry. . . . Its power over me is genuine, strong, & inspir[es] a sort of reverence.*

Martineau's effusion reveals the truth of the observation that reading a new text "catches us up within a historical process that can appear congealed in the order of established facts and achieved meanings or become the dynamic confrontation of memory and hope with the world as it is," that is, of the past and of prospects for the future with present social reality (Brenkman, 4). Martineau's experience of her friend's poetry clearly belongs to the second category. She predicts that Barrett's work, in all the originality of its emerging ideological elements, will eventually be disseminated through the apparatuses of the dominant culture after becoming established in the silent depths of the social subject: it will be "carried out into critical literature hereafter, from chambers & nooks of meditation & tête à tête."

That Elizabeth Barrett was blind to the perceived level of originality and to the often subtle cultural politics operating in her poems of 1838 and 1844 is especially surprising given that these are the attributes of her work that ultimately empowered her as the foremost female poet in mid-Victorian England. Her blindness is, therefore, from the viewpoint of cultural criticism, both a curious and a profoundly important aspect of her poetic productions and career. Analysis of her work from 1828 to 1844 would necessarily feature the struggle within it between an apparent acceptance of dominant, institutionalized value systems (as these were embedded in the discourses of aesthetics, love, religion, and motherhood) and opposition to those systems.[3] The conflicted cultural ideologies at work in this poetry can perhaps best be explained by viewing it as a material embodiment of developing structures of feeling within highly educated and aspiring middle-class Victorian women. (Others similarly positioned would include figures such as Harriet Martineau, Florence Nightingale, and Barbara Bodichon.) These structures of feeling reveal emergent ideological strains within the dominant culture and generate what we might describe as transitional subjectivities and therefore visibly conflicted forms of self-expression. As Raymond Williams has observed, "The actual alternative to the received and produced fixed forms is not silence: not the absence, the unconscious, which bourgeois culture has mythicized. It is a kind of feeling and thinking which is indeed social and material, but each in an embryonic phase before it can become fully articulate and defined exchange. Its relations with the already articulate and defined are then exceptionally complex" (*Marxism*, 131). Manifestations of "embryonic" challenges to dominant cultural values and aesthetic practice make Barrett's work from 1828 to 1844 of special interest as default cultural critique, that is, critique not yet brought to full consciousness.

Barrett's obliviousness to the operations of her work of this period in the arena of cultural politics is especially apparent from her retention and extension throughout that work and her commentaries upon it of the transcendentalist—that is, utopian and nonpolitical—view of her poetry that she had formulated in earlier years. This view emerges even in a sentimental narrative poem like "Isobel's Child." As Isobel meditates on her infant's future, one prospective occupation she considers for him is that of the poet. (Throughout her meditation she denies his irrepressible attraction to "the happy heavenly air," which impels his death wish.) This figure and his work in the world is wholly idealized. Isobel conceives that the poet

> broadly [spreads]
> The golden immortalities
> Of [his] soul on nature's lorn
> And poor of such, them all to guard
> From their decay,—beneath [his] treading,
> Earth's flowers recovering hues of Eden,—
> And stars, drawn downward by [his] looks
> To shine ascendant in his books.

(*Works*,
2:20)

This poet is a Wordsworthian Christ figure come to redeem mankind and the fallen world. His goal is magically accomplished through aesthetic discourse, "his books."

Such a view of the poet is reinforced by Barrett's fatalism with regard to the success or failure of her own poetry in 1844. Having seen only a few reviews of *A Drama of Exile and Other Poems*, all positive, Barrett wrote tellingly to Mary Russell Mitford: "Poetry, if worth anything, will make its own way,—& if *not* worth anything, will fail & die, ultimately— and I do not even *wish* the general law to be reversed on my account. It is a righteous law" (Browning and Browning, 9:125). True "poetry" for her is clearly an essentialist abstraction, unrelated to the particular cultural conditions that produce it. Its operations, in her view, transcend the sociopolitical world.

Unlike poetry by her female contemporaries, however, Barrett's innovative work can be seen to have highly visible effects in that world, as

Harriet Martineau observed. For one thing, her poems' erudition, allusiveness, and formal complexities appeal to readers' intellects as well as their feelings (as even the title poem of her 1826 volume, *An Essay on Mind*, makes clear). Midcentury commentaries dependably make distinctions between poetry by men and poetry by women. These are especially instructive in the case of Barrett's first two (unsigned) volumes, which would have seemed anomalous to her readers had they known the gender of their author. Frederick Rowton in 1853 expressed the common wisdom:

> *While man's intellect is meant to make the world stronger and wiser, Woman's is intended to make it purer and better. . . . How rarely our Female Poets have addressed themselves to the mere understanding, and on the other hand how constantly they have sought to impress the feelings of the race; how little they have endeavoured to increase our wisdom, and how much they have laboured to promote our virtue. It is for man to ameliorate our condition; it is for woman to amend our character. Man's Poetry teaches us Politics; Woman's Morality.* (Williamsson, xxxix)

This passage makes assumptions prescribed by ideology: not only that separate spheres of activity are constitutionally determined for men and women but also that "wisdom" (a male attainment) is separable from "purity" (an aspect of womanhood) and politics (a masculine sphere of activity) is separable from morality (associated with the woman's sphere). In the preface to *An Essay on Mind* Barrett clearly opposes some of these general assumptions and subscribes to others when she acknowledges that "while we behold in poetry, the inspiritings to political feeling . . . we are loth to believe her unequal to the higher walks of intellect. . . . Poetry is the enthusiasm of the understanding; and, as Milton finely expresses it, there is 'a high reason in her fancies'" (*Works*, 1: 56–57). As both Rowton's and Barrett's comments remind us, it was a commonplace of early Victorian aesthetic culture to assert the superiority of "virtue" and "high reason" (the basis of virtue) over "political feeling." Yet, in affirming this transcendentalist ideal of poetry *as a woman* (and implicitly comparing herself to Milton) Barrett is in fact making a political statement and taking a political stance. Moreover, with several of the poems from her 1838 volume, including "The Young Queen" and "Victoria's Tears," Barrett does compose verse on what normally would be seen as political subjects, but these poems, unlike Tennyson's first published in the same year, employ nonpolitical discourse to accomplish ideological effects.

In letters written during the years in which she was composing most of the poems published in *The Seraphim* Barrett in fact defines herself as a thoroughly political woman, in spite of her hermetic life as an invalid: she was keenly aware of the tumultuous political events taking place during the impressionable years of her young adulthood. The first Reform Bill, much discussed in the Barrett household, was passed when she was twenty-six. The abolition of slavery throughout the empire was finally effected with the passage of Lord Stanley's bill in 1834, when she was twenty-eight. (Barrett's deep concern with the issues surrounding this bill would be powerfully displayed sixteen years later, in "The Runaway Slave at Pilgrim's Point.") Both the New Poor Law Amendment of 1834 and the Factory Act of the previous year, especially designed to restrict child labor in a manner that was enforceable (unlike the acts of 1802 and 1819), were hotly debated and, judging from "The Cry of the Children" and other poems of 1844, must have been of equally great importance to Barrett. Throughout the period from 1828 to 1844 as well, her republican sympathies were ignited by the activities of the Chartist movement, a highly controversial topic of political discourse in these years.

Yet in her letters Barrett repeatedly claims to renounce her political interests, just as she renounces poetic ambitions. In fact she is irretrievably captive to both. In 1837, for instance, concluding a letter dense with political commentary, she exclaims, "I would rather . . . write of any other subject than politics—altho' you may not think so, after all this!" (Browning and Browning, 3:217). In the days before passage of the first Reform Bill her father was a constant source of news on political topics (3:22), and even after its passage she confesses to "fits of politics, & to states of reaction." She nurtures a special "affection for the republican radicals" (3:66). Indeed, she is as radical and original in her politics as in her poetry of 1838. Writing to Mary Russell Mitford early in 1837, she explains how "Papa & my brothers go . . . to the full length of radicalism: but whenever I talk politics before *them* . . . I am sure to be called Quixotic & impracticable, because I go so much beyond them into republican depths" (3:225). Though her political ideals may have appeared to Barrett more extreme than her ostensibly conservative and unexceptionable ideals of poetry, both were influenced by an inherent radicalism often subtly demonstrated through her poems' engagement with ostensibly nonpolitical discourses. Such is the case with her two poems celebrating Victoria's ascension to the throne in 1837.

The companion poems "The Young Queen" and "Victoria's Tears" commemorate two new political births, those of a monarch and of her self-authorized laureate, Elizabeth Barrett. Elsewhere I have discussed the complex ideological transpositions that take place in both works, as Barrett describes Victoria's transformation from a fantasized Wordsworthian child of nature into the mother of the nation (*Victorian Poets*, 116–19). Although the queen "Perhaps . . . Remembers what has been—/ Her childhood's rest by loving heart, and sport on grassy sod" (Browning, *Works*, 2:107), her nation now looks to her "For steadfast sympathy." Thus, with some presumptuousness, the poem's speaker instructs the Queen: "as thy mother joys in thee, in them shalt *thou* rejoice" (2:108). Radically extending the Victorian domestic ideology and its exaltation of women's sensitivity and angelic spirituality, Barrett makes clear in "Victoria's Tears" that the new queen's extraordinary adoration by her people and attainment to a degree of power beyond that of (presumably male) tyrants depends exclusively upon her woman's "nature," specifically her "tender heart":

> God save thee, weeping Queen!
> Thou shalt be well beloved!
> The tyrant's sceptre cannot move,
> As those pure tears have moved!   (2:109)
> The nature in thine eyes we see,
> That tyrants cannot own—
> The love that guardeth liberties!

The radical implications of this final description cannot be exaggerated: liberty, the foundational value of Britain's constitutional monarchy, is best protected and preserved by womanly virtues rather than by "manly" (i.e., tyrannical) behavior.

With these poems, both published in the *Athenaeum* within two weeks of Victoria's accession on 20 June 1837, Barrett had resolved a dilemma described in a letter to Mary Russell Mitford: the conflict between her radical, democratic proclivities and her patriotic respect for the monarchy. "Dont [*sic*] you see what a strait I am in?" she laments. "How can loyalty & republicanism be brought together 'into a consistency,'—particularly when Miss Martineau is writing, that kings have ceased to be necessary evils?" (Browning and Browning, 3:261). Ultimately her bind is resolved precisely because the monarchist "loyalty" her republican principles would have her repudiate is, in large part, gender determined and the queen's feminine and motherly, loving nature is instinctively democratic, as Barrett argues in the same letter: "The young Queen is very interesting to me—[with] those tears, wept not only amidst the multitudes at the proclamation, but in the silence of the dead midnight. . . . [Yet] there is something hardening, I fear, in power. . . . the coldnesses of state etiquette gather too nearly round the heart, not to chill it, often! But our young Queen wears still a very tender heart! and long may its natural emotions lie warm within it!" (Browning and Browning, 3:261). If Elizabeth Barrett's poems enable her to usurp a poetic throne by aligning herself as a *woman* poet with a new queen, they do so not only by redefining the monarch's role in terms of a domestic ideology that privileges motherhood but also by adopting a motherly stance and tone, as the title of her first ode suggests. That is, Barrett's poems here appropriate the discourse of idealized motherhood with the effect of empowering the poet. In both poems on Victoria, Barrett repeatedly depicts the queen as "youthful," indeed as a "maiden" who has barely emerged from childhood. We understand the historical importance of such descriptions only insofar as we recognize the general response to Victoria's accession in 1837 touched on in the previous chapter.

Richard Stein has recently reminded us that when she came to the throne, "the new Queen's subjects were less than confident that something important was beginning and less than certain about the prospects for the future." Of course "Victoria herself had not yet become a public symbol, nor was it clear she would become one." Late Victorians as disparate as Lytton Strachey and Walter Besant observed in retrospect that "she was almost entirely unknown to her subjects." In fact, as the *Times* noted in June 1837, the powerful demonstrations of feeling that attended her coronation were directed not so much at Victoria as at the institution she embodied (Stein, 4–5, 61). The *Times* leader only hesitantly endorsed her, "on trust"; she was "in some measure on her trial" (61). Similarly, the *Westminster Review* expected little of her, disparagingly emphasizing her youth, inexperience, and her presumed incompetence as a woman: "Common sense points [to] but one course for her majesty to adopt: in conformity with the example of her predecessors, which her own extreme youth renders it particularly advisable that she should imitate; that is, the course of leaving things as she finds them, taking the advice of [her] ministers . . . and allowing her youthful will and judgment to make their influence on public affairs as little perceptible as possible" (62). In her poems on Victoria, Barrett thus confronted the need to garner sympathy and respect for the queen before she could authorize herself as the proper poet to make Victoria familiar to the nation and to define the true origins of the new monarch's power: her womanhood. Implementing a strategy to accomplish these goals, Elizabeth Barrett's odes implicitly recognize that the year 1838 would constitute "a trial of strength" for both her and the queen.

In her poems from 1828 forward Barrett's radical impulse is irrepressible. Like "The Young Queen" and "Victoria's Tears," many poems from *The Seraphim* employ dominant cultural discourses in ways that generate innovative ideological effects through their subtextual operations. Like the title poem, a number of these works treat religious themes and thus would appear to reinforce Protestant religious values and biblical traditions. (I will discuss such poems shortly.) Other works from this volume, however, also operate in subtle oppositional ways unnoticed by previous critics, and they manipulate the discourses of institutionalized amatory, aesthetic, and domestic ideologies to do so. These works include "The Poet's Vow," which, as we have seen, appears to enforce ideals of universal humanity and romantic love; a variety of works, including "Felicia Hemans" and "Cowper's Grave," that appear to underwrite traditional, idealized valuations of poetry itself; and the poems on Queen Victoria, which not only celebrate traditions of English political authority but also, simultaneously, invoke Romantic idealizations of childhood and Victorian idealizations of motherhood. At the most general level, the subversiveness of these poems results from their reification of patriarchally authorized cultural mythologies from the revisionary perspective of a woman. That is, by reconfiguring them in feminist terms Barrett's poems generated irruptions in the discourses through which particular systems of value and belief had attained ideological dominance. Such poetry was radically novel at the time of its appearance because it engaged comfortably familiar value systems and idealities in ways that ostensibly embraced them but in fact reconstituted the discourses through which they existed and were disseminated. As detailed analysis of additional poems from the 1838 volume reveals, however, her work deploys other effective revisionary strategies that result in self-authorization and self-empowerment for their author. Nearly all of these poems operate, as well, to undercut transcendentalist poetic ideals.

A New Kind of Poetess

Crucial to Elizabeth Barrett's success as a new and original poet were her historical circumstances. She was able to succeed because she appeared on the literary scene at a moment in English cultural history specially suited to her talents and ambitions. Barrett came to maturity at the beginning of a female monarch's reign over the most wealthy and powerful nation in the world—a nation with highly particularized systems of value and belief concerning the nature, roles, and social importance of women. These circumstances liberated her extraordinary talent from the constraints confining precursory and contemporary "poetesses" alike and enabled her to generate what Mermin has termed "a new poetry," which elevated her to a position of unprecedented moral, spiritual, and artistic influence by 1850. Barrett's poetry, as we have begun to see, engaged pervasive Victorian belief systems—the domestic ideology, the cult of motherhood, and the idealization of women's spiritual purity, their humility, passivity, weakness, and sensitivity—in a fashion that empowered their author and led to her early canonization.

Hans Robert Jauss's reception theory once again helps us understand how Barrett's "new poetry" succeeded. Jauss establishes opposed poles of familiarity (or conventionality) and novelty for literary works at the historical moment of their production and reception: "The distance between the horizon of expectations and the work, between the familiarity of previous aesthetic experience and the 'horizonal change' demanded by the reception of the new work, determines [its] artistic character." To the extent that "this distance decreases, and no turn toward the horizon of yet-unknown experience is demanded of the receiving consciousness," he explains, "the work [approaches] the sphere of entertainment art," which does not require any horizonal change at all but rather fulfills "the expectations prescribed by a ruling standard of taste." That is, "it satisfies the desire for the reproduction of the familiarly beautiful; confirms familiar sentiments; sanctions wishful notions; makes unusual experiences enjoyable as 'sensations'; or even raises moral problems, but only to 'solve' them in an edifying manner as predecided questions" (25). Poems by Barrett published in 1838, such as "The Seraphim," "The Poet's Vow," "Felicia Hemans," and "Victoria's Tears," functioned in precisely this way, but they simultaneously opposed or challenged expectations of their original audience, creating what Jauss describes as an "aesthetic distance . . . at first experienced as a pleasing or alienating new perspective" (25). Thus, Barrett's work operates between the poles of the familiar and the alien, often reinforcing conventional values while revising and redirecting them. Despite her aesthetic essentialism, Barrett's technical abilities, her wit, her unusually sophisticated education, and her imaginative capacities—as these appeared to readers inseparable from her gender—yielded to her a level of poetic authority ordinarily denied to women, even the most successful of her predecessors, L.E.L. and Felicia Hemans.

Discussing the poet's mission in her 1844 preface, she acknowledges that she wishes to demonstrate "the obvious truth . . . that if knowledge is power, suffering should be acceptable as part of knowledge" (*Works*, 2:147). In Victorian England suffering, as a manifestation of emotional and spiritual sensitivity, was accepted as the special province of women and a special mode of female subjectivity in the fallen world. Implicitly, therefore, the female poet who aestheticized her subjectivity had access to a special form of power. A number of poems from *The Seraphim* illustrate the complexity of Barrett's first major works and demonstrate her power as an artist. This "trial of strength" should be seen as the inaugural stage of a poetic project that succeeded in wresting authority from contemporaries and precursors alike and established E.B.B. as the natural female spokes-poet for the middle classes in the age of Victoria.

Analysis of these poems reveals a variety of strategies operating in Barrett's work that served, for many of her contemporaries, to define her as the ideal woman poet, a figure she herself had described early in her career as "the feminine of Homer" (Browning and Browning, 1:352). The overtly religious poems in particular, such as "The Seraphim," "An

Island," "The Soul's Travelling," and the four hymns that appear in the volume, as well as the elegy, "Cowper's Grave," transpose widely accepted elements of dissident theology and thus deftly manipulate one of early Victorian England's most influential religious ideologies. "The Virgin Mary to the Child Jesus" engages the same system of values, along with the Victorian cult of motherhood, to dethrone Milton from the patriarchal eminence of English poetry and replace him, through a sleight of ideology, with a woman poet (and potential mother of redemptive children), Barrett herself. By contrast with these religious works, "The Poet's Vow," as we have seen, employs sentimental romantic strategies to expose the human deficiencies of solipsistic Wordsworthian Romanticism. "Felicia Hemans," an elegy, damns with faint praise two representative and popular poetesses, laying the spirit of their poetic aspirations to rest and endorsing those of the elegist. And positioned strategically near the end of the volume, the two poems on the coronation of Queen Victoria commemorate her rise to power, as we have also seen; in them Barrett seizes the opportunity to hail the new queen and aligns the monarch's maternal powers with the prophetic authority of the female poet.

Moving toward the conclusion of her preface to *The Seraphim*, Elizabeth Barrett asserts, concerning the poems in her volume, "I need not defend them for being religious in their general character." She proceeds to cite Burns as her authority: "'An irreligious poet,' said Burns, meaning an undevotional one, 'is a monster.'" But she extends his point. "An irreligious poet, he might have said, is no poet at all" (Browning, *Works*, 1:169). She affirms the connection between religious discourse and poetry in letters of the same period, which repeatedly demonstrate her sincere piety and, like her poems, substantiate reviewers' observations on it. The *Monthly Review* announced that "sacred subjects are her themes, and Miss Barrett can soar aloft and happily seize upon them" (Browning and Browning, 4:385). The *Athenaeum*'s commentator (presumably writing with the controversy over the Oxford movement in mind), was less positive and criticized her devotional extremism. "She addresses herself to sacred song," he admonishes, "with a devotional ecstasy suiting rather the Sister Celestines and Angelicas of Port-Royal, than the religious poets of our sober protestant communities" (Browning and Browning, 4:375).

Occasionally in letters, Barrett herself jokingly worries over her "fa-naticism,"[4] but in more serious moments she insists upon the identifica-tion, formulated in the preface to her 1838 volume, between poetic and religious discourse, two spheres of social activity that had by then become feminized for the Victorian middle classes. In 1836 she writes to Mary Russell Mitford, "Oh what an unspeakable poetry there is in Christ's re-ligion! But like the lovely poetry of inferior things, men look on it coldly because without understanding" (Browning and Browning, 3 : 179). The association of religious virtues, morality, and sensitivity with the femi-nine in early Victorian England empowered women in definable ways, as Sarah Stickney Ellis's familiar thesis in *The Women of England* (1839) and innumerable similar commentaries make clear: women, "clothed in moral beauty," are repositories of "spiritual counsel" and have "secret influence." She explains that "the long-established customs of [England] have placed in their hands the high and holy duty of cherishing and protecting the minor morals of life, from whence springs all that is elevated in purpose, and glorious in action." The language employed in these observations clearly derives from religious discourse (and thus implies far more than it says explicitly); Ellis assumes her reader's under-standing of the meaning of abstract phrases like "moral beauty," "spiritual value," "secret influence," "holy duty," and "all that is elevated" (73–74). Elizabeth Barrett's poetry of 1838 often engages the semiotic codes of such religious discourse and illustrates their operations.

A logical extension of Ellis's view would have placed women in the pulpits of English churches and cathedrals, a position to which some aspired but which most were denied.[5] As Baptist William Landels wrote in *Women's Sphere and Work*, "It were strange if, while on his reception of the gospel, man's less susceptible nature is moved to effort for its diffusion, woman could be content to enjoy its blessings without communicating them to others. It would be a violation of every womanly instinct . . . her greater sensitiveness, her deeper and quicker sympathies" especially (Hel-singer, Sheets, and Veeder, 2 : 177). Frequently in her letters of the 1830s Elizabeth Barrett does in fact mount the pulpit, only sometimes apolo-gizing for "seeming, or seeming to try, to be a sermon writer" (Browning and Browning, 3 : 162–63). In her poems, however, as her preface to *The Seraphim* makes clear, no apologies are needed, not only because of the identification between poetry and religion that she asserts there but also because women's "nature" as well as their inherent spirituality—what the Victorians conceived of as their religious "instinct"—provided a basis among radical writers like Barrett for asserting a further and more profoundly empowering identification: between their own suffering and Christ's. For such women, "literature allow[ed] the sharing in and even the coopting of ministerial functions" (Helsinger, Sheets, and Veeder, 2: 183). Many poems in *The Seraphim* do precisely this.

"The Seraphim" itself is a thousand-line poem on Christ's crucifixion made up mostly of dialogue between two seraphim witnessing the event, one of them incredulous at the horror and apparent injustice of it. Although reviewers tended to gloss over this ambitious poem introducing the volume, it is fascinating for a number of reasons apart from its aesthetic virtues or deficiencies: Barrett positioned it strategically, as her book's most important work, in a sense defining the terms of her "trial of strength" as a poet; she titled the book accordingly; she chose as its subject—from the many religious *topoi* available to her—the events on Calvary; and she appended an epilogue that is at once an apologia and an assertion of her privileged religious vision as a female poet.

The drama's effectiveness lies in its power to render the intensity of Christ's passion, "The naked hands and feet transfixed stark, / The countenance of patient anguish white" (Browning, *Works*, 1 : 199) and the

(1 : 194)
> woe . . . heavy on his head,
> Pressing inward on his brain
> With a hot and clinging pain

At its climax the seraph Zerah laments,

(1 : 194–95)
> No rod, no sceptre is
> Holden in his fingers pale;
> They close instead upon the nail,
> Concealing the sharp dole,
> Never stirring to put by
> The fair hair peaked with blood,
> Drooping forward from the rood
> Helplessly, heavily.

The vividness with which Christ's suffering and the seraphim's responses to it are depicted is central to the empowering operations of this poem

(as they are in "The Virgin Mary to the Child Jesus") and supply a pre-
emptive answer to the question upon which Barrett focuses her epilogue:

> —ah! what am I
> To counterfeit, with faculty earth-darkened,
>   Seraphic brows of light
> And seraph language never used nor hearkened?
> Ah me! what word that seraphs say, could come
>
> From mouth so used to sighs, so soon to lie
> Sighless, because then breathless, in the tomb?

(1:204)

Framed simply, the answer to this complex question is that as a woman,
"used to" suffering and supremely sensitive to her own mortality, she
possesses privileged visionary capacities in spiritual matters. She shares
with Christ the paradoxical strength that arises from weakness. Hence
she can conclude with a prophecy that is corollary to the vision of the
past she has already presented: "that the weak, like me, / Before [Christ's]
heavenly throne should walk in white" (1:205). In their socially prescribed roles as patient, long suffering, and self-sacrificing—"weak"—
beings Victorian women enacted the *imitatio Christi*, a fact lost on few of
them, including Elizabeth Barrett. In a letter to Julia Martin in 1836 she
insists on "a recognition of the oneness of the human nature of [the]
devine [*sic*] Saviour who ever liveth, with ours which perishes & sorrows
so" (Browning and Browning, 3:162). Awareness of that "oneness" is an
essential attribute of women, she asserts in another letter when denounc-
ing Frances Trollope's new novel, *The Vicar of Wrexhill*, which she thinks
irreligious. "What a lamentable book," she exclaims, "& to be written by
a woman—who from the weakness and softness of her nature should so
feel the need & the beauty of that strength & surpassing tenderness found
in the religion of Jesus Christ & only there!" (3:288). The spiritual role
assigned to women in early Victorian culture enabled Barrett to assume
some of that strength, not only in "The Seraphim" but in the other religious poems scattered throughout the volume.

In the concluding stanza of "The Soul's Travelling," for instance,
the speaker dons priestly poetic garments in order to adjure Christ
to recall lapsed souls who wander aimlessly in the world "From city-
pavement to untrodden sward." She pronounces

(Browning, . . . very vain
Works,   The greatest speed of all these souls of men
2:56)   Unless they travel upward to [Thy] throne

where she boldly envisions "the archangel," who,

     . . . raising
(2:56)   Unto Thy face his full ecstatic gazing,
     Forgets the rush and rapture of his wings.

With this, the poem's final and climactic image, Barrett enables a virtual experience of the rapture through a compelling depiction of the archangelic gaze. She is implicitly authorized to do so by her role as a *woman* poet. A later reviewer's comment on one of her religious sonnets reveals the power of the Victorian feminization of spirituality, and it applies to this poem as well: "No MAN could have written [it]. It rises . . . from the heart of a Christian woman" (Browning and Browning, 9:351).

  Barrett's elegy on Cowper is concerned to identify her precursor as no lapsed soul but a pious poet who did not need redirection and was not finally deserted by his savior (as he had feared he would be). Like "The Soul's Travelling," "Cowper's Grave" concludes with a privileged vision of rapture, his "awaking" to "the new immortal throb of soul from body parted." The strength of the poem emerges, however, not only from this image but also from the breathtaking self-assertion of his elegist in her final stanza. Citing Christ's last words (echoed by Cowper), she makes the claim that Christ uttered them not only "That earth's worst phrenzies, marring hope, should mar not hope's fruition," but also that "I, on Cowper's grave, should see his rapture in a vision" (Browning, *Works*, 2:121). This poem, like other religious works in the volume, asserts its author's possession of exclusive spiritual capacities by literalizing and extending Victorian ideals of both poetry and woman's "religious nature." "The Virgin Mary to the Child Jesus" carries this strategy even further.

  In "The Virgin Mary" Barrett produced a meditative and irregular Horatian ode that, like the later *Drama of Exile*, announces the poet's identity as a contemporary prophet, one, however, whose abilities are based in her *un*exceptional nature, that is, her identity as an ordinary woman. The poem lays claim to a uniquely female poetic authority to bear the word of a redemptive domestic ideology focused in the Victorian cult of motherhood. Through her epigraph from Milton's *On the Morning of Christ's Nativity* Barrett is able implicitly to wrest that authority from England's most eminent religious poet in the patriarchal tradition. This new woman poet—a lineal descendant not of Eve but of the Virgin Mary, as the poem suggests—inescapably identifies herself with her heroine, the speaking subject of this text who bore God's Word as flesh to save mankind. This poem thus reconstitutes the myth of the Virgin Mary as transmitter of God's Word, a myth upon which the Victorian cult of motherhood, and the discourse in which it issued, was founded. It does so by lifting "the interdict on Mary's own manipulation of language that forms a conspicuous part of the myth" (Homans, 158).

With this poem Barrett enters, during its earliest stages and on the most radically feminist side, the Victorian debate over the extent of Mary's power and importance in redeeming mankind.[6] This debate constitutes one discursive strand woven into two overlapping discursive formations of the period: those surrounding religion (focused on Christianity) and motherhood. The exaltation of motherhood by the Victorians is a familiar fact of their social history, as is the complexity of women's maternal role when viewed whole, that is, in the context of power relations between men and women in Victorian society.[7] Uncontroversial, however, is the fact that an essential foundation of idealized motherhood is the analogy between all mothers and the Virgin Mary. Charles Merivale reflected a belief widely accepted by the middle classes in mid-Victorian England when he asserted, "The Mother of Jesus is the type and pattern of [all mothers]—the type of true female purity, loving, trusting, accepting, realizing" (Helsinger, Sheets, and Veeder, 2:200). "The Virgin Mary" extends this pervasive belief. The poem exemplifies an array of ideological values that constitute the discourse of motherhood, constructing a spiritual "reality" out of its narrator's and her heroine's represented traits of purity, love, trust, and acceptance (along with their additional virtue of humility).

Barrett's ode begins where Milton's poem ends, that is, with an epigraph from his final stanza: "But see! The Virgin blest / Hath laid her Babe to rest." The tone of Mary's monologue is at once awed and intimate as she watches Jesus sleep while contemplating the "light celestial from his wings and head" and speculating on the "glory" of his "dream."

From the images of these opening stanzas it is clear that the poem implies its own potential to supersede Milton but also to redirect and thus correct the secular lapses of Wordsworth's Intimations ode, which recovers "celestial light" and "the glory and the freshness of a dream" through radically unorthodox spiritual maneuvering. With the fourth stanza, however, the gaze of the poem refocuses on Mary and, through a sleight of identification, on the poet who generates this image of her: "The slumber of his lips meseems to run / Through *my* lips to mine heart." The Word is silent, while the Virgin Mother speaks of Christ's birth and its meaning through the "lips" of a Victorian woman poet. In the fifth stanza she recalls the events at Bethlehem. In stanzas 6 and 7 she abases herself before God, insisting on her humility, her vileness, her ignorance, and, perhaps most importantly, her weakness from which this strength has emerged ("God knows that I am feeble like the rest!"). In the eighth stanza, nonetheless, Mary calls for the crowning of her son as king in an imperative whose chiastic syntax serves to identify her with him. "Come, crown me Him a King!" she says, but then she immediately acknowledges the impotence of her voice:

> What is my word? Each empyreal star
> Sits in a sphere afar
> In shining ambuscade:
> The child-brow crowned by none,
> Keeps its unchildlike shade.

In his somber sleep, this child is—more complexly, paradoxically, and conventionally than in Wordsworth's parable—father of the man who redeems mankind. In being identified with his weakness, both Mary and the poet who ventriloquizes her monologue are empowered.

This is so because the poem is built upon a triple dialectic. Oppositions between Mary's humility and her exaltation, between Christ's omnipotence and Mary's weakness, between the stature of the canonized Virgin and that of the belated poet who gives her a voice, are all resolved in the crucial first line of stanza 11: "It is enough to bear" (Browning, *Works*, 2:78). In this sentence all dichotomous identities merge in the triple entendre of a pivotal verb: Mary gives birth to Christ, the Word of God, who endures suffering to redeem mankind, while the poet prophetically bears Mary's voice to a future generation whose cultural focus is as much on the Mother as the Son.[8] The monologue culminates in this stanza, which stands typographically and prosodically in relief, using trimeter lines in its long, first sentence at once to generate and to accent its emotional force:

> It is enough to bear
> This image still and fair,
> This holier in sleep
> Than a saint at prayer,
> This aspect of a child
> Who never sinned or smiled;   (2:78)
> This Presence in an infant's face;
> This sadness most like love,
> This love than love more deep,
> This weakness like omnipotence,
> It is so strong to move.

Here power ultimately accrues to the poet, who conveys to her Victorian audience this double image of strength and endurance in a series of appositions that serve to conflate the oppositions on which the poem has been constructed. If Mary is like her child in his weakness, the woman poet is like both of them in her power "to bear" their images. Here the patriarchal focus of traditional religious discourse (that exemplified by Milton) is subtly redirected. The ideological effect of doing so is to privilege the value and roles of women in the accomplishment of mankind's salvation (an effect, it can be argued, that also issues from Barrett's *A Drama of Exile*).

Other poems from Barrett's 1838 volume also adroitly engage components of nonreligious, but equally familiar, Victorian discourses, as we have seen, and they do so in ways that set emergent ideologies of the period in relief. Ultimately, however, analysis of the cultural politics of works like "The Poet's Vow" and the religious poems of Barrett's 1838 volume affirm Helen Cooper's assertion that "the central issue in Barrett Browning's work is how a woman poet empowers herself to speak" (5). As both Cooper and Mermin have made clear in their pathbreaking books, that issue is often inseparable from the challenge Elizabeth Barrett faced of positioning herself in relation to popular women poets of her day. Whereas recent feminist theorists often stress the difficulty of establishing an identity, not to mention a tradition, for women writers compelled to employ "the language of the father" (a fundamentally patriarchal linguistics), Barrett's concerns originate at an earlier stage of inquiry into the cultural politics of literary inheritance and self-assertion. She aspired to raise the general level of poetic discourse for women and by women at a time when the extraordinary potential of women's poetry was, as she claimed, "lowered . . . to uses" particular to the socialized roles, values, behaviors, and expectations of Victorian women (Browning and Browning, 1 : 232). In Barrett's view—a strikingly modern one—the quality of poetry by women in her era was limited by the narrowness of their education, their works' subject matter, and their aspirations.[9]

Such was, for her, the distressing case with two of her eminent contemporaries, Laetitia Landon and Felicia Hemans, whose work is frequently echoed and improved upon in her own poetry.[10] Barrett intimated to her close friend Mary Russell Mitford the problems she found with each poet's work in language that makes clear her belief that she possessed talents and "powers" superior to those of the two most successful women poets of her day:

(Browning, Letters, 1 : 235)
> *If I had those two powers to choose from . . . I mean the* raw bare powers *. . . I wd choose Miss Landon's. I surmise that it was more elastic, more various, of a stronger web. I fancy it wd have worked out better—had it been* worked out—*with the right moral & intellectual influences in application. As it is, Mrs. Hemans had left the finer poems. Of that there can be no question. But . . . there is a sense of sameness which goes with the sense of excellence [in her work]—a feeling [that] "this writer has written her best,"—or "It is very well—but it can never be better."*

In these comments Barrett's feeling of disappointment is as unmistakable as her astute perception of her contemporaries' poetic failings. Their work lacks moral depth as well as intellectual sophistication and complexity, and it is boringly repetitive. Barrett directly addresses these deficiencies in a single work of her 1838 volume; in doing so, she is admiring and respectful but also canny.

Barrett's strategy for vanquishing her perceived rivals in "Felicia

Hemans" is both politic and highly original. The elegy was first published in the *Monthly Magazine* under the self-consciously intertextual title "Stanzas Addressed to Miss Landon, and Suggested by Her 'Stanzas on the Death of Mrs. Hemans.'" Both there and as retitled in 1838, the poem foregrounds its multivalent parodic effects. (The subtitle in 1838 became, "To L.E.L. / Referring to Her Monody on the Poetess.") In the poem Barrett appropriates the genre of the pastoral elegy adopted by Laetitia Landon to eulogize Hemans, but she does so at a significantly higher level of generic self-consciousness than Landon's poem demonstrates. Whereas the main object of Landon's eulogy is to bewail the suffering of Hemans's life and to praise her achievement, Barrett's poem is designed as a corrective to Landon's emphases (Mermin, 74–75). But in the process Barrett also exploits the genre to discuss the value and function of poetry by women in her contemporary world. She thus "corrects" Landon not only by explaining the inappropriateness of particular imperatives articulated in her eulogy but also, and more importantly, by illustrating the proper historical uses of the English elegy as these resonate, for example, from Milton's *Lycidas* and Shelley's *Adonais*. Barrett's poem further parodies Landon's, as Mermin has observed, by appropriating her stanzaic form but improving upon it; Barrett makes stately four-line stanzas out of the more diffuse eight-line stanzas used by Landon.

What ultimately defines "Felicia Hemans" as a revisionary elegy is a strong element of realism. Landon's instruction to "bring flowers" to "crown the 'cup and lute'" and "flowers to greet the 'bride'" of Christ alludes to Hemans's poem "The Grave of a Poetess," in which Hemans acknowledges how her subject gave "a vain love to passing flowers." Whereas Landon thereby suggests the vanity of Hemans's own nature worship, Barrett stingingly corrects her and commands Landon not to "bring . . . near the solemn corse a type of human seeming" but rather to "Lay only dust's stern verity upon the dust undreaming." She advises against the traditional laying on of flowers but also attempts to dispel Landon's (artificial) grief: "Be happy, crowned and living one!" And by an implicitly invidious comparison of Landon's poems with those of Hemans, Barrett suggests a new direction for Landon's narrowly amatory work. Hemans, she insists, "never wronged that mystic breath which breathed in all her breathing, / Which drew, from rocky earth and man, abstractions high and moving." And Barrett concludes with an even

more damning critique of Landon, who has nonetheless been deferen-
tially introduced in the first stanza as "the bay-crowned living One." She
suggests to Landon that a less shrill and less brazen style might be learned
from Hemans's example. She expresses hope that when Landon's "dust
decayeth,"

> May thine own England say for thee what now for
>   [Hemans] it sayeth—
> "Albeit softly in our ears her silver song was ringing,
> The foot-fall of her parting soul is softer than her
>   singing."

In these last lines Barrett is, by implication, killing off her remaining rival
by prematurely inscribing her epitaph. This is, one might say, a *practical*
effect of the poem, but it is one with ideological ramifications. This work
self-consciously intervenes in the literary culture of its day by adapting
the discourse of mourning—with its imagery of weeping, graveside attendance, and a laying on of flowers, as traditionally manipulated in the
poetic form of the pastoral elegy—to idealize the "mystic breath" of the
poet who generates "abstractions high and moving," that is, once again
to reify a transcendental poetic ideal. But the worldly power struggles
among the three poets that surface in the course of this attempt ultimately
betray that ideal and suggest that the fame ("May thine own England
say") that accompanies successful poetic endeavors is ideologically effi-
cacious because it enables its subject to shape and generate discourse.

In a letter written to her friend Julia Martin four months before the publication of *The Seraphim and Other Poems* Barrett admits to a striking character trait. Responding to Martin's praise of her chronic cheerfulness and
peace of mind, she confides, "Perhaps my contentedness arises a good
deal out of merely this, which many people might . . . call discontent-
edness,—that is, out of seeing, instead of 'good in everything,' the evil of
all things" (Browning and Browning, 3:217). This world-view goes far
toward explaining both the idealist impetus of Barrett's 1838 poems and
the reforming zeal apparent in the revisionist strategies they deploy. It
also helps to explain her unusual anxiety about the reception of her first
book of poems not published anonymously.

In the event, her apprehensions were unwarranted. The reviews
were generally effusive. The *Athenaeum* does worry over an only half-

successful oracular mission visible in the poems but also comments from the outset that "this is an extraordinary volume—especially welcome as an evidence of female . . . accomplishment. . . . Miss Barrett's genius is of a high order: active, vigorous, and versatile" (Browning and Browning, 4:375). *Blackwoods* predicts that she will "some day shine forth with conspicuous splendour" and greets the volume "with love and admiration." John Wilson finds the preface seductive—"pregnant with lofty thoughts" appropriate, one surmises, to an unmarried and devout woman. "Yet," he insists, "her heart [is] humble withal—and she wins her way into ours" (Browning and Browning, 4:379). The *Sunbeam's* observations on Barrett's "masculine genius" (4:390) might explain Wilson's sense of being emotionally and spiritually penetrated by these poems, but they also acknowledge, as if with surprise, the genuine power and originality of Barrett's art for early Victorian readers. The extent of her triumph with *The Seraphim* volume can in fact be measured not only by the common admission that she is "a genuine poetess, of no common order" (4:375), but also by the fact that reviewers compare her, most often, not to other women poets but to male contemporaries, especially Wordsworth and Tennyson. The *Sunbeam* in 1838 asserted that "her style . . . is frequently like [that of] Alfred Tennyson, but she is capable of sustaining a more prolonged flight and pours herself out with greater emotion, enthusiasm and more intense feeling" (4:400). (Barrett nonetheless despised being placed, as she often was, in the "school of Tennyson.") [11] The *Metropolitan Magazine* went so far as to insist that "one or two of Miss Barrett's minor pieces might be mistaken for the productions of the greatest of our poets since Milton" (5:383), that is, for works by Wordsworth. In fact a striking aspect of most of the 1838 reviews is the strain they display when trying to position this "fair author" who possesses "masculine" intellectual strength within existing categories of poets. At every move they are challenged by her self-presentations and the unconventional conventionality of her art.

The praise accorded *The Seraphim* is therefore nearly always qualified. Reviewers display the caution typical of readers who approach new works possessing unexpected virtues and power. Despite strong commendations of her poetry, for instance, the *Athenaeum* finally pronounced the volume "not entirely successful" (4:376) and the *Examiner*, while admitting that Barrett possesses "many of the highest qualities of the divine art" of poetry, worried that she was "in danger of being spoiled by overambition" (4:375). Thus, as Jauss observes, "A literary work, even when it appears to be new, does not present itself as something absolutely new in an informational vacuum, but predisposes its audience to a very specific kind of reception by announcements, overt and covert signals, familiar characteristics, or . . . allusions. It awakens memories of that which was already read, [and] brings the reader to a specific emotional attitude," as we have observed Barrett's 1838 poems doing (23). As a result, eventually even what is, in such works, "at first experienced as [an] alienating perspective, can disappear for later readers, to the extent that the original negativity of the work has . . . entered into the horizon of future aesthetic experience, as a henceforth familiar expectation" (25). Judging from commentaries on Barrett's 1844 poems, within only a few years she had achieved precisely this effect.

The tributes that her work elicited from reviewers and readers alike in that year are familiar by now, but a brief review of several will demonstrate the extent and the quality of the cultural power that had accrued to Elizabeth Barrett by midcareer. *Blackwoods* reflects the general tone of the 1844 reviews when it magisterially pronounces that "among the living poets of England [Elizabeth Barrett] enjoys a very eminent position. Her writings are of such a character as to exert a powerful influence among the imaginative, the religious, and the reflecting portions of the reading public" (Browning and Browning, 9:374). In short, few readers are exempt from the ideological effects of her work, but this influence clearly depends to a significant extent upon her gender. Because poetry was, for the Victorians, a form of social experience that attended specifically to the culture of the emotions—as John Stuart Mill's testimony avers—and because women were universally believed to have greater emotional depth, sensitivity, and range than men, poems produced by a woman had proportionally greater potential to exert "influence" on the subjective life of their audience. The *Blackwoods* reviewer therefore means even more than he says when he describes Barrett as "a woman whose powers appear to . . . extend over a wider and profounder range of thought and feeling than ever before fell within the intellectual compass of any of the softer sex." Another reviewer confirms the judgment: "In Miss Barrett's poems there are frequent evidences of a truer and deeper sensibility than has ever yet been exhibited by any female writer in the language" (9:350, 374). But *Blackwoods* also indicates how crucial the repeated emphasis on Barrett's female subjectivity is to her canonization by contemporaries when he comments on her sonnet "Comfort": "How profound and yet how feminine is the sentiment . . . [it] overflows with feelings more gracious and more graceful than ever man's can be" (9:351).

Such commentaries are typical of Barrett's reception by 1844. The reviews more often than not echoed one another, and the result was virtual obeisance at the aesthetic altar of England's singular sage poetess, as we see from a review in the *League*: "We receive her volumes not as works to criticise, but as lessons of holy wisdom which it is our duty not less than our delight to 'read, mark, learn, and inwardly digest'" (9:379). In a similar vein, the *Atlas* describes Barrett as the "priestess" of an order of poets characterized by "their endurance—their trustfulness in supreme goodness—their confidence in individual and social improvement—their large-hearted humanity . . . their belief in virtue—their assurance in the regenerating forces now acting upon society—their assertion of the law of progress—their alliance of truth and beauty as the grand source of happiness—and, above all, their entire devotion to their art, as a serious, a sacred, a most holy thing" (9:326–27). Here, if anywhere, are tributes to the ideological efficacy of Barrett's poetry. For this last reviewer in particular, her work successfully intervenes in virtually every field of social discourse, from the philosophical and the religious to the political and the aesthetic.

The artistic and ideological success of Elizabeth Barrett's poems of 1838 and 1844 yielded her a form and degree of social power intuited by Harriet Martineau and some of the reviewers of 1844 but to which Barrett herself remained relatively oblivious because she did not yet comprehend, or could not risk the assertion, that in mid-Victorian bourgeois culture the aesthetic was a very important locus of ideology and power. By 1850, however, in part as the effect of discussions with Robert Browning and in part as a matter of her maturing intellectual awareness, she had clearly come to realize the political and ideological dimensions of her art: with her poems of that year she began, for the first time with a high degree of self-consciousness, to assert and exploit her power. And by the time she published *Aurora Leigh* in 1856, she could revel in the "triumph of the poet," who utters speech that "burns you through / With special revelation," and "shakes the heart / Of all the men and women in the world" (1:902–7).[12]

IV

Matthew Arnold's Gipsies: Ideology and the Discourse of the Other

In spite of his immense wisdom and his mysterious breadth,
[the gipsy] had a human weight, an earthly condition that
kept him involved in the minuscule problems of daily life.
Gabriel García Marquez, *One Hundred Years of Solitude*

Byron found our nation, after its long and victorious struggle
with revolutionary France, fixed in a system of established
facts and dominant ideas which revolted him. The mental
bondage of the most powerful part of our nation, of its strong
middle class, to a narrow and false system of this kind is what
we call British Philistinism. That bondage is unbroken to this
hour. . . . [But] as the inevitable break-up of the old order
comes, as the English middle class slowly awakens from its
intellectual sleep of two centuries, as our actual present world,
to which this sleep has condemned us, shows itself more
clearly,—our world of an aristocracy materialised and null,
a middle class purblind and hideous, a lower class crude and
brutal,—we shall turn our eyes again . . . upon this passion-
ate and dauntless soldier of a forlorn hope.
Matthew Arnold, "Byron" (1881)

IN 1881 MATTHEW ARNOLD could, remarkably, still identify with Byron as a poet-gipsy, an outcast wandering Europe and writing verses in futile rebellion against the values and behavior of the social class that had produced him. But if Arnold's image of Byron as a revolutionary on the ideological margins—"this passionate and dauntless soldier of a for-lorn hope"—is not entirely a sentimental idealization of the real man and poet, Arnold's implicit identification with him is both sentimental and disingenuous. Approaching the age of sixty in this year, Arnold had served two five-year terms as professor of poetry at Oxford and was only three years away from the chief inspectorship of schools and just two from a Civil List pension given "in public recognition of service to the poetry and literature of England." With a score of influential books behind him, Matthew Arnold had become a public institution, a cultural force unprecedented in Victorian England. Arnold was able to attain this position in large part because of his extraordinarily complex sensitivity to the interactions of discourse and ideology in his society; in particular, he strove ceaselessly in his writings against "the mental bondage of the most powerful part of our nation, of its strong middle class, to a narrow and false system" of "established facts and dominant ideas."

Arnold's identification with the position of social rebel dates from his earliest days. Park Honan describes Arnold passing his fourteenth year (the year he first read Byron) "in the grandest juvenile defiance of the fact that he was an Arnold" (Honan, 26). His rebellious inclinations, notorious during his Oxford years, were never quelled but were profitably channeled as he aged. Consistently challenging the dominant (materialist and, in his estimate, spiritually barren) ideologies of his era, he gradually emerged as the preeminent intellectual authority of late Victorian England.

By this account it is perhaps unsurprising that a central, indeed mythic figure in Arnold's poetry written between 1843 and 1866 is the gipsy, a cultural outsider. In "To a Gipsy Child by the Sea-Shore" (begun in 1843 or 1844), "Resignation" (begun in 1843), "The Scholar-Gipsy" (begun in 1848), and his great elegy "Thyrsis" (1866), varied but prominent images of gipsies—who were coming increasingly under public scrutiny at midcentury—take on totemic value.[1] These figures have more than merely personal and temperamental significance for Arnold and his poetry. They serve him, ultimately, as crucial ideological tropes that engage conventional stereotypes of a threatening alien Other in Victorian England. As is clear from the first appearance of a gipsy figure in his work, Arnold imbued these cultural outcasts with a special burden of not only sociological but also intertextual and philosophical significance.

Investigating the historical and literary contexts surrounding the production of Arnold's poems that feature images of gipsies provides a partial set of answers to the kind of question that a historicist critic might well ask but that seems not to have occurred to commentators with other orientations: Why gipsies?[2] Exploring the implications of those contexts reveals that an implied gipsy trope operates throughout Arnold's cultural criticism, as well as his poetry, to position and define him as a writer whose power—like that of Byron—accrues in part from the equivocal quality of his professed estrangement from a society he, unlike Byron, desired not to escape but to transform. Arnold's poetic assaults on the false values of that society begin with a challenge to its most formidable literary titan from the 1840s, William Wordsworth. They quickly proceed, however, to capitalize on the burgeoning popular interest in gipsies during the 1850s and 1860s, one strand in a discourse of the period notable for its simultaneous fascination with and chauvinist attacks upon the alien Other.[3]

In this chapter I focus at first on the intertextual aspects of Arnold's earliest gipsy poems. These works should be viewed as critical responses to works by Wordsworth (particularly the Intimations ode and "Gipsies"), as well as to his poetic procedures and ideological inconsistencies. I then discuss an array of fictional and nonfictional texts available to Arnold that purported to report facts about gipsies but more often actually employed the discourse of the Other to promulgate myths about them. These texts circulated with unusual frequency in early to mid-Victorian England: they influenced parliamentary investigations, blue books, and ultimately the passage of laws directly related to gipsy life and culture. Similarly, I remark on the economic circumstances—the progress of capitalism—that helped to generate such texts and laws. Matthew Arnold's gipsy poems were thus produced in the contexts of particular literary, social, and political discourses operating in early and mid-Victorian England. His central trope in four major poems is appropriated, as I hope to demonstrate, not only from his well-known reading of Glanvill's *The Vanity of Dogmatizing* but also from an important controversy that attracted a great deal of public discussion during the period in which the poems were written and published (1843–66).

Examining the operations of the gipsy trope in Arnold's poetry and in his culture, we observe how his work engaged the mid-Victorian discourse of the Other to great advantage. The crucial strategic beginnings of these engagements appear in Arnold's adoption of a mask of estrangement (as early as in his rebellious teens). Constituting the voice of his poems as alien allowed his work to appropriate and eventually reconstruct the discourse of the Other, which had been most often a colloquy of fascinated repugnance, in *positive* terms and to construct the image (an illusion) of a poet positioned at the margins of all (corrupt) discourses through which social subjects normally define themselves and live their lives, discourses that normally strive to represent cultural values associated with the Other as misguided and threatening. Embracing this position was for Arnold, simultaneously, to represent his own stance as one outside of history: Arnold fully understood the ideological operations of discourse and the historical particularity of discursive formations, as his prose writings consistently demonstrate. He saw history as the grounds of cultural exegesis, yet he was thoroughly aware of the textuality of history, the narrative and fictive elements visible in even documentary discussions of any particular historical moment. (A close reading of *Culture and Anarchy*, for instance, would make this clear.) Arnold appears also to have understood that conclusions reached by historians, including cultural historians, are inevitably tentative and contingent upon gaps in the narrative that remain to be filled. After 1852 his poetry employs this perspective on narratives, which we now loosely term *deconstructive*, as a rhetorical strategy in the gipsy trope so as to *resist* ideological consistency and commitment and to intervene in social discourses in ways that might reshape their ideological effects. Matthew Arnold, professor of poetry at Oxford, through such means succeeded in accruing cultural power over the middle classes, those single-minded adherents to "established facts and dominant ideas."

Intertextual Matters

Arnold's earliest gipsy poem, "To A Gipsy Child by the Sea-Shore," is a pessimistic, if not morose, elegy that visibly reinscribes and transvalues Wordsworth's "Ode: Intimations of Immortality Recollected from Early Childhood." Arnold's gipsy child, with its "gloom" and "meditative guise," is at once muse and philosophical father of the man who speaks in this poem: "With eyes which sought thine eyes thou didst converse, / And that soul-searching vision fell on me" (ll. 15–16). The infant's postlapsarian "vision" of the world, as the speaker projects it, is complete: the child has "foreknown the vanity of hope" and "foreseen

[its] harvest" yet endures with a "funereal aspect" and "the calm . . . of stoic souls," "drugging pain by patience" (ll. 39–40, 46, 29, 13). Unlike Wordsworth's child, who trails "clouds of glory" into this world, Arnold's already possesses the sober eye of maturity, its "slight brow" surrounded by "clouds of doom" (l. 4). And even as the speaker imagines the gipsy child growing up, possibly to forget its stoical infant wisdom, he makes no mention of any precorporeal "joy," the real subject of Wordsworth's poem and object of his speaker's "obstinate questionings." In his own visions of the child's prospective getting and spending—Arnold's "winning" in the "throng'd fields" (l. 58) of a Darwinian existence—the speaker refuses to accept the possibility that the child will ever wholly forget its present "majesty of grief" (l. 68). The most positive memory the speaker can evoke for this infant employs metaphors of the Fall:

Not daily labour's dull, Lethean spring,

(ll. 54–56)   Oblivion in lost angels can infuse

Of the soil'd glory, and the trailing wing.

Arnold's reinscription of Wordsworth ("trailing clouds of glory do we come") appropriates his images, his abstract and weighty diction, and the syntactic movement of his lines only to reject his precursor's proclaimed faith in a joy at the heart of human existence. This child's thoughts, unlike those of Wordsworth in his Ode, are not disturbed by "longings vain" or any "superfluity of joy" (ll. 9–10). The gipsy child thus becomes a cipher through whom Arnold's speaker can ventriloquize his nihilism, anticipating the ideological critique of Wordsworth articulated in the preface to Arnold's edition of Wordsworth's poetry published thirty-four years later: "His poetry is the reality, his philosophy . . . is the illusion" (Arnold, *Prose Works*, 4:48). Arnold further explains that "the 'intimations' of the famous 'Ode,' those corner-stones of the supposed philosophic system of Wordsworth,—the idea of the high instincts and affections coming out in childhood, testifying of a divine home recently left, and fading away as our life proceeds,—this idea, of undeniable beauty as a play of fancy, has itself not the character of poetic truth of the best kind; it has no real solidity" (4:49).

Arnold's intertextual assault upon Wordsworth in his gipsy poems is, however, more complex than this reading of the language in "A Gipsy Child" indicates. For Wordsworth had also written about gipsies and viewed them in clearly ideological terms. Arnold, who belatedly proclaimed himself a Wordsworthian, certainly knew Wordsworth's poem "Gipsies." The 1807 version reads in full:

> Yet are they here?—the same unbroken knot
> Of human Beings, in the self-same spot!
> Men, Women, Children, yea the frame
> Of the whole Spectacle the same!
> Only their fire seems bolder, yielding light:
> Now deep and red, the colouring of night;
> That on their Gipsy-faces falls,
> Their bed of straw and blanket-walls.
> —Twelve hours, twelve bounteous hours, are gone while I
> Have been a Traveller under open sky,
> Much witnessing of change and chear,
> Yet as I left I find them here!
> The weary Sun betook himself to rest.
>
> (Wordsworth, *Poems*, 211–12)[4]
>
> —Then issued Vesper from the fulgent West.
> Outshining like a visible God
> The glorious path in which he trod.
> And now, ascending, after one dark hour,
> And one night's diminution of her power,
> Behold the mighty Moon! this way
> She looks as if at them—but they
> Regard not her:—oh better wrong and strife
> Better vain deeds or evil than such life!
> The silent Heavens have goings on;
> The stars have tasks—but these have none.

This is an extraordinary work from the pen of the professedly empathetic poet of the "primary affections of the human heart," a poem that reflects, as Arnold might well have observed, a wholly Philistine provincialism and lack of curiosity, along with a suffocating captivity to the puritan values of "Hebraism." This poem clearly betrays the liberal, humanitarian ethos that Wordsworth's 1798 poems and his famous preface to the *Lyrical Ballads* define as fundamental to valuable poetry.

The speaker in "Gipsies" begins openly uncomprehending: these people, their customs and their reason for being, are wholly alien to him, as is their community, which Wordsworth describes as a mere "knot." They constitute a "Spectacle," always a disparaging term in his lexicon.[5] As a "Traveller under open sky, / Much witnessing," the speaker contrasts his own energetic activity with the gipsies' apparent immobility and passivity, his sensitivity to the natural world with their obliviousness to it: "they regard [it] not." Although an admitted outsider who has only the slightest acquaintance with the gipsy sociality, he sits in judgment upon them. This poem's coda is stridently didactic. Wordsworth's bourgeois arrogance and insularity, qualities Arnold consistently condemns, are obvious here, and, more importantly, so is the basis of his judgment in the entirely external aspects of the gipsies' lives rather than in their *inward* qualities as "human Beings." In this poem we find Wordsworth demonstrating none of the compassion for his fellows that elsewhere, especially in pieces from the *Lyrical Ballads*, energizes his work. Indeed, the racist overtones of "Gipsies" subvert Wordsworth's early liberal and Romantic poetic ethos, which Arnold in his maturity appropriated and revised along classical lines.

The speaker's ideological stance in this lyric radically diverges from the ideal of human perfection Arnold articulates in his later essays on culture. That ideal, we recall, requires "an inward spiritual activity, having for its characters increased sweetness, increased light, increased life, increased sympathy" (*Prose Works*, 5 : 108). Refusing any real contact with the gipsies, Wordsworth in this poem hardly embodies Arnold's premier *social* idea, namely, that "the men of culture are the true apostles of equality . . . those who have had a passion for diffusing, for making prevail, for carrying from one end of society to the other, the best knowledge, the best ideas of their time," that is, for "humanising" knowledge (5 : 113). It comes, then, as no surprise that early in his essay on Wordsworth Arnold insists that "composing moral and didactic poems . . . brings us but a very little way in poetry" (4 : 45).

Yet the impact "Gipsies" made upon Arnold is apparent from linguistic echoes of the poem and revaluations of its critique of gipsies that appear in "Resignation," begun in 1843 but not published until 1849. A formal and structural revision of "Tintern Abbey," this philosophical lyric, written not in blank verse but rather in rigid iambic tetrameter couplets, finally advocates the supreme value of the poet's life, "resigned" in several senses: detached or withdrawn from the world; willing to accept all vicissitudes; and willing also to accept the fate of reinscription (re-signing), a fate here enacted upon Wordsworthian texts by Arnold himself. The life of the gipsies in "Resignation" is contrasted with that of the contemplative poet, who attains "not [Wordsworthian] joy, but peace," a consequence of "His sad lucidity of soul" (ll. 192, 198):

> Before him he sees life unroll,
> A placid and continuous whole—
> That general life which does not cease   (ll. 189–97)
> Whose secret is not joy, but peace;
> That life . . . Fate gave.

Unlike this idealized poet, the gipsies—who, as in Wordsworth's poem, "In dark knots crouch round the wild flame" (l. 118)—appear constitutionally unable to attain tranquillity and detachment. They cannot compare past and present, nor can they "reason" about mortality ("time's busy touch") and the inevitable "decay" of their own culture, as "Crowded and keen the country grows," with "The law [growing] stronger every day" (ll. 133–35). Inaccessible to the higher poetic consciousness,

> . . . they rubb'd through yesterday
> In their hereditary way,
> And they will rub through, if they can,
> To-morrow on the self-same plan,   (ll. 138–43)
> Till death arrive to supersede,
> For them, vicissitude and need.

This, despite the fact that

> Signs are not wanting, which might raise
> The ghost in them of former days—
> Signs are not wanting, if they would   (ll. 123–26)
> Suggestions to disquietude.

Although this speaker claims to possess high levels of both semiotic and historical awareness ("Signs . . . might raise / The ghost . . . of former days"), and although he is not (as Wordsworth's speaker is) wholly unsympathetic to the gipsies' plight, his attitude toward the gipsies remains equivocal. He generates an image of their mindless passivity and fatalism in order to aggrandize the stature of the idealized poet. In doing so, he suppresses any consciousness that their situation is socially and economically determined. As a "migratory" underclass (whose westward trek from India began about A.D. 1000), they lack the speaker's privileges of education, leisure, and wealth. They are in no position to make serious life choices at all. Yet Arnold's speaker is aware that their "decay" or displacement from the countryside is both a sign and product of the economic times, a result of an expansion of the Anglo-Saxon population directly tied to industrial capitalism. Unlike the speaker of Wordsworth's "Gipsies," Arnold's speaker is sensitive to social and political developments that pose a threat to traditional gipsy culture, and to the extent that they are endangered wandering outcasts he identifies with them. Like him (and Fausta, his auditor),

> They, too, have long roam'd to and fro;
> They ramble, leaving, where they pass
> Their fragments on the cumber'd grass.
> And often to some kindly place
> Chance guides the migratory race,
> Where, though long wanderings intervene,
> They recognise a former scene.
> The dingy tents are pitched . . .
> They see their shackled beasts again
> Move, browsing, up the gray-wall'd lane.

(ll. 109–21)

The speaker in this poem exposes his limited political understanding and inadequate social vision, rhetorically urging the gipsies to recover the "fragments" of their past in order to reconstitute their present and future lives as a "placid and continuous whole." This he attempts to persuade "Fausta" to do and apparently has himself done. Finally, for him as for Wordsworth these alien people remain ciphers, despite his partial identification with and incomplete compassion for them. The attitude toward the gipsies expressed in this poem, hovering somewhat obtusely between idealization and criticism, in fact replicates the extremes of contemporary response to "the gipsy problem" in England during the 1840s and 1850s. Ironically, through its critique of gipsy culture, as well as its intertextual resonances, Arnold's position calls attention to the self-righteous provincialism of Wordsworth's poetic commentary on the gipsies some forty years earlier. But Arnold's ambivalent perspective in "Resignation" allows for important re-visions of gipsy figures (and gipsy culture) in his poems of 1853 and 1866.

Victorian Gipsies and "The Scholar-Gipsy"

In a familiar letter to Arthur Hough Clough, written on 23 September 1849, the year "Resignation" was published and the year during which "The Scholar-Gipsy" was partly composed (*Poems*, 356), Arnold laments his sense of personal isolation, angst, distraction, and immobility. He sees himself as a representative product of a corrupt society: "These are damned times—everything is against one—the height to which knowledge is come, the spread of luxury, our physical enervation, the absence of great *natures*, the unavoidable contact with millions of small ones, newspapers, cities, light profligate friends, moral desperadoes like Carlyle, our own selves, and the sickening consciousness of our difficulties: but for God's sake let us neither be fanatics nor yet chalf blown by the wind" (Arnold, *Letters*, 156). The substance of this critique is of course central to "The Scholar-Gipsy," a poem that laments "this strange disease of modern life," with its "sick fatigue," "its languid doubt," its manifold "disappointments," "its sick hurry, its divided aims," and "Its heads o'ertax'd." In a distinct turn from his equivocal use of the gipsy figure in "Resignation," Arnold now—some six years after the initial composition of that poem—presents the gipsy as an idealized alien Other, the speaker's imaginary hero, whom he warns to

> . . . fly our paths, our feverish contact fly!
> For strong the infection of our mental strife,
> Which, though it gives no bliss, yet spoils for rest;   (ll. 221–25)
> And we should win thee from thy own fair life,
> Like us distracted, and like us unblest.

By 1849 the placid and harmonious, distanced perspective on life maintained by the ideal poet of "Resignation" was beyond the grasp of Arnold, who immersed himself compulsively in the public issues of the day. The similarly idealized Scholar-Gipsy is, however, immune to such issues because he is alien to the society plagued by them. Arnold envied such immunity. In the same letter to Clough he explains: "When I come to town I tell you beforehand I will have a real effort at managing myself as to newspapers and the talk of the day. Why the devil do I read about Ld. Grey's sending convicts to the Cape, and excite myself thereby, when I can thereby produce no possible good. But public opinion consists in a multitude of such excitements" (*Letters*, 156–57). Perhaps less incendiary than Lord Grey's proposal to establish a penal colony at the Cape of Good Hope, the controversy over the status and future of the gipsies in English society had constituted one such "excitement" for the British public since the early 1840s. By 1852 the directions of the public discussion, both in the periodical press and in fiction, had changed significantly.

Beginning in 1842 "the gipsy problem" was much in the news. A long controversy—one prominent feature of a discourse of the Other that also included debates about colonialism and imperialism—simmered over this "intriguing people who from time out of mind had flouted convention" (Behlmer, 231). As Arnold must have been aware, the gipsy presence in England "struck some reformers as an intolerable affront to the values of modern civilization," precisely those Hebraic middle-class values (industry, wealth, pragmatism, respectability) that Arnold attacks as Philistine throughout his prose works of the 1860s. Attitudes toward the mysterious gipsies generally reflect the social values and cultural dispositions of those who discuss them. During the second half of the century gipsies became the objects of both romantic idealization and systematic harassment in England. Widely considered an "'alien' race and culture," the gipsies "existed on the fringes of society, and of the economic and political spheres, and this marginality to, or rejection of, a conventional, settled mode of life made them suspect and unwelcome." They represented a threatening cultural Other, "to be feared for the implicit threat their existence posed to a method of thinking that was increasingly to stress immobility and regularity, and to be resented for remaining apart from the pressures towards conformity, whether legal, institutional, cultural or [social]. . . . Yet they were also envied for managing to retain some independence and individuality" (Mayall, 92).

In 1842 the *Times* featured a number of articles on the gipsies, reflecting the public's inconsistent attitude toward gipsy culture. On 12 October readers were reassured that "the New Forest Gypsies were an honest lot who, in return for a little straw to cushion their beds, acted as farmers' watchdogs against poachers." But a month later "the same tribe stood accused of suffocating sheep by forcing wool down their throats."

That autumn two sensational articles described the "stately funerals and shunning ceremonies in which Gypsy renegades were banished from their tribes" (Behlmer, 234–35). Even more noteworthy was the retirement in 1847 of the Reverend James Crabbe from his exotic and well-known mission at Southampton (begun in 1829), where he had attempted to care for but also to convert the New Forest gipsies.

The gipsies remained in the news as much for the threat they posed to the values of the respectable middle classes (and the scenery of the English landscape) as for the mysteriousness of their customs and social organization. They were special targets of repression in 1849, when "England's new county constabularies launched a campaign against mendicancy in all its forms," and also several years later, when "rural police redoubled their efforts to drive all Gypsy tents off public land" (Behlmer, 235–36). Gipsies were much discussed in the reports of the Select Committee on Police of 1852 and 1853. In 1856, when the County Constabulary Act was passed, "methods of surveillance, harassment and persecution became increasingly efficient, and there are many references to the constant pressures exerted by the police on [gipsy] travellers, driving them from the rural roads into the towns. On occasions, camps were raided and the people persecuted simply on suspicion they might have stolen something" (Mayall, 155).

Books and periodical essays about the gipsies appeared regularly throughout the forties, fifties, and sixties, when Arnold was composing most of his poetry. These works exerted a strong influence on popular opinion. In 1843 Crabbe himself published *A Condensed History of the Gipsies*. The previous year the fifth edition of Samuel Roberts's popular book *The Gipsies; their Origins, Continuance, and Destination* (first published in 1836) had appeared, and in the following year the Reverend J. West's *A Plea for the Education of the Children of the Gipsies* came out. Also in 1844, William Howitt's *The Rural Life of England* focused on the lifestyle and movements of English gipsy tribes. During the 1840s articles on gipsy life were to be found in a wide variety of magazines and institutional organs, from *Fraser's* (which often published essays by Thomas Arnold), the *New Edinburgh Review*, and *Sharpe's London Magazine* to the *Church of England Magazine*.[6]

The public interest in gipsy life and customs is most fully revealed by the success between 1841 and 1851 of fictional and semifictional works by George Borrow.[7] *The Zincali; or, An Account of the Gypsies of Spain* (1841), though published by John Murray in a small edition, was hailed as the "prize book" of the season by the *Dublin University Magazine* and went through two additional printings in 1843, when Borrow's new book, *The Bible of Spain*, became an enormous popular success, establishing itself as "one of the great books of mid-century Britain" (Collie, 183) and drawing further attention to *The Zincali*.[8] *The Bible of Spain* also raised strong expectations for Borrow's second major work about gipsies, *Lavengro*, published in 1851. Although reviews of *Lavengro* were uniformly bad, they were numerous, and, for better or worse, among Victorian readers of fiction Borrow had by midcentury aroused a powerful interest in gipsy life, language, and customs.[9]

Inspired in part by Borrow's work, a number of major literary figures, including Carlyle, Bulwer-Lytton, Robert Browning, Swinburne, and George Eliot (who published her poem *The Spanish Gipsy* in 1868), became fascinated with gipsies. Matthew Arnold was, it seems, even more intimately familiar with Borrow than these writers. Arnold's "The Forsaken Merman," which appeared along with "A Gipsy Child by the Sea-Shore" in his 1849 volume of poems, for example, makes use of George Borrow's version of the story from his 1825 review of J. M. Thiele's *Danske Folkesagen* (Honan, 89).

The Zincali appeared during Arnold's first year at Oxford, with its second and third printings coming in 1843, the year Arnold won the Newdigate prize with his poem "Cromwell" and "settled on poetry as his *vocation*. . . . his calling, his star, his reason for being. . . . He reconciled this [newly] serious view of himself with his idle Oxford days, and though still looking for time-wasting pursuits he also wrote" and read voraciously (Honan, 70). In 1844 Arnold picked up a copy of Joseph Glanvill's *The Vanity of Dogmatizing*, which discusses the Oxford "lad" he memorialized as the Scholar-Gipsy. At the time, similarities between Borrow's descriptions of his early life with the gipsies and Glanvill's myth would have struck Arnold with uncanny force.[10] The experiences of this student, as Glanvill describes them, remarkably prefigure those George Borrow mythologized in his much-discussed *Lavengro* in passages that often replicate material from *The Zincali*, which begins, "I can remember no period when the mentioning of the name of Gipsy did not awaken feelings . . . hard to be described, but in which a strange pleasure predominated." Like Arnold's Scholar-Gipsy, Borrow felt a natural kinship with the gipsies and studied their culture extensively:

> *Throughout his youth he had frequently come across and spent time*
> *with groups of gipsies. . . . he had consorted with them on Mouse-*
> *hold Heath and other such places near Norwich; had met them at*
> *horse-fairs and prizefights; had lived with them, sometimes, and*
> *been accepted by them. . . . In all these places, he had been [em-*   (Collie,
> *braced] by the gipsies, partly because he had taken the trouble to*   162–63)
> *learn their language . . . and partly because of a scarcely definable*
> *feeling of kinship he and many gipsies immediately felt for one*
> *another.*

Thus, Arnold's scholar is a particular student of "the secret [of the gipsy] art" of ruling "as they desired / The workings of men's brains" so that they "can bind them to what thoughts they will" (ll. 45–48). His "*one* aim, *one* business, *one* desire," once the long-awaited "spark from heaven" has fallen, is to impart that secret to the world (ll. 152, 120). In the meantime, this mythical figure remains elusive: in and out of the public eye and the social world, glimpsed on occasion by maidens, farmers, housewives, and possibly even by the poem's "dreaming" speaker, who ultimately admonishes the phantom gipsy to flee all contact with those contaminated by "this strange disease of modern life" (l. 203). Arnold's poem clearly suppresses the sensational and threatening elements of the public controversy over gipsies during the 1840s to emphasize the ideal and exotic features of gipsy mythology featured in the fiction of the period.

If we read "The Scholar-Gipsy" (originally titled "The Wandering Mesmerist") in the dual contexts of Arnold's other works that feature gipsies and public discourse, both factual and fictional, surrounding "the gipsy problem" in mid-Victorian England, coming to terms with this difficult poem is increasingly complicated. As David Riede has recently argued, the poem is, on the one hand, so deeply resonant of various literary intertexts—including Milton, Wordsworth, and Keats—that its vision is "relegated to a literary never-never land where it can have no real contact with modern life" (Riede, *Arnold*, 142). On the other hand, as we have seen, the poem is topical. It presents a comprehensive and damning, albeit highly generalized critique of the cultural values that dominate the historical moment of its composition. A transitional poem, "The Scholar-Gipsy" wholly suppresses the historical particulars in which it is grounded, and it does so in the service of overtly ideological commentary. Its subject is the attainment of benign power in the social world. Yet any reader of 1853 even superficially acquainted with public issues of the day would have read "The Scholar-Gipsy" (as well as Arnold's other gipsy poems) with an awareness of the controversy over English gipsies and seen it as a peculiar extension of the romantic interest elicited by images of gipsies in recent literature, especially the work of Borrow.

Far more than today's readers, those who picked up the poem then would inevitably also have been struck by the process of historical elision that dominates the last two stanzas. (These have wholly perplexed modern critics.) On first reading, the narrative presented here of the Tyrian trader fleeing from the "merry Grecian coaster" evokes mythical, rather than historical, resonances. Or, if viewed as distantly historical, the descriptions are so antiqued as to have acquired more imaginative force than topical interest. Yet the questions raised on second and subsequent readings of these difficult stanzas do elicit a concern with contemporaneous events whose existence they seem to deny. This is especially the case because of the stark contrast between the images they present and the emotionally fraught obsession of the preceding stanzas with modernity and its malaises. How, one asks, do the Tyrians and the Greeks stand in for the Scholar-Gipsy and the modern narrator? What exactly do the cargoes of the trader and coaster, described in such loving detail, signify? Metaphorical equivalences quickly break down as geographical details take on prominence. The trader sails

> O'er the blue Midland waters with the gale,
> Betwixt the Syrtes and soft Sicily,
>   To where the Atlantic raves
> Outside the western straits . . . where
>   Shy traffickers, the dark Iberians come.

What issues are actually raised in these stanzas relevant to those that occupy the rest of the poem? Several, in fact, and all point to a fairly tumultuous European present that this imaginative tableau of the distant past would appear to suppress. When the veneer of Keatsian description is penetrated, the poem's culminating simile is seen, at the general level, to concern itself with problems of territorial invasion, the maintenance of cultural autonomy, threats of conflict, and the success of economic relations between nations, all issues of great moment during the period in which "The Scholar-Gipsy" was composed (1848–52).

After the European countries shattered by revolution or the threat of it in 1848 and 1849 became stabilized, the standoff between major powers—England, France, Russia, Austria, Prussia, and Turkey—all eager to usurp territory or protect what they already possessed, dominated political discourse in Europe. The German provinces were at issue between Austria and Prussia; France desired more land along the Rhine; Italy rankled under the "protection" of Austria; and a conflict between Russia and Turkey in the Near East seemed inevitable. A host of stopgap treaties and protocols prevented the outbreak of any full-scale conflict until Britain and France declared war on Russia in February 1854 and inaugurated the Crimean debacle.[12] This was the tense political situation in Europe, which, as we have seen, Arnold typically would have been unable to ignore. Yet the metaphorical strategies and Keatsian stylistic devices that dominate the last two stanzas of "The Scholar-Gipsy" artistically reconstitute such historical particulars, which served in part to define what it meant to be a "modern" European at midcentury and which are thus also responsible for the poem's mood of estrangement, its idealization of gipsies, and its various refusals of reality. These elements of the poem, all of which have ideological implications, are generated through the work's engagement with the contemporary discourse of the Other. Glanvill's scholar-gipsy explains how his gipsy-mentors "could do wonders by the power of *Imagination*." The concluding stanzas of Arnold's poem do not merely replicate its escapist themes; they demonstrate a process of elision and imaginative transfiguration that Arnold may well have viewed as a prospective cure for this "strange disease of modern life."

The Acquisition of Cultural Power

Riede suggests that Arnold's removal of his Scholar-Gipsy from the "gradual furnace of the world" so that he might live forever "may anticipate Arnold's later critical strategy of disinterestedness, of removing oneself from the fray to preserve a sense of the ideal, but it also anticipates the problem of that strategy: anyone so distanced from society cannot be effective or meaningful within it. By corporealizing his ideal in such a tangible form as the Gipsy, Arnold cut off the possibility of absorbing it. The Gipsy and the ideal are preserved, but only on the outskirts of society. Poetic reverie is, in a sense, banished or outlawed, or at the very least rendered irrelevant. It can have no practical influence on life" (142). But as Arnold repeatedly emphasizes, most notably in "The Function of Criticism at the Present Time," practical influence is, from the perspective of the ideal critic—who is also a critic of the culturally hegemonic frameworks of meaning and value we know as ideology—the least desirable kind of influence to have: "The critic must keep out of the region of immediate practice in the political, social, humanitarian sphere if he wants to make a beginning for that more free speculative treatment of things, which may perhaps one day make its benefits felt even in this sphere, but in a natural and thence irresistible manner" (*Prose Works*, 3 : 275). Throughout his critical writings Arnold, by his example, insists precisely on the need for remaining outside the sphere of practice, that is, for remaining culturally alien, Other. He does so through a strategy of equivocation, espousing the value of a free play of ideas on all subjects, which disallows the taking of rigid ideological positions and allows for changes of mind and heart. Insofar as "The Scholar-Gipsy" presents a generalized condemnation of frameworks of value and modes of behavior characterized as "modern," it also implicitly repudiates, through its ambiguous metaphors, all varieties of doctrinalism. It may thus be read as a poetic manifesto that prefigures the central beliefs and procedures of Arnold's most important works of criticism.

From the outset of the preface to *Poems* (1853), in which "The Scholar-Gipsy" first appeared, Arnold decries "modern problems" and the consequent "doubts" and "discouragement" that afflict his contemporaries. "The confusion of the present times is great," he acknowledges (*Prose Works*, 1 : 8), and he therefore concludes by idealizing writers who, like him, with steady and composed judgments, reject their own historical eras as "wanting in moral grandeur"; these are ages of "spiritual discomfort." Like the speaker of "The Scholar-Gipsy," Arnold the critic laments that "it is impossible for us, under the circumstances amidst which we live, to think clearly, to feel nobly . . . to delineate firmly" (1 : 15), and therefore to write significant poetry. It is precisely the failure of his eponymous hero Empedocles to do these things and therefore of the poem in which he figures to depict "an excellent action" that compels Arnold to remove his greatest work from *Poems*, 1853. "The Scholar-Gipsy," as one of the poems that supplants *Empedocles*, however does little more to fulfill his ideal of a poetry that "shall inspirit and rejoice the reader."

The "circumstances" Arnold cites in his preface as responsible for the modern malaise ("sick hurry," "divided aims") result in part from industrial capitalism, an obviously dominant Victorian social ideology whose effects preoccupied him just as "The Scholar-Gipsy" was being conceived. A letter of 1 March 1848 to Arthur Hugh Clough demonstrates Arnold's concern with "relations between labour & capital" and the crisis of alienation spawned by capitalism that is destabilizing his culture: "What are called the *fair profits* of capital which if it does not realize it will leave it's [*sic*] seat & go elsewhere, have surely no absolute amount, but depend on the view the capitalist takes of the matter. If the rule is— everyone must get all he can—the capitalist understands by *fair profits* such as will enable him to live like a colossal Nob: & Lancashire artisans knowing if they will not let him make these, Yorkshire artisans will, tacent & sweat" (*Letters*, 86–87). Industrial capitalism has produced profound social fractures and conflicts, as well as a uniquely modern variety of individual malaise, in an era wholly dominated by a materialistic middle class. This is the class whose values and behavior Arnold repeatedly disparages in his later essays but out of which he himself emerged. As he acknowledges in *Culture and Anarchy*, "Almost all my attention has naturally been concentrated on my own class, the middle class, with which I am in closest sympathy, and which has been, besides, the great power of our day" (*Prose Works*, 5:139). Beginning with his prose works of the 1850s, it is of course Arnold's ambition to reform and regenerate, indeed to assist in refining and "perfecting," the middle class so that its power in the world may be justified. As John Storey has observed, unlike Marx, who "attacked the middle class as representatives of an oppressive and exploitatitve system[,] Arnold attacked them to change them, in order to secure their future—not to close it" (221).

In *A French Eton* (1864) Arnold envisions the day when his goals will have been accomplished:

(*Prose Works*,
2:322)

> *In that great class strong by its numbers, its energy, its industry, strong*
> *by its freedom from frivolity, not by any law of nature prone to immo-*
> *bility of mind . . . in that class, liberalised by an ampler culture, admit-*
> *ted to a wider sphere of thought, living by larger ideas, with its provin-*
> *cialism dissipated, its intolerance cured, its pettiness purged away—*
> *what a power there will be, what an element of new life for England!*
> *Then let the middle class rule, then let it affirm its own spirit, when it*
> *has thus perfected itself.*

But it is Arnold, representing himself as a presumably perfected cultural outsider—tolerant, intellectually sophisticated, broad minded, living by large ideas—who will orchestrate the discourse that will impel that process of reform. Like his mysterious Scholar-Gipsy, Arnold was, through his engagements with particular Victorian social and political discourses, eventually able to attain a position of enormous ideological influence, influence over middle-class values, behavior, and tastes. That is, he was enabled in surprising ways to "rule . . . / The workings of men's brains." Edward Said has astutely asserted that Arnold appears to have viewed society "as a process and perhaps also an entity capable of being guided, controlled, even taken over. What Arnold always understood is that to be able to set a force or a system of ideas called 'culture' over society is to have understood that the stakes played for are an identification of society with culture, and consequently the acquisition of a very formidable power" (10).

Arnold's appetite for such power becomes, to some extent, suppressed in his prose writings, but it is explicit in a letter to Clough in 1853, the year of the preface, "The Scholar-Gipsy," and his altered sense of vocation: "I catch myself desiring now at times political life . . . and I say to myself— you do not desire these things because you are really adapted to them, and therefore the desire for them is merely contemptible" (*Letters*, 263). After 1853 Arnold's desire for "political" activity and influence expressed itself in an alternate and finally more secure, prestigious, and enduring line of work to which he *was* adapted: that of cultural sage and prophet. In that work Arnold immediately hit upon the characteristic discursive mode and critical stance that we have already witnessed in the equivocal relationship established between himself and his Philistine middle-class audience in both his poems and his prose works.

The gipsy, as Arnold deploys that figure in his poems, develops as a proleptic metaphor for this relationship and for Arnold's self-positioning in his prose works of cultural criticism. The trope initially embodies Arnold's stoicism and early skepticism (in "Gipsy Child"). It then serves as a contrast to his image of the ideal poet detached from worldly activity ("Resignation"). By 1853, however, it projects his realization that attaining power over men's minds requires not merely poetic detachment but an often ostensibly self-contradictory stance of simultaneous estrangement from society and involvement with it ("The Scholar-Gipsy"). Thus, the midcentury interest in gipsies and the discourse surrounding their cultural past and social future at first provided Arnold with an important and intertextually sanctioned poetic metaphor but eventually suggested an invaluable critical identity whose essential feature was elusiveness and whose central rhetorical strategy was mystification, that is, textual "mesmerism."

The value of the gipsy trope in understanding Arnold's success becomes especially clear if we recall the portions of Glanvill's text that Arnold *omits* in his own note to "The Scholar-Gipsy":

> *In the practice of [the gipsies'* Mystery]*, by the pregnancy of his wit and parts, [the scholar] soon grew so good a proficient, as to be able to out-do his Instructors. . . . [Upon meeting with two former class-mates, he] told them, that the people he went with were not such* Impostours *as they were taken for, but that they had a* tradi-tional *kind of* learning *among them, and could do wonders by the power of* Imagination, *and that himself had learnt much of their Art, and improved it further then themselves could. . . . [Later, to explain how he knew his friends' exact words spoken in his absence, the scholar told them] that what he did was by the power of* Imagination, *his Phancy binding theirs; and that himself had* dictated *to them the discourse, they held to-gether, while he was from them.*
>
> (Tinker and Lowry, 206, my emphasis)

For Arnold the "secret" of the gipsies' "art" is inseparable from their position as cultural aliens, their peregrine lifestyle, and their uncertain origins, in short, the exotic aura surrounding them that confounds expectations of predictability in their behavior.

In another context, Wendell Harris has demonstrated how Arnold himself cultivates precisely such an aura in the self-representations of his prose works. By promoting singularly elusive values in these works Arnold was able to gain unprecedented influence over the directions of Anglo-American culture in the late nineteenth and early twentieth centuries. Further, the power he acquired was in direct proportion to the gipsylike, mesmeric qualities as well as the elusiveness of cultural doctrines whose "secret" force lay ultimately in their refusal to acknowledge their own desired ideological effects. As we shall see, Arnold's strategy for attaining a position to "perfect" the middle classes is exposed in his last major poem dominated by a gipsy trope, "Thyrsis."

In his helpful discussion of nineteenth-century and contemporary responses to Arnold's cultural criticism, Harris has analyzed the consequences of Arnold's often self-contradictory and mystifying prose: above all, it has succeeded in "binding" generations of middle-class readers and thinkers to a liberal humanist system of values. "Arnold," he acknowledges, "has offered any number of hostages to denizens of the deconstructive abyss. If we wish to demonstrate that the significant words in any discourse appeal to a hierarchy that might be reversed in another discourse, or are employed in several senses, or necessarily imply the existence of their opposites, or are indeterminate in meaning outside the context of each use, Arnold has almost done the work for us" (122). In other words, the central precepts of Arnold's critical writings are self-deconstructing, consciously deferring precise meaning to such an extent that the ideals and values he propounds in a given essay—such as "The Function of Criticism at the Present Time"—constitute a "rich range of perspectives that finally refuse to coalesce" (124). Notions such as "seeing the object as in itself it really is" and measuring all ideas by "the best that has been known and thought in the world" leave themselves open to a wide variety of interpretations, subject only to Arnold's overarching emphasis on "a free play of ideas." Thus, Harris can lament that "Arnold's manifest failure to bring his major arguments into a convincing unity— not a unity to defy the deconstructionist, but simply one to satisfy our ordinary practical sense of coherence—has seemed to authorize readers to detach whatever single slogan especially appeals to them and develop it for their own purposes" (125). The articulation of values and ideals in Arnold's prose after 1853 becomes a process of continual deferral, displacement, and redefinition in which, as Marjorie Levinson has argued in connection with Wordsworth's poetry, "the constitutive and deconstructive moments" are inseparable (647).

But Arnold's elusive abstractions conform to his wholly relativistic view that social and cultural criticism of genuine value must always operate both synchronically and diachronically. He thus writes for the future as well as the present, engaged with issues of the moment but from a desired perspective of "timeless" detachment. He is aware of his captivity to "the present age," while—like Byron's heroes—defiantly resisting, indeed repudiating, that situatedness. As a result, his work is self-reflexive in its use of a language of historical and ideological relativism: "The Arnoldian program decrees that no one ideology, no one scheme of social reformation, can be exempt from continual comparative evaluation. Nor can any one critical evaluator—Arnold included—be presumed infallible. . . . Precisely because all values and beliefs are ideological, no single mode of thought can replace the free play of mind" (Harris, 130).

Because "the free play of mind" must, ideally, be incessant, the notion expressed in "The Scholar-Gipsy" that it might end with the appearance of a singular "light from heaven"—followed by the revelation of a "secret" to "control men's brains" and diffuse that light—is fallacious, as Arnold makes clear in "Thyrsis," where the figure of the scholar-gipsy reemerges. In 1853 Arnold's estranged and mysterious hero had appeared in eternal pursuit of the ultimate ideology. Yet thirteen years later, in "Thyrsis," a reconceptualization of this quest is voiced, one that appears to accommodate the gipsy stance Arnold has adopted as a cultural critic during those years. Placing supreme value on the free play of ideas, the poem, like much of Arnold's prose of the 1860s, projects a set of indeterminate and mystifying ideals that constitute an anti-ideology defined metaphorically as "A fugitive and gracious light . . . / Shy to illumine" ("Thyrsis," ll. 201–2). In confessing that "I must seek it too," the poet insists upon the extent to which this symbol wholly eschews Philistine cultural values:

> This does not come with houses or with gold,
> With place, with honour, and a flattering crew;   (ll. 203–5)
> 'Tis not in the world's market bought and sold.

Ultimately, Arnold's power over the future was realized in "the world's market," where diverse ideologies compete for dominance, largely by means of claims implied in major poems and made directly throughout his prose works that he occupied a position outside of that market. In other words, Arnold's ideological triumph resulted from an ostensible rejection of ideology as power.

Through his works' deployment of a discourse of the Other, typified in his gipsy poems, Arnold became a "ruler" of the structure and values of Anglo-American educational institutions and other cultural apparatuses, not only during his own lifetime but also with later generations. As Park Honan has observed, "In his poetry and critical prose, Arnold introduced a new, subtle, comparative attitude to central problems in Western society and culture, and helped to form the modern consciousness. An understanding of him is really more useful to us than an understanding of any other Englishman of the last century. . . . He is a very great critic: *every* English and American critic of distinction since his time has felt his impact" (vii–viii). Like the original scholar-gipsy from Glanvill's text, Arnold was able to "dictate" the cultural discourse of his own and later historical eras, in part by appropriating the mysterious influence popular images of the gipsies had attained over the Victorian imagination.[13]

V

Christina Rossetti: Renunciation as Intervention

Rossetti, Religious Discourse, and Feminist High Anglicanism

[W]hile knowledge runs apace, ignorance keeps ahead of knowledge: and all which the deepest students know proves to themselves, yet more convincingly than to others, that much more exists which still they know not. As saints in relation to spiritual wisdom, so sages in relation to intellectual wisdom, eating they yet hunger and drinking they yet thirst.

It may never indeed in this world be [God's] pleasure to grant us previsions of seers and forecastings of prophets: but He will assuredly vouchsafe us so much foresight and illumination as should suffice to keep us on the watch with loins girded and lamps burning; not with hearts meanwhile failing us.

Christina Rossetti, *Seek and Find*

IF, FOR STRATEGIC RHETORICAL PURPOSES in his writings, Matthew Arnold frequently adopted a pose of ideological estrangement from society, it can be argued that Christina Rossetti wrote her works from a genuinely marginalized ideological position, that is, a position fundamentally opposed to the moral, economic, and political values that effectively dominated her culture. Her prose writings and her poetry engage various discourses—aesthetic, amatory, domestic, and capitalist—in which these values were embedded so as repeatedly to challenge them and to repudiate the social roles they entailed. We therefore come to understand the radical ideological effects of Rossetti's substantial body of work only when it is positioned in its proper discursive contexts. The most important among these surround religious belief: at the time of her death

Rossetti was canonized by admiring critics because her work was based wholly in Christian orthodoxy (Lootens, 158–82), an almost universally accepted belief system that, if seriously adopted, in fact opposed political, economic, and amatory values generally embraced by her contemporaries.

Three months before she died of cancer in December 1894, Rossetti wrote to her close friend Frederick Shields in order to bid "good-bye for this life" and request his "prayers for a poor sinful woman who has dared to speak to others and is herself what God knows her to be."[1] Ironically, by the date of this letter Rossetti had a reputation in both England and America as a saintly, reclusive author of highly wrought and effective poems (both secular and devotional) as well as six widely read books of religious commentary. Edmund Gosse, one of England's foremost literary intellectuals of the period, had a year earlier described Rossetti as an artist "severely true to herself, [a poet] of conscientiousness as high as her skill is exquisite. . . . one of the most perfect poets of the age." He insists that she is "a writer to whom we may not unreasonably expect that students of English literature in the twenty-fourth century may look back as the critics of Alexandria did toward Sappho and toward Erinna" (21–12). Nearly two decades later Ford Madox Ford praised the work of Rossetti at the expense not only of her famous brother, painter and poet Dante Gabriel, but also of Arnold, Tennyson, and the Brownings. "Christina Rossetti," he pronounced, "seems to us to be the most valuable poet that the Victorian Age produced" (Ford, 179). The exalted regard in which Rossetti was held by these two critics was widely shared: A. C. Swinburne, Gerard Manley Hopkins, Richard Le Gallienne, Oscar Wilde, Arthur Symons, Lionel Johnson, Theodore Watts-Dunton, and Virginia Woolf all admired her art enormously.

In her poetry, but especially in her books of devotional prose, Rossetti "dared to speak to others" in a characteristically humble but nonetheless firmly sagacious, indeed often prophetic voice. Commentators toward the end of the century commonly acknowledge the intellectual and spiritual power of Rossetti's writings, which for them is inseparable from her religious piety. "She is an inspired prophetess or priestess," according to one reviewer ("Christina Rossetti's Poems," 129). For another she is a "poet and saint" who "lived a life of sacrifice . . . [and] unreluctantly endured the pains of her spirituality" (Meynell, 206). One eulogy acknowledges that "her language was always that of Christian assurance and of simple . . . faith in her Saviour. . . . her life was one of transcendent humility" ("Late Miss Rossetti"). After the turn of the century, we are told that Rossetti "needed not to pray, for her life was an unbroken communion with God" (More, 820).

Rossetti's reputation as a devout "prophetess" and saintly woman, along with consistently strong reviews of her work, attracted a remarkable audience, as other commentators late in her career indicate. A long essay in *Harper's* for May 1888 insists that "Christina Rossetti's deeply spiritual poems are known even more widely than those of her more famous brother" (Bowker, 827). Two years earlier William Sharp had acknowledged that "the youngest of the Rossetti family has, as a poet, a much wider reputation and a much larger circle of readers than even her brother Gabriel, for in England, and much more markedly in America, the name of Christina Rossetti is known intimately where perhaps that of the author of the House of Life is but a name and nothing more" (Sharp, 427). Reviewing Mackenzie Bell's biography of Rossetti in 1898, a writer for *The Nation* noted that her income rapidly increased during the last years of her life "less because of a growing appreciation of her poetry than because of her manuals of piety," which "secured her an extensive following" (Review of *Christina Rossetti*, 272). And a writer for the *Dial* remarked that Rossetti's "devotional books . . . have both found and deserved a large and appreciative audience" ("Christina Rossetti," 37). Such observations appear to confirm a widespread agreement among the Victorian reading public that "there is no higher form [of Christianity] than that of a highly educated, devout English woman."[2]

As these commentaries also suggest, Rossetti's prose, unlike her highly symbolic, sometimes allegorical poetry, is often patently didactic. In that respect it resembles the sage discourse of Carlyle, Ruskin, Tennyson, and even Arnold at times, but the language she speaks, the stances she most often adopts, and the intended audience of her devotional books are uniquely "feminine" (according to Victorian stereotypes) and otherworldly. Rossetti's perspective on the values and behavior of her contemporaries was thus unavailable to male writers of the era, and it enabled her to launch a quietly comprehensive attack on a network of patriarchal values (especially those embedded in the discourses of love and marriage) that even the most stringent social critics of her day normally accepted without question. Surprisingly, and it may seem paradoxically, Rossetti was able to accomplish this goal by positioning herself as a devout adherent of High Anglican religious doctrine and, ostensibly, as an advocate of the more widespread Victorian ideology of the "woman's sphere." By embracing religious values with a uniquely radical fervor, however, Rossetti's work ultimately undercuts the domestic ideology of middle- and upper-class Victorians and vigorously rejects both the patriarchal values dominant in Victorian England and their extension in industrial capitalism. If we view Victorian High Anglican religious doctrine from the 1850s to 1893 as a relatively stable discursive formation—in which oppositional elements were nonetheless continually at work—we can observe how Rossetti's radically religious poetry and prose works accomplish some surprising ideological effects.

Historically, criticism of Rossetti has properly emphasized her renunciatory mindset. *Vanitas mundi* is her most frequent theme, and no work better illustrates her employment of it than the sonnet "The World" (1854):

> By day she woos me, soft, exceeding fair:
> But all night as the moon so changeth she;
> Loathsome and foul with hideous leprosy
> And subtle serpents gliding in her hair.
> By day she wooes me to the outer air,
> Ripe fruits, sweet flowers, and full satiety:
> But thro' the night, a beast she grins at me,
> A very monster void of love and prayer.
> By day she stands a lie; by night she stands
> In all the naked horror of the truth
> With pushing horns and clawed and clutching hands.
> Is this a friend indeed; that I should sell
> My soul to her, give her my life and youth,
> Till my feet, cloven too, take hold on hell?

(*Poems,* 1:76–77)

Rossetti's use here of image patterns from religious and classical sources is striking, as is her craftsmanship. But that the poem personifies as a duplicitous woman the world it repudiates is of even greater interest because Rossetti's procedure in this sonnet is typical of her poetry as well as her prose works. This text appropriates traditional antifeminist (medusan) iconography in order to highlight its patriarchal origins by conflating the image of the "foul" seductress with that of her male counterpart from Christian tradition, Satan. The speaker employs these representational traditions of "the world" not only to expose the materialism, hedonism, and false amatory ideologies that they serve but also to renounce the degraded constructions of woman's nature and her accepted roles that these ideologies depend upon and perpetuate. Clearly, the wholly fallen, "loathsome and foul" world that is disparaged includes the stereotypes that have been associated with duplicity and corruption ever since the myths of Medusa and Eve were generated within patriarchal cultures.

Much of Rossetti's poetry and nearly all of her devotional writings anticipated a largely female audience and exploit an array of assumptions about women's social and moral roles that were fundamental to the Victorian ideology of the "woman's sphere." This domestic ideology, familiar to all students of the period, insisted that a middle-class woman, as a leisured Angel in the House, occupy her life in domestic management and ministering to the moral and spiritual needs of her father and brothers (if unmarried) and her husband and children (if married) while undertaking hours of leisure tasks that were largely ornamental (embroidering, arranging flowers, playing music). Retaining her spiritual purity by at least appearing to transcend all worldly concerns was essential to the Victorian woman's success as a spiritual minister. Joan Burstyn has offered a rationale for the inculcation of this stereotype and the assumptions on which it was based:

> *[According] to this ideal, women played a crucial part in providing stability for men who were torn by doubts and faced by insoluble problems. Few people were prepared to confront social, economic and intellectual changes in society by changing their own terms of thought, which was what the psychological crisis of the age called for;* (102)
> *most Victorians turned, instead, to an intensification of personal relationships and an exaggerated adherence to domestic virtues. Religious writers, in their exaggeration of domestic virtues, described women as saviours of society. Men might be assailed by religious scepticism, but women never.*

Rossetti's work consistently engages this system of beliefs in its clear connections with the material seductions of the world and insists, in effect, that both be renounced. In the works of less radical writers commentaries like Rossetti's would appear merely to reinforce middle-class Victorian ideals of the woman's sphere. But as I will demonstrate, the stance that her works take regarding worldly renunciation is far more militant than that of most of her contemporaries, and it ultimately undercuts the material assumptions upon which the stereotypical roles of middle-class women were based.

One aim of the domestic ideology in Victorian England was to compensate for the almost complete usurpation by men of economic activities previously undertaken by women of all classes (e.g., spinning, sewing, and other domestic labors). These activities had provided women with social status and a degree of economic independence unavailable to them in Victorian England. Judith Lowder Newton has examined how "the ideology of woman's sphere . . . served the interests of industrial capitalism by insuring the continuing domination of middle-class women by middle-class men and, through its mitigation of the harshness of economic transition, by insuring the continuing domination of male bourgeoisie in relation to working class men and women as a whole." The domestic ideology assured women "that they *did* have work, power, and status" in the world after all (19–20). Through her insistent advocacy of worldly renunciation, however, Rossetti implicitly repudiates the fundamental economic and political values of industrial capitalism and actively challenges the ideology of the "woman's sphere," which operated in the service of those values.

Rossetti's most fervent monitions are associated, in the predictably orthodox manner of "The World," with the figure of Satan. In *Time Flies* (1885), for instance, she decries the fact that "over and over again we are influenced and constrained by the hollow momentary world we behold . . . while utterly obtuse as regards the substantial eternal world no less present around us though disregarded" (36). At one point she compares this "hollow momentary world" to a funnel-shaped spider's web: "It exhibits beauty, ingenuity, intricacy. Imagine it in the early morning jewelled with dewdrops, and each of these at sunny moments a spark of light or a section of rainbow. Woven, too, as no man could weave it, fine and flexible, frail and tenacious. Yet are its beauties of brilliancy and colour no real part of it. The dew evaporates, the tints and sparkle vanish, the tenacity remains, and at the bottom of all lurks a spider" (82). The spider is of course Satan, who, according to Rossetti's theological literalism, owns this world: "It must be perilously difficult to set up one's tent amid Satan's own surroundings and continue in no way the worse for that neighborhood. The world and the flesh flaunt themselves in very uncompromising forms in the devil's own territory. And all the power and the glory of them set in array before a man whose work forces him to face and sift them day and night, may well make such an one tremble" (267). In the event,

> Earth is half spent and rotting at the core,
> Here hollow death's heads mock us with a grin,
> Here heartiest laughter leaves us tired and sore.
> Men heap up pleasures and enlarge desire,
> Outlive desire, and famished evermore
> Consume themselves within the undying fire.

(116)

In order to assist readers in avoiding such a fate, in her devotional works Rossetti typically presents them with parables. In the approximately two thousand pages of religious commentary she published between 1874 and 1892 Rossetti instructively discusses an extraordinary range of topics from the perspective of a fervent adherent of High Anglican devotionalist doctrine.[3] These include such matters as what and how to read; the probability of Christian election; the possibilities for self-perfection through the imitation of Christ; prospects for immortality; varieties of love; the necessity of patience, obedience, and humility; the maintenance of moral purity, or the controversy over virginity; the need for empathy and charity; the difficulty of knowing truth in a fallen world; the achievement of harmony with the divine will; the necessity of faith; the inevitability of suffering; the multitude of temptations in the world (especially the problem of vanity); and the constitution of true happiness. Rossetti usually approaches such issues through an analysis of religious texts, the lives of saints, or personal experiences rendered figuratively. Because she clearly anticipated a female audience for her devotional works, the treatment of all these subjects bears ultimately on her perception of socially prescribed roles and the operations of domestic discourse for Victorian women.

Early in *Seek and Find* (1879) Rossetti makes explicit her intent to address a variety of issues derived from the Benedicite primarily in connection with "the feminine lot" (30). Here as elsewhere throughout her devotional prose Rossetti insists upon the spiritual superiority of women by comparing expectations of their behavior with the example of Christ. More complexly, however, she is able to reconcile herself to women's subordination to men in worldly affairs only by looking forward to an eventual equality of the sexes in heaven. Her radical strategy at the start is to establish an identity between Christ and woman. "In many points," she explains,

> *the feminine lot copies very closely the voluntarily assumed position*
> *of our Lord and Pattern. Woman must obey: and Christ "learned obe-*
> *dience" (Gen. 3. 16; Heb. 5. 8). She must be fruitful, but in sorrow:*
> *and He, symbolised by a corn of wheat, had not brought forth much*
> *fruit except He had died (Gen. 3. 16; St. John 12. 24). She*
> *by natural constitution is adapted not to assert herself, but to be sub-*
> *ordinate: and He came not to be ministered unto but to minister; He*
> *was among His own "as he that serveth" (I St. Peter 3. 7; I Tim. 2. 2,*
> *12; St. Mark 10. 45; St. Luke 22. 27). Her office is to be man's help-*
> *meet: and concerning Christ God saith, "I have laid help upon One*
> *that is mighty" (Gen. 2. 18, 21, 22; Ps 89. 19). And well may she*
> *glory, inasmuch as one of the tenderest of divine promises takes (so to*
> *say) the feminine form: "As one whom his mother comforteth, so will*
> *I comfort you" (Is. 66. 13).*

Upon the foundation of this identity between Christ and the feminine Rossetti builds a view of the social subordination of women that is undercut by her insistence upon the irrelevance of women's secondary status to spiritual matters, which are of ultimate importance:

> *In the case of the twofold Law of Love, we are taught to call one Com-*
> *mandment "first and great," yet to esteem the second as "like unto it"*
> *(St. Matt. 22. 37–39). The man is the head of the woman, the woman*
(30–32) *the glory of the man (1 Cor. 11. 3, 7). . . . But if our [women's pride]*
> *will after all not be stayed, or at any rate not be allayed (for stayed [it]*
> *must be) by the limit of God's ordinance governing our sex, one final*
> *consolation yet remains to careful and troubled hearts: in Christ there is*
> *neither male nor female, for we are all one (Gal. 3. 28).*

Clearly Rossetti herself has a "careful and troubled" heart when considering these vexed matters. I quote this lengthy passage in full because its rhetorical strategies mark a conflict within the patriarchal religious doctrine to which Rossetti subscribes. Repeatedly in her poetry, her prose works, and her letters she wrestles with the glaring contradiction between her culture's insistence upon the inferior social status of women and their spiritual exaltation. She obediently and humbly claims to accept the illogic of this contradiction. But as in this passage, her ultimate subordination of power relations in this world to expectations for the afterlife challenges the domestic ideology that her exegetical discourse would appear to serve. The final purpose of her prose works is to ensure that women, deemed "last" in the affairs of this world, will be "first" in heaven and thereby to inspire each of her female readers to give "all diligence to make her own personal calling and election sure" (224). Rossetti's general procedure is to translate "symbols, parables, analogies, inferences" into "words of the wise which are as goads" (223). Her aim is that, as a result of such efforts as her own, "we [women] shall demean ourselves charitably, decorously according to our station; we shall reflect honour on those from whom we derive honour; out of the abundance of our heart our mouth will speak wisdom; kindness will govern our tongue, and justice our enactments; thus shall it be with us even now, and much more in the supreme day of rising up, the Day of Resurrection" (223).

This prose passage and many of her poems—from "Goblin Market," "A Triad," and "Maude Clare" to "The Lowest Room," "The Prince's Progress," and "Monna Innominata"—adapt a discourse of gender relations (including power struggles) to the language and formulas of religious doctrine. That is, within the conventional language of such passages that clearly accept the patriarchally ordained position of women a deliberate subtext of resistance to cultural determinations operates. Such a strategy appears again in *Time Flies*, in the entry for March 23: "In common parlance Strong and Weak are merely relative terms: thus the 'strong' of one sentence will be the 'weak' of another. We behold the strong appointed to help the weak: Angels who 'excel in strength,' men. And equally the weak the Strong: woman 'the weaker vessel,' man. This, though it should not inflate any, may fairly buoy us all up" (57). Ultimately, Rossetti believed in the potential of all women to be "elect," as the title of her volume published in 1882, *Called to Be Saints*, indicates. In *The Face of the Deep* (1892) she explains, "Now the saints are they who know not their names, however they name each other. Thus Patience will not discern herself, but will identify a neighbour as Charity, who in turn will recognize not herself, but mild Patience; and they both shall know some fellow Christian, as Hope or Prudence or Faith; and every one of these shall be sure of the others, only not of herself" (73).

A materialist reading of such passages from Rossetti's work would conclude that she is merely a tool of hegemonic Victorian middle-class ideology, embracing with all her intellectual and emotional energies the discourse of a system of religious belief that privileges the patriarchy, employs religious doctrine to subjugate women, and calls for no alterations in the legal, political, or economic status of women. But Rossetti's self-representations are always radically and insistently antimaterialist, and the predominantly spiritual values promulgated in her work culminate in advocacy of a hermetic female community as an alternate sociality to that which dominates "the world" she so vehemently renounces. This direction is unmistakable in her work, from lyrics such as "An Apple-Gathering" to narratives such as "The Convent Threshold," "Goblin Market," and "The Prince's Progress" as well as the passages I have cited from her books of devotional prose. In her life it is visible in her refusal ever to marry (despite two offers), her work with the women of the Highgate Penitentiary for Fallen Women, and her de facto commitment after 1875 to a self-sufficient female household that included herself, her mother, and her two aunts. For Rossetti "the world" was a sphere of male activity, alien and corrupt. Her life imitated the doctrine of its repudiation advocated everywhere in her poetry and prose, which as cultural critique nonetheless constitutes a significant attempt to intervene in that world.

Very often in Rossetti's writings the rhetoric of orthodoxy and acquiescence gradually modulates into a rhetoric of resistance. Her writing is "a mode of social strategy" and "a form of struggle," as Newton has described certain Victorian novels, directed to a specific literary and religious subculture in Victorian England that by extension and projection assumes a degree of solidarity and sisterhood.[4] Elaine Showalter was the first to discuss this "feminist" phenomenon in connection with the literature of the period, emphasizing that "it is important to understand the female subculture not only as . . . a set of opinions, prejudices, tastes, and values prescribed for a subordinate group to perpetuate its subordination—but also as a thriving and positive entity" (13–14). Rossetti's particular position illustrates Nancy Cott's view that "women's group consciousness [is] a subculture uniquely divided against itself by ties to the dominant culture. While the ties to the dominant culture are the informing and restricting ones, they provoke within the subculture certain strengths as well as weaknesses, enduring values as well as accommodations" (quoted in Showalter, 14). In assaulting her dominant culture's primary social and material frameworks of value and meaning through a critique based in the religious beliefs that traditionally complemented and served them Rossetti's work deploys subversive strategies of extraordinary power and complexity.

In order fully to understand the operations of these strategies it is crucial to explore the special sociohistorical contexts of her work in some detail. As I have suggested, Rossetti's adherence to Victorian High Anglicanism as a discursive formation that embodied a culturally specific framework of religious values actually reinforced the potential for feminist subversiveness in her writing, and it is in these beliefs that both her poetry and devotional prose find their primary inspiration.

Rossetti's agnostic brother, William Michael, described her as "an Anglo-Catholic, and, among Anglo-Catholics, a Puritan" (Rossetti, *Poetical Works*, lxiv). In this century, Raymond Chapman has successfully argued a case "for seeing Christina Rossetti as directly and fully a product of the Oxford Movement," and he insists that she is "the true inheritor of the Tractarian devotional mode in poetry" (175–96). More recently, George B. Tennyson and others have extended Chapman's argument, and the history of Rossetti's involvement with High Anglican churches and church figures has been documented thoroughly by her biographers (Tennyson, 1980; Marsh). In 1843, at the impressionable age of twelve, Rossetti began regular attendance at Christ Church, Albany Street, "noted at the time for the incendiary sermons of the Reverend William Dodsworth, one of the chief preachers of the Oxford Movement, a man closely associated with both [John Henry] Newman and [Edward] Pusey" (Packer, *Rossetti*, 6). As Lona Mosk Packer notes, citing an article from the *Edinburgh Review*, this church was becoming "a principal centre of High Church religionism in the metropolis" (7). Rossetti's early religious education in this environment and her lifelong involvement with major figures from the later days of High Anglicanism profoundly influenced her particular appropriations of a system of religious beliefs that pervaded every aspect of her existence: "For Christina this form of religion came to be, quite simply and without question, the most important thing in her life" (Battiscombe, 31).

Readers of Rossetti's works today tend to forget the extent to which Anglo-Catholicism was perceived in midcentury as a radical movement. As Packer explains, "This exhilarating . . . Tractarian Renascence" was "an avant-garde movement accepted alike by the Regent's Park worthies and the Albany Street literati" (*Rossetti*, 7). Rossetti's involvement with institutional extensions of this movement, such as the Highgate Penitentiary, continued and deepened throughout her life. All but one of her books of devotional prose were published by the Society for Promoting Christian Knowledge, a press with close ties to Anglo-Catholicism.

More significantly, Rossetti developed important connections with the High Anglican movement to resurrect sisterhoods, conventual institutions that many Victorians found threatening because they undercut the roles and functions widely accepted for middle-class women. One Anglican convent opened about 1850 a few doors from Christ Church. "Founded and directed by Dr. Pusey, who chose the Albany Street church as the scene of a novel experiment, . . . the religious community of women caused amazement and consternation even in a parish as radical as [William] Dodsworth's. 'The special vocation of a Sister,' wrote Pusey's biographer, 'the character involved and the claims of such a character, were altogether unknown. . . . That young ladies [of good families] should shrink from society, and entertain thoughts of a vow of celibacy in the face of an eligible marriage was almost inconceivable'" (Packer, *Rossetti*, 55). In 1874 Rossetti's sister Maria, to whom she was extremely close, joined the All Saints' Sisterhood in Margaret Street. Two decades earlier Christina Rossetti had been composing poems, such as "Three Nuns" and "The Convent Threshold," that clearly reflect her fascination with these new institutions that liberated women from the temptations of "the world," especially the world of the Victorian marriage market (attacked parodically in "Goblin Market") and the domestic ideology.

Rossetti's sonnet "A Triad" concisely exposes the unsatisfactory vocational alternatives for Victorian women.

Three sang of love together; one with lips
Crimson, with cheeks and bosom in a glow,
Flushed to the yellow hair and finger tips;
And one there sang who soft and smooth as snow
Bloomed like a tinted hyacinth at a show;
And one was blue with famine after love,
Who like a harpstring snapped rang harsh and low
The burden of what those were singing of.
One shamed herself in love; one temperately
Grew gross in soulless love, a sluggish wife;
One famished died for love. Thus two of three
Took death for love and won him after strife;
All on the threshold, yet all short of life.

(*Poems*, 1 : 29)

For Rossetti, Christ was the only lover whose "threshold" it was worthy to be carried over; becoming his bride the only rejuvenating alternative to the stereotypical roles of prostitute, wife, and lovelorn spinster, and it is one she advocates repeatedly in her poems and devotional works, sometimes with extraordinary passion. Unequivocal renunciation of the world, with all its misguided social institutions and material temptations, is the unique route to self-fulfillment, as is made clear through the powerful images of desolation and emptiness in "A Better Resurrection":

My life is like a faded leaf,
    My harvest dwindled to a husk;
Truly my life is void and brief
    And tedious in the barren dusk;
My life is like a frozen thing,
    No bud nor greenness can I see:
Yet rise it shall—the sap of Spring;
    O Jesus, rise in me.
My life is like a broken bowl,
    A broken bowl that cannot hold
One drop of water for my soul
    Or cordial in the searching cold.

These elegiac images merely prepare, however, for metaphors of self-destruction and reconstruction embedded in a series of vigorous imperatives that culminate with a surprising and rapturous, if not erotic, appropriation of communion imagery:

(1:68)

> Cast in the fire the perished thing,
> Melt and remould it, till it be
> A royal cup for Him my King:
> O Jesus, drink of me.

One might expect such a passion for renunciation to result in a yearning for the conventual life. Rossetti herself never joined a sisterhood, however, in part because of a compulsion to exercise whatever influence she could through her writings so as to expose and challenge a culturally dominant system of values that denied genuine fulfillment for women. She did so by advocating strict, devotional alternatives.[5] (Unexpectedly, at one point in *Time Flies* she wryly interjects, "But Bishops should write for me, not I for Bishops!" [123].) Nonetheless, Rossetti did become an associate at one of the many Anglican Church–related homes founded at midcentury for the redemption of prostitutes and sexually abused women and girls. She worked regularly at St. Mary Magdalene's on Highgate Hill until her health broke down in the late 1860s. As Martha Vicinus has observed, the "reform of fallen women" was one of the three major tasks undertaken by the Anglican sisterhood (74). Rossetti's involvement in it had visible effects on her many poems about fallen women (including "Goblin Market," "The Convent Threshold," and "An Apple-Gathering") as well as on her devotional prose works.

Rossetti's intimate connections with the newly developing Anglican sisterhoods, although she remained outside their conventual restrictions, gave her a unique position from which to present a critique of her society. These institutions, conservative as they might appear in the late twentieth century, were in fact radically liberating for the women who became involved with them. As an extension of the Oxford movement, the convents "played an important initial role in the emancipation of women in England," presenting "a wide variety of opportunities to women in the fields of teaching, nursing, social work, and community organization." Vicinus has traced the origins, development, and social influence of the Anglican sisterhoods, emphasizing the extent to which they empowered Victorian women: the "sisters carved out an area of expertise and power within their male-dominated churches. . . . [They] were clearly in the

vanguard of single-sex organizations, in both their organizational autonomy and their insistence upon women's right to a separate religious
life." Vicinus also remarks upon the varieties of freedom offered to Victorian women through the sisterhoods, some of "the most important
women's communities in the nineteenth century." These communities
"were among the first to insist upon a woman's right to choose celibacy,
to live communally, and to do meaningful work. They demanded and
received great loyalty from their members and were in turn deeply sup-
portive of each other . . . . the orders maintained a very high standard of
religious life, proving convincingly that women could lead women, live
together, and work for the greater good of the church, the people, and
God" (83). One sister's commentary suggests the radicalism of the Anglican sisterhood movement: "It was a wonderful thing at that period to be
young among young comrades. . . . It was an era of religion and faith,
and at the same time of intellectual challenge. We read, discussed, debated
and experimented and felt that all life lay before us to be changed and
moulded by our vision and desire" (81).

Rossetti could not have been unaware of the potentially liberating
effects of Anglican sisterhoods upon Victorian women and of the fact that
these sisterhoods were perceived to represent a disturbing challenge to
dominant patriarchal ideologies, including that of the woman's sphere.
John Shelton Reed has discussed the public controversy that swirled
around the sisterhoods. He explains that "there was widespread uneasi-
ness about the development of sisterhoods" because they clearly presented an "affront to Victorian family values." For instance, "Prebendary
Gresley of Lichfield, a sober Tractarian . . . gave the anglo-catholic view
when he remarked matter-of-factly that 'Home and comfort have been
too long the idols of Englishmen, a settlement and establishment in life
the *summum bonum* of Englishwomen. It is a great point to have it admitted that there may be something nobler and more desirable than these
acknowledged blessings'" (229). Earlier, Florence Nightingale, a heroine
of Rossetti's early adulthood, had described the Victorian domestic ideology derisively as a "Fetich": "'Family'—the idol they have made of it.
It is a kind of Fetichism. . . . They acknowledge no God, for all they say
to the contrary, but this Fetich" (quoted in Reed, 238). Sisterhoods
strongly threatened this idol. Conventual life "took women out of their
homes. It gave important work and sometimes great responsibility. It

replaced their ties to fathers, husbands, and brothers by loyalties to church and sisterhood. It demonstrated that there were callings for women of the upper and middle classes other than those of wife, daughter, and 'charitable spinster,'" offering "an alternative to a life of idleness or drudgery—exotic, but safely exotic, and cloaked in the respectability of religion" (Reed, 130–31).

But as Reed has demonstrated, the sisterhood was only one of many Anglo-Catholic innovations that threatened the social and economic values of the Victorian patriarchy. The revival of auricular confession and the establishment of "free and open seating" in the churches (as opposed to privately rented family pews), among other Anglo-Catholic alterations of church ritual, were also seen as powerfully subversive, especially because these changes were strongly supported by women like Rossetti, who, as most observers agreed, were drawn to Anglo-Catholicism in disproportionate numbers. One commentator complained that "the Ritual movement is a lay movement . . . but it is more than that; it is a female movement. . . . The Ritualistic clergyman is led, or rather misled, by a few ladies" (203). In fact the religious movement to which Rossetti fervently committed herself and the audience to whom she directed her devotional prose commentaries and poems must finally be seen as feminist: "By its sometimes studied disregard for conventional standards of manliness and by its revaluation of celibacy, the movement issued a series of subtle but continual challenges to received patriarchal values. That these challenges were heard and understood by the movement's male opponents is evident in their denigration of women's part in the movement, and in the alarm and contempt evoked in them by the movement's 'effeminacy'" (213).

As I have remarked, the quality of Rossetti's own devotionalist feminism is complicated and often disguised by her ostensible subscription to orthodox notions of male supremacy, especially in her prose writings. (Her poems, however, are full of male villains.) But a number of passages from her devotional books, letters, and unpublished remarks expose a radically feminist bent. Rossetti's insistence that women patiently endure this life in expectation of the life to come upholds the dogmas of the patriarchy, but only in anticipation of the ultimate dissolution of these dogmas in that afterlife which is a "flowering land of love" where men and women will be "happy equals" ("Monna Innominata," Rossetti, *Poems*, 2 : 89). Typical is her modulation in a discussion of St. Hilary from an acceptance of an "unknown" wife's subordinate position in matters of worldly reputation to an insistence on her ultimate equality with her spouse: "Now of St. Hilary's wife I read nothing further, beyond such a hint of her career as is involved in that of her husband. Wherefore of her I am free to think of as one 'unknown and yet well known'; on earth of less dignified name than her husband. . . . in Paradise it may well be of equal account" (*Time Flies*, 11–12).

Rossetti's discussions of marriage and of marital relations between the sexes are most often cautiously critical in her devotional works. Her poems almost never broach the topic except to renounce the prospects of marital union, to depict betrayed or disappointed love, or to celebrate the prospect of marital union with Christ in the afterlife. (In the preface to "Monna Innominata" she goes so far as to suggest that Elizabeth Barrett Browning would have written better sonnets had she been "unhappy, rather than happy in love" [*Poems*, 2:86]). Because worldly marriages for Rossetti most often require that women "grow gross in soulless love," she often implicitly disdains the institution. In one passage from *Letter and Spirit* she acknowledges that "a wife's paramount duty is indeed to her husband, superseding all other human obligations" (43).[6] But she immediately proceeds to oppose the patriarchal ideology underlying that dogma: "Yet to assume this duty, free-will has first stepped in with its liability to err." In short, the choice to marry is mistaken: "In this connexion woman has to reap as she has sown, be the crop what it may: while in the filial relation all is safe and flawless, for all is of Divine ordaining" (43).

When discussing prospects for immortality in particular or for moral virtue and purity in general Rossetti frequently recurs to Christ's commandments regarding marriage:

> *Change and vicissitude are confined to this life and this world: once safe in the next world the saved are safe for ever and ever. So our Lord deigned to effect to teach us all, when answering certain Saducees, He said: "The children of this world marry, and are given in marriage: but they which shall be accounted worthy to obtain that world, and the resurrection from the dead, neither marry, nor are given in marriage: neither can they die any more: for they are equal unto the angels. . . ." And further we gather hence by implication that not all shall "obtain . . . the resurrection from the dead."*

(*Face*, 100)

The clear implication here is that the unmarried are more likely to be saved than those who succumb to this worldly institution. Earlier in *The Face of the Deep*, when discussing how "the precarious purity of mortal life shall become the indefectible purity of the immortal" (93), Rossetti compares the individual who succumbs to the world's temptations to trodden snow, which turns to mud. By contrast, those who remain pure are like snow on "mountain summits," which "endures alone": "Even so chaste virgins choose solitude for a bower" (93). Such implicit attacks upon marriage culminate when Rossetti asserts that "Eve, the representative woman received as part of her sentence 'desire': the assigned object of her desire being such that satisfaction must depend not on herself but on one stronger than she, who might grant or might deny" (312). That is, woman's "desire" to attain fulfillment in a relationship with a man is a sign of sinfulness rather than of angelic propensities; it is one punishment for her "desire" to eat the forbidden fruit. If we recall that marriage was the single dominant ambition of young middle- and upper-class Victorian women, then the extreme radicalism of Rossetti's next remarks stands out. Women who do not marry, she insists, are "no losers if they exchange desire for aspiration, the corruptible for the incorruptible. . . . 'Give me children or else I die,' was a foolish speech: the childless who make themselves nursing mothers of Christ's little ones are the true mothers of Israel" (312). These sentences constitute an extraordinary challenge to Victorian social values, especially the "Fetich" of the family and its extension in the ideology of the "woman's sphere." It was a challenge that took on institutional form in the revival of the Anglican sisterhoods.

Because Rossetti positions herself strategically on the margins of "the world" in her prose works, focusing her commentaries on preparing for the afterlife, the cultural critiques she presents often take on circumspect, parabolic forms. In her secular poems, however, especially the dozens that employ the discourse of romantic love to expose patriarchal amatory ideologies that victimize women, she is more outspoken; but even many of these works (including "Goblin Market," "The Prince's Progress," and "Dream-Love") operate allegorically.[7] Occasionally Rossetti's letters also demonstrate the feminist directions of her thought quite explicitly. One in particular, written to the widely published poet and suffragist Augusta Webster, reveals Rossetti's view of sexual roles as artificial "barriers" that are exclusively this-worldly in their provenance. Rossetti responds (probably in 1878) to a request from Webster that she support the suffragist movement: "You express yourself with such cordial openness that I feel encouraged to endeavour also after self-expression," Rossetti explains candidly, as she begins a discussion of the appointed roles of the sexes that modulates into a speculation on their power relations (Bell, 111). I quote the rest of this extraordinary letter in full:

> *Does it not appear as if the Bible was based upon an understood unalterable distinction between men and women, their position, duties, privileges? Not arrogating to myself but most earnestly desiring to attain to the character of a humble orthodox Xian, so it does appear to me; not merely under the Old but also under the New Dispensation. The fact of the Priesthood being exclusively man's, leaves me in no doubt that the highest functions are not in this world open to both sexes: and if not all, then a selection must be made and a line drawn somewhere. On the other hand if female rights are sure to be overborne for lack of female voting influence, then I confess I feel* (111–12, my emphasis) *disposed to shoot ahead of my instructresses, and to assert that female M.P.'s are only right and reasonable. Also I take exceptions at the exclusion of married women from the suffrage, for who so apt as Mothers—all previous arguments allowed for the moment—to protect the interests of themselves and of their offspring? I do think if anything ever does sweep away the barrier of sex, and make the female not a giantess or a heroine but at once and full grown a hero and giant, it is that mighty maternal love which makes little birds and little beasts as well as little women matches for very big adversaries.*

Rossetti begins with an unquestioning acceptance of the dogmas of patriarchal orthodoxy. But her fear, irrepressible in this letter as in so many of her poems, that men cannot be expected, finally, to protect "female rights" inspires her to take a line that is, even at the end of the century, distinctly radical.

That radical bent emerges in part from Rossetti's customary exaltation of motherhood, which, significantly, indicates only a partial acceptance of the ideology of the "woman's sphere." (Most often in her work Rossetti elides any discussion of husbands and marriage as a necessary prelude to the production of children.) But her radicalism also results from a literal acceptance of a basic premise of the domestic ideology: that men are inevitably seduced and sullied by involvement with "the world." Although Rossetti acknowledges that women are men's helpmates (the "weaker vessels" appointed to assist "the strong"), it becomes clear in this letter and throughout her secular poetry that "goblin" men will prove difficult, if not impossible, to redeem, participating as they do in the "loathsome and foul" world controlled by Satan.[8] Hence, the most consistently positive relationships among characters in Rossetti's poems are between mothers and daughters or between sisters. These relationships reinforce a spirit of subcultural solidarity that, ultimately, can deal with "the world" only by wholly renouncing it.[9]

Rossetti's "prophetic" devotional texts always advocate renunciation and resistance. Addressing a female audience whose values, like her own, had been molded primarily by patriarchal religious, amatory, and domestic ideologies, her work consistently appropriates the discourses that serve those ideologies so as to expose their inability to fulfill the spiritual, moral, and even intellectual needs of Victorian women. In response to the misguided values of "the world," her prose writings urge the acceptance of alternative, radically devotionalist ideals whose origins are avowedly patriarchal but whose otherworldly goal for adherents is an eventual assumption into a genderless, egalitarian utopia—Paradise.

Despite the unwavering strength of her faith and the consistency of her vision of the fallen world, Rossetti was characteristically humble and cautious, especially in her prose works, when she assumed the authoritative role of sage that her reformist impulses demanded of her. In *The Face of the Deep*, her last major work, she comes to final terms with the spiritual dangers and ideological difficulties facing any Victorian woman engaged in sage discourse. As usual, however, a prospectively feminist self-confidence emerges in the very act of self-effacement: "Far be it from me to think to unfold mysteries or interpret prophecies. But I trust that to gaze in whatever ignorance on what God reveals, is so far to do His will. If ignorance breed humility, it will not debar from wisdom. If ignorance betake itself to prayer, it will lay hold on grace. . . . at least I . . . may deepen awe, and stir up desire by a contemplation of things inevitable, momentous, transcendent" (146).

Rossetti and the Romantics

In the ways I have described, Christina Rossetti's works of devotional prose make use of traditional Christian beliefs and their foundational texts to critique the social values they are normally seen to serve. Her poems also operate as oppositional texts, and they often do so by appropriating works by Romantic poets and the literary mythologies they propagate in order to extend their spiritual insights (Blake) or expose their spiritual deficiencies (Coleridge, Wordsworth, and Keats), that is, to expose the extent to which they actively participate in the corrupt values of "the world." By the early 1850s, when Rossetti began to see herself as a serious poet, the cultural assimilation of some of these texts and mythologies (particularly those associated with Wordsworth and Coleridge) was deep and widespread, as conventional criticism of Victorian poetry everywhere demonstrates.

One of her earliest letters accompanying a group of poems she was submitting for publication, written to William Edmonstoune Aytoun, editor of *Blackwood's Magazine*, on 1 August 1854, reveals the missionary spirit in which Rossetti wrote to correct her misguided precursors: "My love for what is good in the works of others teaches one that there is something above the despicable in mine; poetry is with me, not a mechanism, but an impulse and a reality; and that I know my aims in writing to be pure, and directed to that which is true and right. I do not blush to confess that, with these feelings and beliefs, it would afford me some gratification to place my productions before others" (Rossetti, *Letters*, 98). Purity, truth, righteousness—these are the linguistic abstractions, the covering angels, under which she makes public her revisionist, devotional system of beliefs. Embedded in every poem she wrote, such values are imbricated in an ideology that is antipositivist, anticapitalist, antipatriarchal, antimaterialist, and ultimately anti-Romantic. Everywhere in her poetic works we see Rossetti employing the discourses of Romanticism—especially those that mystify amatory desire and love relationships, on the one hand, and those that present secular ideals of nature, on the other—in the service of religious values that challenge those discourses.

The "works of others" that Rossetti truly admired were relatively few. She was not a voracious, but rather a focused, reader. Apart from the Bible, Thomas á Kempis, St. Augustine, Plato, Homer, and the classics in Italian, her adult reading was largely in the religious literature and the fiction of her day (Rossetti, *Poetical Works*, lxix–lxx).[10] She appears not to have been influenced by a number of authors and works we would expect her to have appropriated. References to Shakespeare and Milton, for instance, are scant in her writing, and in 1870 she acknowledged to a close friend that she was still "the rare Englishwoman not to have read [Tennyson's] the Holy Grail" (*Letters*, 339). Yet her copy of Keble's *The Christian Year* was dog-eared by the time of her death in 1894. She read widely in Tractarian literature, as this fact, her sonnet on John Henry Newman, and the theological content of her books of devotional prose make clear.

Rossetti also read the Romantics. Unlike poetry by the other Pre-Raphaelites, however, her work reveals no ideological debt to them. Instead her poems most often stand as powerful correctives to what she saw as the inadequate or wholly corrupt amatory, spiritual, and political values—the secular ideologies—of those Romantics most important to her: Blake, Coleridge, Wordsworth, and Keats. Throughout Rossetti's poetry we find stylistic and thematic echoes as well as structural resonances of work by these writers, whom she often deliberately parodies. Rossetti's genius is in fact partly visible in her ability to rework a variety of Romantic styles and topoi in order to empower orthodox Christian beliefs in a world where dangerously secular values were increasingly parading themselves in attractive poetic garments.[11]

Misreading her transpositions of Romantic discourses of nature, love, and spirituality has often produced a view of Rossetti as a failed or obstructed Romantic. More than forty years ago Maurice Bowra observed in her "a truly Romantic temperament, trained to look for beauty in mysterious realms of experience, and able to find it without any strain or forcing of herself. She might have been a purely secular poet, so great were her gifts for the interpretation of strange corners of life and fancy. But her taste for this world was countered by a belief in God" (246). For Bowra, Rossetti "presents in a remarkable manner the case of a poet whose naturally Romantic tendencies were turned into a different channel by the intensity of her religious faith," so that she "passed beyond the Romantic spirit" (269). As more recent criticism has begun to suggest, however, Rossetti's work does not merely glance off "the Romantic spirit"; rather, her poetry operates in dialogue with it and constitutes a challenge to it: whereas echoes of Blake and Coleridge in some of her works reveal appropriation and a limited acceptance of their religious values, other poems by Rossetti seek to undercut, overturn, and expose as false or inadequate the secular world-views propagated in the poetry of Wordsworth and Keats. Although responses to Blake, Coleridge, and Wordsworth often emerge in her poems, Keats was the Romantic whose attraction Rossetti felt most powerfully. Her deeply conflicted responses to his poetry are visible both in the strength of his stylistic influence over her work and in Rossetti's unrelenting attempts, in her mature years, to disavow a youthful commitment to Keatsian idealizations of erotic love. These threatened her adherence to the framework of High Anglican religious values that she relied upon for emotional and psychological strength throughout her adult life.

The starkness and passion of Rossetti's religiosity, visible not only in her six books of devotional commentary but also in hundreds of her poems, helps to explain the complexity of her assault upon the works of some Romantic writers. Rossetti's poems, like her prose works, are homiletic and prophetic. Her treatment of erotic love, for instance, consistently demonstrates its illusory nature, its transitoriness, or its inability to fulfill the needs of the "craving heart." Her obsession with death results from her impassioned anticipation of the afterlife. Her interest in the objects of nature is typological: they symbolize a host of religious truths and teach lessons in piety or virtue. Like "The World," dozens of Rossetti's poems reiterate her central theme of *contemptus mundi*:

> This Life is full of numbness and of balk,
> Of haltingness and baffled short-coming,
> Of promise unfulfilled, of everything
> That is puffed vanity and empty talk . . .
> This Life we live is dead for all its breath[.]

*(Poems,
2:149)*

The conceptual framework and the metaphors in this sonnet from *Later Life* (1881) are typical. Images of betrayal, failure, inadequacy, illusion, and disappointment are the commonplaces of Rossetti's work, and they are usually borrowed either from nature or from the Bible. It is her uncompromising belief in the truths these images serve to formulate that allows Rossetti to appropriate motifs, language, structural patterns, and metaphors from Romantic poetry exclusively to reject any hope of happiness or fulfillment in this world. She adopts the various discourses of Romanticism most often to expose its ideological mirages and to supplant them with a view of meaningful human experience grounded in a particular religious ideology. Analysis of intertextual relations in her work therefore allows us to reconceive it as the site of a discursive conflict whose stakes are, according to this ideology, as high as they can be.

Blake: Infants, Shepherds, and Little Lambs

On 12 November 1848 Christina Rossetti wrote a parody of Blake's "A Cradle Song" that remained unpublished for 142 years. The lyric enacts a strategy of revisionism common in her work that alludes to Romantic pre-texts. Her title quotes two lines from Blake's poem: "Sleep, sleep, happy child; / All creation slept and smiled." "A Cradle Song" (from *Songs of Innocence*, 1789) celebrates innocent infants as types of Christ:

(Blake, 12)

> Sweet babe in thy face,
> Holy image I can trace.
> Sweet babe once like thee,
> Thy maker lay and wept for me.
>   . . . . .
>
> Infant smiles are his own smiles.
> Heaven & earth to peace beguiles.

Blake's song was written in a year of the French Revolution, and it obliquely acknowledges its own historicity in its turn to Christ's birth, "beguiling" the world to peace, as the ultimate solution to social turmoil and war. Blake's infant slumbers, moans, and sighs in its singing mother's arms, promising happiness in mankind's future. By contrast, the infant (also a Christ type) in Rossetti's responsive lyric, written in another year of revolution, is dead. Describing its "slumber," the poet leaps rhetorically from Christ's birth, to the crucifixion, to the apocalypse:

(Rossetti, *Poems*, 3:165)

> There is no more aching now
> In thy heart or in thy brow.
> The red blood upon thy breast
> Cannot scare away thy rest.
>   . . . . .

> Sleep, sleep; what quietness
> After the world's noise is this!
> . . . . .
> Sleep on until the morn
> Of another Advent dawn.

That by the conclusion of these stanzas "the world's noise" is subsumed as immaterial to the generation of a new world is extraordinary considering the tumultuous events taking place around Rossetti in 1848. In this, her eighteenth year Rossetti became engaged to James Collinson, the Pre-Raphaelite Brotherhood was formed (with her as its solitary, unofficial "sister"), England was in the throes of Chartist demonstrations, and the politics of revolution in Europe, and especially in Italy, were explosive. As we saw in chapter 1, living in the Rossetti household at this time would have made it impossible for Christina to ignore political events and the social conditions that spawned them, which were constantly under discussion there. But this poem suppresses such matters, not, as in her brother's work, to draw attention to aesthetic surfaces but rather to position the reader in an estranged ideological context. The poem ruthlessly deploys what for child-worshiping Victorians would have been a powerfully brutal image, that of a bloodied infant, precisely to shock readers, to destabilize familiar domestic values, and to force upon them a perspective on worldly experience that wholly devalues it: at the Last Judgment, "another Advent dawn," the "noise" of this existence, whether personal or political, will evaporate in a rapturous process previewed by the operations of this poem. Rossetti here, as elsewhere in poems that echo Blake, extends the religious content of his work eschatologically.

Familiar with Blake's engravings as well as his early poems, Rossetti would have felt that she was challenging neither his work nor his theology. *Time Flies* reveals her sense of theological kinship with Blake: "There is a design by William Blake symbolic of the Resurrection. In it I behold the descending soul and the arising body rushing together in an indissoluble embrace: and this design, among all I recollect to have seen, stands alone in expressing the rapture of that reunion" (88). Rossetti's poetry nonetheless demonstrates little interest in Blake's works after 1789, including his prophetic books. The image patterns she appropriates are exclusively from the *Songs of Innocence*: mothers and infants, shepherds and lambs, roses and thorns, sunflowers. All of these appear in brief lyrics, many of them from *Sing-Song* (1872). These poems also replicate the simple forms of Blake's *Songs*. As William Michael Rossetti told his sister's biographer, Mackenzie Bell, "It would . . . be an error to suppose that C[hristina] at any time read B[lake] much or constantly [though] . . . certainly she prized the little she did read" (Bell, 308).

Rossetti's own simple songs often reply overtly to Blake's. "Rejoice with Me," for instance, problematizes Blake's "The Lamb," an ontological poem that celebrates Christ as creator and redeemer:

> Little Lamb who made thee
> Dost thou know who made thee
> Gave thee life & bid thee feed.
>   . . . . .
>
> Little Lamb I'll tell thee,
> Little Lamb I'll tell thee!
> He is called by thy name,
> For he calls himself a Lamb:
> He is meek & he is mild
> He became a little child:
> I a child & thou a lamb,
> We are called by his name.

(Blake, 8–9)

Echoing Blake's anaphora, Rossetti produces a sophisticated, emotionally intense lyric whose dramatic situation reflects what Packer has described as Rossetti's Coleridgean, existential religious faith ("Existentialism," 214). "Rejoice with Me" in fact reinscribes Blake's song of innocence as a personalized (rather than generalized) song of penitence, guilt, and gratitude:

> Little Lamb, who lost thee?—
> I myself, none other.—
> Little Lamb, who found thee?—
>   Jesus, Shepherd, Brother.
> Ah, Lord, what I cost Thee!
>   Canst Thou still desire?—
> Still Mine arms surround thee,
>   Still I lift thee higher,
> Draw thee nigher.

(Rossetti, *Poems*, 2:196–97)

Whereas Blake's song is benedictory, suppressing awareness of sin and man's fallen condition, Rossetti's is confessional and amatory (as is much of her religious verse). This lamb of Christ, this Everywoman, despite her betrayal of God the Shepherd, remains the object of his passion (in every sense) and becomes a bride of Christ; here their marriage approaches the "rapture" of its consummation.

Less radically revisionist are a number of lyrics from *Sing-Song* in which Rossetti appears to take delight both in reworking Blakean figures of guardianship and in Blakean wordplay, as she does in the following poem:

> A motherless soft lambkin
> Alone upon a hill;
> No mother's fleece to shelter him
> And wrap him from the cold:—
> I'll run to him and comfort him,
> I'll fetch him, that I will;
>
> I'll care for him and feed him
> Until he's strong and bold.

(Poems, 2:33–34)

This poem's resonances of Blake's "The Shepherd" and "The Little Black Boy" playfully reinforce the efficacy of shepherding in this world. Rossetti appropriates Blake's images as authoritative, using simple metrical and prosodic techniques to extend the work he began. The poem's final emphasis on the assonantal rhyme word "bold," for instance, suggests not only the condition of the revived lamb but also the indelible character of the Shepherd (not to mention that of the parodic poet, the shepherd of pastoral literary tradition).

More subtle effects emerge from Rossetti's generalized allusions to the rose imagery pervasive in Blake's *Songs*. Echoes of "The Sick Rose," "My Pretty Rose Tree," and "The Lily" in one quatrain from *Sing-Song* suggest that Rossetti learned important symbolist techniques from Blake.

> I have but one rose in the world,
> And my one rose stands a-drooping:
> Oh when my single rose is dead
> There'll be but thorns for stooping.

(2:39)

The statement communicated symbolically here is complex, though the metaphors used are both simple and common, demonstrating how

Rossetti's poetry often deliberately inhabits a space of linguistic ambiguity. By the poem's final line it is clear that the rose is at once a unique flower, a beloved, and Christ. The second and third lines refigure the crucifixion, enabling the fourth to dramatize the incarnation (Christ "stooping" to become man) and its culmination in his passion, while homiletically announcing the rewards of Christian humility.

In such poems as these brief lyrics Rossetti reveals her admiration for Blake's stylistic and prosodic accomplishments, as well as his early and innocent prophetic impulses, which she extends by heightening the Low Church liberalism implicit throughout his *Songs*. That Blake's work was little known during the period in which poems she wrote allude to it suggests the "purity" of her motive to promote and extend what she viewed as a shared religious ideology.

Coleridge, Wordsworth, and Tractarian Aesthetics

Reviewing *Goblin Market and Other Poems* (1862), Caroline Norton observed thematic and temperamental affinities between Christina Rossetti and Coleridge.[12] These, in fact, reinforce the techniques she appropriated from the early work of Blake. Norton insists that *Goblin Market* is "incomparably the best of [Rossetti's] compositions" and argues that it "may vie with Coleridge's 'Ancient Mariner' . . . for the vivid and wonderful power by which things unreal and mystic are made to blend and link themselves with the everyday images and events of common life" (404). Later commentators also acknowledge similarities between the symbolist techniques that operate in both poems or between the moral purposes such techniques serve. Richard Le Gallienne, arguing for Rossetti's preeminence among women poets in 1891, asserts that "she is . . . our one imaginative descendant of the magician of 'Kubla Khan'" (130). B. Ifor Evans, some forty years later, worries that "the same problems are raised [by *Goblin Market*] as by *The Ancient Mariner*; a theme and movement, suggesting many things and not assignable to one source, a concluding moral acting as an anti–climax to the glamour and magic which precede it" (156). Packer goes considerably further than these critics, however, locating not only thematic echoes and temperamental affinities but also structural allusions to Coleridgean poems in works by Rossetti as diverse as "The Convent Threshold," "From House to Home," and "Cobwebs"

(*Rossetti,* 132, 135). Less convincingly, she also insists that the theology that dominates Rossetti's work, poetry and devotional prose alike, is the same "kind of Protestant existentialism found also in Coleridge" ("Existentialism," 214).

Thus, although particular stylistic or prosodic echoes of Coleridge in Rossetti's poetry are rare, structural patterns, a variety of motifs and settings, as well as religious and moral dicta, resonate between their works. For instance, sensitivity to all creatures great and small is a recurrent theme in poems such as "Brother Bruin" (Rossetti, *Poems,* 2:168) and a number of lyrics from *Sing-Song,* where in one poem Rossetti admonishes, "Hurt no living thing," and she catalogues sacred creatures, from ladybirds and moths to "harmless worms that creep" (2:44). Extending into real life the Coleridgean tradition epitomized in the moral tag that concludes *The Rime of the Ancient Mariner,* Rossetti became a passionate antivivisectionist.

Other echoes of *The Rime of the Ancient Mariner* emerge in poems such as "Sleep at Sea," in which "White shapes flit to and fro / From mast to mast" shouting "to one another / Upon the blast." Their ship "drives apace" while these sleeping spirits "Bewail their case." Like Coleridge's *Rime,* this poem displays supernatural elements and pyrotechnic effects, but only in order to resolve the complexities of its precursor with an allusion to *Ecclesiastes* that is a commonplace of Rossetti's devotional poetry. Coleridge's Mariner reenters the world to instruct it; Rossetti's poem, typically, advocates renouncing the world altogether. Her mariners "sleep to death in dreaming / Of length of days" as the poem's narrative voice concludes,

> Vanity of vanities,
>   The Preacher says:
> Vanity is the end
>   Of all their ways.

(1:81–82)

The poetic kinship between Rossetti and Coleridge goes deeper than thematic, structural, and situational echoes, however. Its basis is a shared aesthetic ideology, derived from Coleridge's prose rather than from his poetry. This ideology had been sanctioned for Rossetti by the example of the writers of the Oxford movement, especially Keble.[13] As George Tennyson has demonstrated, "Coleridgean ideas permeate Tractarian thinking on aesthetic subjects and . . . probably color Tractarian poetics more than those of any other single figure. The main point of contact between the Tractarians and Coleridge lies in their dispositions to regard religion and aesthetics as kindred fields" (17−18). One feature of Coleridgean aesthetics fundamental to the operations of Rossetti's poetry is his natural supernaturalism, his apparent belief in the continuity of objects in the natural world with spiritual forces. This belief is expressed in a definition of the primary imagination that employs religious terms: "a repetition in the finite mind of the eternal act of creation in the infinite I AM" (Coleridge, *Biographia*, 304). Tennyson's reading of this definition is a generally accepted one: "The human mind in its limited sphere recapitulates, because it participates in, the divine mind in its infinite sphere." But he further observes that it "is the basis for [the] religiously based aesthetic ultimately developed by the Tractarians" (Tennyson, 19). This aesthetic includes the Tractarian doctrine of Analogy, which pervades Rossetti's poems and prose works. According to this concept, God veils himself behind the natural surfaces of this world, as Rossetti argues in *Seek and Find*: "All the world over, visible things typify things invisible. . . . common things continually at hand, wind or windfall or budding bough, acquire a sacred association, and cross our path under aspects at once familiar and transfigured, and preach to our spirits while they serve our bodies" (244, 203). "Consider the Lilies of the Field" formulates the doctrine poetically, asserting that "Flowers preach to us if we will hear": the rose and the lilies say, "Behold how we / Preach without words of purity." Even

	The merest grass
(Poems,	Along the roadside where we pass,
1:76)	Lichen and moss and sturdy weed,
	Tell of His love who sends the dew.

As this poem indicates, Rossetti, like Keble and Newman, would have had severe reservations about the philosophically idealistic treatment of nature in much of Coleridge's poetry, as well as in Wordsworth's. *Dejection: An Ode* is characteristic:

(Coleridge,	O Lady! we receive but what we give,
Works,	And in our life alone does Nature live:
365)	Ours is her wedding garment, ours her shroud!

> And would we aught behold, of higher worth,
> Than that inanimate cold world allowed
>   Ah! from the soul itself must issue forth
> A light, a glory, a fair luminous cloud
>   Enveloping the Earth—
> And from the soul itself must there be sent
>   A sweet and potent voice, of its own birth,
> Of all sweet sounds the life and element!

In such poems the speaker's alienation from nature reflects his sense of unfulfillment and joylessness and bespeaks the need for rejuvenation. In lamenting these problems *Dejection* is of course a response to the first four stanzas of Wordsworth's Intimations ode. The "existential" issues central to these great poems are also at the heart of Rossetti's work, but the resolution to them is inevitably that of Tractarian theology,[14] which Rossetti's poetry implicitly presents as a corrective to the misguided secular philosophies formulated by Wordsworth and Coleridge and contributing heavily to the particular Romantic discourse of nature, which insists that "in our life alone does Nature live."

For Rossetti genuine joy, as well as amatory and spiritual fulfillment, can be found exclusively in union with Christ and the resurrected hosts in Paradise, described in the "Monna Innominata" as "the flowering land of love." Lines from a sonnet written in 1849 (but unpublished during her lifetime) make the point: "Some say that love and joy are one: and so / They are indeed in heaven, but not on earth" (*Poems*, 3 : 171). In this sonnet, as in "The Thread of Life," "Three Stages," and *An Old-World Thicket*, Rossetti addresses the problems of alienation, unfulfillment, and joylessness that inspired the Intimations ode and *Dejection*.[15] The pivotal issue in all of these works is expressed in the second sonnet of *The Thread of Life*, a three-sonnet sequence—the form is significantly trinitarian— in which the speaker laments her self-imprisonment, feeling "Everything / Around me free and sunny and at ease." The "gay birds sing," and all "sounds are music," but music that is cacophonous to the ears of the speaker:

> Then gaze I at the merrymaking crew,
> And smile a moment and a moment sigh   (2 : 123)
> Thinking: Why can I not rejoice with you?

This speaker's situation is precisely the same as Wordsworth's in the first four stanzas of the Intimations ode. His alienated persona seeks spiritual unity with the jubilant objects of nature as a defense against mortality. He is able, eventually, to participate in the May Day festival with the birds that "sing a joyous song," the bounding lambs, and the "happy Shepherd boy," but for him nonetheless

(William
Wordsworth,   The Clouds that gather round the setting sun
302)   Do take a sober colouring from an eye
        That hath kept watch o'er man's mortality.

By contrast, Rossetti's speaker rejects as a "foolish fancy" the desire for liberation from self-imprisonment and for the contemplative unity with nature achieved by Wordsworth's speaker, who, through exercise of "the philosophic mind," attains a "faith that looks through death." Such faith, expressed in ambiguous metaphors of "celestial light," "clouds of glory," and "mighty waters," would have appeared suspect to Rossetti, who affirms the necessity of estrangement from "the merrymaking crew" of this world in order eventually to attain genuine, that is, heavenly, liberation.

Rossetti's anti-Wordsworthian poems inevitably acknowledge—as do "Three Stages" and "The Thread of Life"—that

        I cannot crown my head
(Poems,
3:234)   With royal purple blossoms for the feast,
        Nor flush with laughter, nor exult in song.

The very inabilities Wordsworth's speaker in the Intimations ode strives to overcome in fact constitute the basis of self-affirmation in the third sonnet of "The Thread of Life." The alienated, solipsistic self remains "that one only thing / I hold to use or waste, to keep or give." It is

        My sole possession every day I live,
                · · · · ·
        Ever mine own, till Death shall ply his sieve;
        And still mine own, when saints break grave and sing.
(2:123)   And this myself as king unto my King
            I give, to Him Who gave Himself for me;
        He bids me sing: O death, where is thy sting?
            And sing: O grave, where is thy victory?

Death, in orthodox Christian fashion, is an event to be welcomed rather than rationalized. It is the only gateway to Paradise, the only route to fulfillment.

Rossetti thus repudiates a crucial feature of the Romantic (specifically Wordsworthian) discourse of nature: its insistence that a marriage of mind and nature will generate a secular Paradise. Her speakers devote their energies, rather, to becoming brides of Christ. Wordsworth's "Prospectus" to *The Recluse*, we recall, outlines the project of a grand epic poem that will show us exactly how to attain to *his* ideal of the "great consummation."

> Paradise, and groves
> Elysian, fortunate islands, fields like those of old
> In the deep ocean, wherefore should they be
> A History, or but a dream, when minds
> Once wedded to this outward frame of things
> In love, find these the growth of common day.

(*William Wordsworth*, 198)

In "Paradise" Rossetti presents a monitory response to any Wordsworthian seduced by such worldly transcendentalism. For her, during life visions of Paradise can appear only in a dream:

> Once in a dream I saw the flowers
> That bud and bloom in Paradise;
> More fair they are than waking eyes
> Have seen in all this world of ours.

(*Poems*, 1:221)

This poem, like many by Rossetti, transposes lush, Keatsian images of nature—"the perfume-bearing rose," birdsongs "like incense to the skies," and "glassy pools"—to an afterlife distinct and separate from this one. Arguing that only in Heaven can perfection exist and the problem of alienation be overcome, "Paradise" constitutes a direct attack on Wordsworth's anti-orthodox philosophical idealism, and the assault is all the more effective for presenting the afterlife as a palpable reality:

> I hope to see these things again,
> But not as once in dreams by night;
> To see them with my very sight,
> And touch and handle and attain:
> To have all Heaven beneath my feet

(1:222)

> For narrow way that once they trod;
>   To have my part with all the saints,
>   And with my God.

Through intertextual transpositions of issues and images dominant in the poetry of Wordsworth and Coleridge, Rossetti thus intervenes in cultural discourses shaped and propagated by Romantic verse and assimilated by mid-Victorian readers (largely at a preconscious level of experience). The effect of her revisionist strategies is to expose the limiting secularism of those mythologies. The existential crises precipitated by failed (philosophically idealistic) attempts to realize a paradisal ideal in this world are, for Rossetti, inevitable and just. Through their confessional humility but firm doctrinalism her devotional lyrics repeatedly expose the fatuous vanity of such projects and, implicitly, of the misguided poets who have pursued them.

It is crucial to recognize that the ideological effect of Rossetti's poetry that alludes to the Romantic discourse of nature is to dismantle particular subjective patterns of response to the world, patterns that would prompt acculturated readers to discover in "nature" rather than God a special kind of promise and "meaning" that are illusory. By midcentury these patterns had become so widely diffused throughout Victorian culture that they constituted an ideological force of inestimable significance to the "inwardness" of the middle classes.

Keats: Amatory Ideologies

By contrast with both Wordsworth and Rossetti, Keats locates paradise in the bedroom. In *The Eve of St. Agnes*, Porphyro, hiding in a closet, watches Madeline disrobe seductively, say her prayers, and go to bed, where she lies "In a sort of wakeful swoon," "Blissfully havened both from joy and pain" (Keats, 468). "Stolen to this paradise" (469), Porphyro attempts to awaken his "seraph fair" and tells Madeline, "Thou art my heaven, and I thine eremite" (471). He utters these words immediately after "heaping" a table in the room with "spiced dainties" in preparation for seducing his beloved. The irresistible fruits with which he plans to tempt Madeline—"candied apple, quince, and plum, and gourd" among them—are echoed in the early lines of "Goblin Market." The Goblin men tempt Laura and Lizzie to "Come buy . . . Apples and quinces" and other luscious fruits (Rossetti, *Poems*, 1 : 11).

One young reader Keats clearly seduced with his sensual images of an amatory paradise was Christina Rossetti. She discovered Keats at the age of nine, and as Packer explains, "She, and not [Dante] Gabriel or Holman Hunt, was the first 'Pre-Raphaelite' to appreciate" him (*Rossetti*, 14). On Saint Agnes's Eve, 18 January 1849, Rossetti wrote a sonnet to his memory:

> A garden in a garden: a green spot
> Where all is green: most fitting slumber-place
> For the strong man grown weary of a race
> Soon over. Unto him a goodly lot
> Hath fallen in fertile ground; there thorns are not,
> 　But his own daisies: silence, full of grace,
> 　Surely hath shed a quiet on his face:　　　　　*(Poems,*
> His earth is but sweet leaves that fall and rot.　　　　3 : 168)
> What was his record of himself, ere he
> 　Went from us? *Here lies one whose name was writ*
> *In water*: while the chilly shadows flit
> 　Of sweet Saint Agnes' Eve; while basil springs,
> 　His name, in every humble heart that sings,
> Shall be a fountain of love, verily.

The "fountain of love" constituted by Keats's poetry fed the hundreds of amatory poems Rossetti wrote, most of them before her thirty-fifth year. Keats was the single Romantic writer whose influence on her style, her thematic preoccupations, her dominant metaphors, and the dramatic situations of her poems was inescapable during the most productive years of her life.[16]

Throughout the poetry in her three volumes published between 1862 and 1881 Rossetti struggled against the seductive power of Keatsian amatory ideals basic to his work from *Endymion* through the major poems of 1819, including the odes "To Psyche," "On Melancholy," and "On a Grecian Urn," as well as *La Belle Dame sans Merci, Lamia, Isabella,* and of course *The Eve of St. Agnes*. Keats's idealization of love as the world's most potent spiritual force begins with the famous "Pleasure Thermometer" passage from *Endymion*. For Keats, "at the tip-top" of life's "self-destroying" "enthralments" and "entanglements" (Keats, 155–56) is love:

> Its influence,
> Thrown in our eyes, genders a novel sense. . . .
> Nor with aught else can our souls interknit
> So wingedly. . . .
> . . . men, who might have towered in the van
> Of all the congregated world . . .
> Have been content to let occasion die,
> Whilst they did sleep in love's elysium.
> And, truly, I would rather be struck dumb
> Than speak against this ardent listlessness,
> For I have ever thought that it might bless
> The world with benefits unknowingly.

(156)

Keats in effect replaces traditional Christian notions of a beneficent deity with an ideal of "human souls" that "kiss and greet." In her published poems from *Goblin Market* forward Rossetti often adopts Keatsian techniques in ways that challenge such amatory discourse. Like Keats's lovers, Rossetti's are often dreamers, unable to distinguish fantasy from reality (as are Endymion and Madeline in *The Eve of St. Agnes*), or they are victims, betrayed by their beloveds (as is Lycius in *Lamia* or Keats's pale knight-at-arms in *La Belle Dame sans Merci*). But most often they perceive love as "a foretaste of our promised heaven" (Rossetti, *Poems*, 3:134). Typically, Rossetti transvalues eros into agapé and sees passion in life as an experience whose inevitable disappointment prepares us for fulfillment in heaven, where "love [is] all in all;—no more that better part / Purchased, but at the cost of all things here" (2:106). Thus for Rossetti, though "Many have sung of love [as] a root of bane," to her ultimately "a root of balm it is,"

> For love at length breeds love; sufficient bliss
> For life and death and rising up again.
> Surely when light of Heaven makes all things plain,
> Love will grow plain with all its mysteries.

(2:105)

Like Keats, but in a greater number of poems, employing more diverse dramatic situations, Rossetti explores all the mysteries of Keatsian pas-

sion—both desire and its concomitant suffering—most often exposing
it as a dangerously illusory ideal in this world.[17] Her speakers, "tired / Of
longing and desire," discover their "Dreams not worth dreaming," their
scheming "useless," and their treasure "unattainable." Most turn finally
to the "Heavenly Lover" "Beyond all clouds," who will redeem life's
losses and disappointments (2:101). Thus, any promise of fulfillment in
this world is a fantasy, a reason for many of the speakers in her poems who
are betrayed by love or who dishonor its promise to desire death:

> Thus only in a dream we are at one,
> Thus only in a dream we give and take
>   The faith that maketh rich who take or give;   (2:87–88)
> If thus to sleep is sweeter than to wake,
> To die were surely sweeter than to live.

Many of the presumably female voices in Rossetti's poems are—like
the Keatsian persona in the "Ode to a Nightingale"—"half in love with
easeful death," but for markedly different reasons from those of that
speaker. In Keats's odes suicidal speakers are directed to the lush beauties
of this world as a source of comfort. "When the melancholy fit shall fall,"
Keats commands in the "Ode on Melancholy,"

> Then glut thy sorrow on a morning rose,
> Or on the rainbow of the salt sand-wave,   (Keats,
> Or on the wealth of globed peonies[.]   540)

By contrast, Rossetti's desperate speakers either turn their "eyes unto
the hills" to seek aid from God or yield to the comfort of death. The
second speaker in "Three Nuns" (1849) is an unfulfilled lover who ex-
pects a heavenly reward for resisting the temptations of earthly love, and
she therefore desires death: "Oh sweet is death," she repeats, because it
"giveth rest" and "bindeth up / The . . . bleeding heart" (*Poems*, 3:189).
The speaker in "Two Parted" (1853?) is one of Rossetti's rare, betrayed
male lovers, whose passions are sustained by dreams he cannot distinguish
from reality:

> All night I dream you love me well,
> All day I dream that you are cold:
> Which is the dream?

Ultimately he too seeks certainty: to "Know all the gladness or the pain" so that he might "pass into the dreamless tomb" (3:222). "The Heart Knoweth Its Own Bitterness" (1857) powerfully explains why Rossetti repudiated Keats's infatuation with eros:

> How can we say "enough" on earth;
> "Enough" with such a craving heart:
> I have not found it since my birth
> But still have bartered part for part.
> I have not held and hugged the whole,
> But paid the old to gain the new;
> Much have I paid, yet much is due,
> Till I am beggared sense and soul.

(3:265)

Rossetti's economic metaphors here, as in *Goblin Market* and many other poems, significantly align her rejection of love's false promises with the seductions of the marketplace. Rather than blessing "The world with benefits unknowingly" (Keats, 156), investments in worldly passions are ruinous. Rossetti's speaker can "bear to wait" for fulfillment in the after-life because lovers in this world merely "scratch my surface" or "stroke me smooth with hushing breath." To fill her love's capacity she needs one to "pierce . . . nay dig within, / Probe my quick core and sound my depth," as only God can do. Fulfillment comes, as we have seen, not in "This world of perishable stuff," but only afterwards: "I full of Christ and Christ of me" (*Poems*, 3:266).

Rossetti's obsessive revaluations of the Keatsian ideal of love suggest the tenacity of its attractiveness to her, reflected in her appropriation of Keatsian stylistic mannerisms, her common thematic focus on illusory images of ripeness, and her preoccupation with autumnal settings. She insists in her sonnet on Keats that "His earth is but sweet leaves that fall and rot," a line in which postlapsarian resonances reinforce the contrast between the assonantal promise of "sweet leaves" (those of plants, books, valedictions) and the harsh reality stressed in the internal slant rhymes of the concluding verbs.

Whereas in Keats's ode "To Autumn" we discover a world content-edly sated with the "mellow fruitfulness" and the "ripeness" of a declin-ing year, a world willing to abjure the songs of spring, the speaker in

Rossetti's "Autumn" craves the ultimate spring and the surpassing fruits
of Paradise. Her "Autumn" (1850) responds to Keats's ode:

> Go chilly Autumn,
>   Come O Winter cold;
> Let the green things die away
>   Into common mould.
> Birth follows hard on death,
>   Life on withering:
>   Hasten, we shall come the sooner
>   Back to pleasant spring.

(*Poems*,
3:301)

Similarly, in "The World"—with Keatsian eroticism, mellifluousness,
and imagery resonant of "To Autumn"—Rossetti powerfully undercuts
both Keatsian hedonism and his amatory discourse. As is already clear,
this sonnet's portrait of the world as a medusan Lamia, an "exceeding
fair" temptress proferring "Ripe fruits, sweet flowers, and full satiety," is
an illusion whose exposure reveals "all the naked horror of the truth":
the world of natural beauty reconstituted in Keats's poetry is thus neither
"Truth" nor "all we need to know on earth." Rossetti presents an alternate perspective: the world "stands a lie," inviting us to sell our souls "Till
[our] feet, cloven too, take hold on hell" (1:77).

One Keatsian truth Rossetti does embrace is that youth and beauty
die. But she admonishes her readers to forfeit, rather than glut themselves
upon, the pleasures youth and beauty offer. As in her revisionist reworkings of the other Romantics that overturn their valorizations of worldly
experience, Rossetti's response to Keats in "Sweet Death" (1849) argues
for "a better resurrection":

> Better than beauty and than youth
> Are Saints and Angels, a glad company;
>   And Thou, O Lord, our Rest and Ease,
> Art better far than these.

(1:75)

The question with which Rossetti's poetry, resonant of Romantic discourses, thus repeatedly confronts her precursors is, "Why should we
shrink from our full harvest?" (1:75). For her that harvest is not attained
by accepting Keats's vision of life as replete with redemptive possibilities

marked by our sensitivity to beauty and our susceptibility to love ("His name . . . Shall be a fountain of love"). Nor is it accomplished through the Wordsworthian program for transforming the "light of common day" into celestial light, that is, regenerating Paradise by consummating a marriage between mind and nature. Rather, "our full harvest" comes only with death and resurrection, for which we must wait and watch with pious devotion in this world while exercising stern self-discipline to resist its illusory temptations. With such rigidly devotionalist discourse Rossetti positioned herself, as recent critics have acknowledged, not as one of the last Romantics but rather as the preeminent poet of the Tractarian movement in England.[18]

Rossetti was also arguably the most significant woman writer of devotional prose works to emerge from that movement, and these works are also uniformly ideological, as we have seen. They attempt, in ways traditionally associated with the prophetic impulse, to intervene in a culture whose mainstream values—materialist, positivist, capitalist, and patriarchal—she renounced and successfully resisted. And insofar as Rossetti's work identifies the religious values she promulgated uniquely with the spiritual potential of *women*, it overreaches the conventions she appropriates and quietly launches an assault upon the culturally embedded beliefs and behaviors of her contemporaries, an assault that, if successful, would have had fairly apocalyptic consequences for the social world of Victorian England.

Afterword

ALTHOUGH MATTHEW ARNOLD'S INFLUENCE in shaping the discourses of high culture and education has seldom waned since the mid-1860s, that of the other figures discussed in the preceding chapters has clearly fluctuated over the years since their deaths. Tennyson, once a monumental figure and a household name, now has a restricted audience, as does Dante Rossetti. And today only academics read Swinburne. Yet appreciation of works by Elizabeth Barrett Browning and Christina Rossetti is growing rapidly as they are recuperated by contemporary feminist critics and readers who are redefining the cultural *meaning* of these poets' work, both for the present and for the historical moment in which they wrote. Whether their future reputations wax or wane, however, they—like all authors who have enjoyed a significant audience—accrued power as their works entered the field of ideological conflict, where cultural activity and cultural change can be profitably discussed only in the context of socially dominant discourses and the historical particulars to which those discourses relate.

With his newest book, *The Western Canon*, Harold Bloom argues strongly against such a position, staking his reputation as one of America's most eminent literary critics on his belief that the academy has, at least temporarily, become corrupted by "cultural criticism." He finds its egalitarian bent deplorable: the field is "another dismal social science," one that is working to undermine traditional aesthetic values. By contrast, "literary criticism, as an art, always was and always will be an elitist phenomenon" (17). More than a hundred years after his death Matthew Arnold's cultural power clearly remains strong among influential academics like Bloom but also, presumably, among middle-class readers, who are the anticipated audience for Bloom's volume, published not by an academic but by a popular press.

The particular historical and social circumstances that compel Bloom to defend, with flourishes of prophetic and apocalyptic rhetoric, the autonomy of the aesthetic are as visible as those that prompted Matthew Arnold, in his famous preface to *Poems*, 1853, to attack the Keatsian (or Spasmodic) "school" of poets, whom he saw as a direct threat to the success of his own poetry and to the cultural survival of his literary values. Bloom writes in confessedly futile reaction against "Feminists, Afrocentrists, Marxists, Foucault-inspired New Historicists, [and] Deconstructors" (20). For Arnold and Bloom, both apostles of high culture, insistence upon the autonomy of the aesthetic is disingenuously represented as an act of underdog rebellion and a refusal of political inevitability. Like Arnold, Bloom in fact hopes that his magisterial act of critical self-assertion may help to reverse the winds of sociopolitical change that have been sweeping across Anglo-American cultural fields during the last decade and a half.

Although we may locate survivalist motives and defensive rhetorical strategies in the work of both critics, the similarities end there. Whereas Arnold wished to return poetry to the classical purity of form as well as "the calm, the cheerfulness, the disinterested objectivity" of "early Greek genius" (Arnold, *Matthew Arnold*, 172), Bloom presents himself as a neo-aesthete. Whereas Arnold lamented that "the dialogue of the mind with itself has commenced" (172), Bloom vaunts "aesthetic criticism" because it "returns us to the autonomy of imaginative literature and the sovereignty of the solitary soul, the reader not as a person in society but as the deep self, our ultimate inwardness" (11). Arnold extolled the "Greek genius" of the *Iliad* and *Oresteia* (175), while deploring Shakespeare's "mischievous" effects on poetry written by his contemporaries. By contrast, Bloom locates Shakespeare at the "center of the canon" largely because of the "transcendent" aesthetic values that inhere in his work but also in part because "we know next to nothing about [his] social outlook" (45). The "cognitive acuity, linguistic energy, and power of invention" that exalt Shakespeare in Bloom's mind are precisely the sources of his insidious influence according to Arnold: his "gift . . . of happy, abundant, and ingenious expression. . . . has been the mischief" (178).

Even such a sketchy contrast between the aesthetic values of two eminent spokesmen for high culture separated from each other by four generations provides historical perspective. Despite the claims of each critic (implied by Arnold, explicit with Bloom) to a view that poetry transcends sociopolitical circumstance, the beliefs of both are patently shaped by historical (and, if we would seek them out, biographical) particulars from the period of their formulation. Finally we must of course ask whose canon and whose aesthetic values are to be granted validity and on what transcendent or what pragmatic grounds? Alternate canons and systems of aesthetic values on which they rest might be brought to bear for the purposes of this argument. But the conflict between those of Arnold and Bloom easily suggest the extent to which literary criticism is as ideologically charged as the poetry it treats. Through feints of innocence (or acts of repression or genuine naiveté) participants in critical discourse are as deeply immersed in struggles for cultural power as were Victorian poets, employing other social discourses in other literary forms. Such struggles among the critics are no more limited to questions of aesthetic value than the conflicts among those poets were limited to questions of merely aesthetic supremacy (as Bloom would insist they were).

Bloom argues that "the terms 'power' and 'authority' have pragmatically opposed meanings in the realms of politics and . . . 'imaginative literature.' If we have difficulty in seeing the opposition . . . it may be because of the intermediate realm that calls itself 'spiritual.' Spiritual power and spiritual authority notoriously shade over into both politics and poetry. Thus we must distinguish the aesthetic power and authority of the Western Canon from whatever spiritual, political, or even moral consequences it may have fostered" (36). The implications of such an argument are, quite obviously, antisocial (in the broadest sense of the word), as Bloom himself admits: "Aesthetic authority, like aesthetic power, is a trope or figuration for energies that are essentially solitary" (37). For all Bloom's claims to pragmatism, his impulse to separate the aesthetic from the social denies the reality of the social construction of literature and the inevitability of human participation in the social sphere, where "spiritual, political, and moral" forces inescapably operate as ideology. Bloom instead wishes to embrace the idealist Romantic narrative of aesthetic experience best described by Walter Pater, for whom "the whole scope of human observation"—that is, all sensory and mental impressions—is "dwarfed into the narrow chamber of the individual mind." Thus, all experience including the aesthetic is solipsistically "ringed round for each one of us by that thick wall of personality through which no real voice has ever pierced on its way to us, or from us to that which we can only conjecture to be without" (*Appreciations*, 114–15).

In the preceding chapters I have attempted to expose the discursive and ideological operations of Victorian poetry so as to counter such a view of literary experience. No matter what fantasies of aesthetic purity and readerly isolation one wishes to embrace, literary texts *in fact* generate historically particular kinds of meaning, authority, and "political" responses among readers, and thus special kinds of power accrue to those texts and their authors. Inevitably, that power deeply affects the "inextricable web of affinities" we call culture.

Notes

Introduction

1. See Cruse, 174–203, for examples.
2. For Williams's discussion of this important concept, see *Marxism and Literature*, 128–35.
3. McGann (*Ideology*), Chandler, Levinson, and Liu have argued complexly and compellingly that the emphasis in Wordsworth's poems from 1798–1807 on the power of nature to assist in transcending "the fretful stir / Unprofitable, and the fever of the world" ("Tintern Abbey," ll. 52–53) emerges largely out the devastating failure of his engagement with the French Revolution, its philosophical and political underpinnings.

I. Medievalist Discourse and the Ideologies of Victorian Poetry

1. Girouard demonstrates with unprecedented thoroughness how pervasively medievalist values were embedded in Victorian culture.
2. The most subtle, astute, and comprehensive analysis of the "subversive, conservative poetry" of Tennyson's early years appears in Armstrong, *Poetry*, 41–76.
3. See Lindsay, 97–98, for a discussion of the volume's reception. As he observes, "the public response . . . was for the most part hostile or bored" (98).
4. This is so despite Morris's famous comment in a letter to Cormell Price in July 1856: "I can't enter into politico-social subjects with any interest, for on the whole I see that things are in a muddle, and I have no power or vocation to set them right in ever so little a degree. My work is the embodiment of dreams in one form or another" (Morris, 28).
5. See McGann, *Ideology*, for a full discussion of these ideologies.
6. See Harrison, *Victorian Poets*, 90–99.
7. In *Swinburne's Medievalism*; see esp. 1–37 and 54–78.
8. The most incisive commentary to date on Swinburne's treatment of Villon appears in McGann, *Swinburne*, 88–91.
9. See Girouard, esp. 177–274.

II. Merlin and Tennyson

1. As Herbert Tucker has argued, "Poets do not become famous—not on anything like Tennyson's scale in their own lifetime—without imagining and meeting the conditions of their fame; self-fulfilling prophecy, while not a sufficient cause in this matter of luck and labor, surely is a necessary one" (52).
2. Tucker has properly argued that "there have been few poets so conspicuously successful in publication, as a business matter and as a matter of what is not quite the same thing, cultural prestige" (51).

3. Linda Shires suggests the importance of such crucial inconsistencies in his poetry when she interprets "his works and his career as both reproducing and contesting ideologies in a field of multiple and varied discursive relations" and when she observes "important gaps in the cultural hegemony he . . . represents so magisterially" (50). For useful analysis of Tennyson as the "careful architect" of his own career, see Tucker, 180, 183, and 347–48.

4. See esp. Shaw, *Veil*, 188–98; Landow; and Sussman.

5. John Rosenberg begins to approach this conclusion when he argues that "the *Idylls* is not an allegory and . . . those who so read it are forced into simplistic conclusions. . . . [Yet] an allegorical residue remains embedded in the overall symbolic structure of the poem." Most often, however, "this residue results in a certain deficiency of realization" (22).

6. See, e.g., Sinfield, *Tennyson*, 12–35, passim; Tucker; and Lourie.

7. Sinfield (*Tennyson*) presents the fullest discussion to date of this issue: "Rather than closing the gap between sign and referent, Tennyson creates, as it were, a plenitude of the sign. Language cannot be brought closer to the world, but it can be made more full and substantial *in itself*. In Tennyson's writing any particular word has, or appears to have, many reasons for being appropriate: it is linked to other words through effects of sound and rhythm, syntactical parallelism, and figurative associations which may extend through a network of images across hundreds of lines; and passages which seem ornate rather than organic also seem to make the work more substantial in itself. Thus the arbitrariness of language seems to be controlled. And it all works in relative independence of reference to the world: significance begins to seem a property of the poem, not of the world. The poem creates an alternative reality which is bounded entirely by its language. Of course a deception, no doubt benign, is involved here: for if the relationship between sign and referent is in principle arbitrary, then to multiply the facets of that relationship will not help. Twenty kinds of arbitrary relationship, however much they interlock, are still arbitrary. There is—can be—only the *impression* of plenitude" (86).

8. Tennyson was also yet to divide "Enid" into two books.

9. Quoting from Armistead Churchill Gordon, *Memories and Memorials of William Gordon McCabe* (Richmond: Old Dominion Press, 1925), 352–54.

10. For related commentaries on Tennyson's imperialist ideology in connection with *Idylls of the King* see Kiernan and McGuire.

11. Quoting from *Clifton College—Endowed Scholarships and Prizes*, ed. G. H. Wollaston (Oxford: Clarendon, 1914), 18–19.

12. See chapter 1 and notes.

13. Sinfield (*Tennyson*, 166–79) discusses *Maud* as a collaborative response to bourgeois ideology. Armstrong, who more carefully positions the poem within the dual contexts of mid-Victorian militarism and the emerging science of psychiatry, views its ideological stance and cultural critique as more complex and conflicted (*Poetry*, 170–83).

III. *Elizabeth Barrett in 1838*

1. Excluding her privately printed juvenile production, *The Battle of Marathon*.

2. Quoted in Homans, 173.

3. Here and throughout this chapter I grapple with a number of questions also raised

by Deirdre David (97–151): "Possessing no sustaining female poetic tradition, from where does the Victorian woman poet derive her authority to speak? What are the suitable subjects for poetry written by women? Does the Victorian woman poet possess the intellectual strength to perform strong political criticism" (141). The conclusions I reach, however, diverge from David's thesis that Barrett's "entanglement in the ideological matrix of sex, gender, and intelligence that produces the Victorian woman intellectual seems to have determined a firm identification with male modes of political thought and [idealized] aesthetic practice, and whatever feminist sympathies she may be said to possess are . . . thereby strongly compromised" (98). I argue that Barrett's poetic texts and the ideologies that operate within them are internally conflicted in ways that undercut David's positioning of her, using Gramscian categories, as a "traditional intellectual."

4. See, e.g., Browning and Browning, 3:51, 78, 85, 89, and 98.
5. See Helsinger, Sheets, and Veeder, 2:174–211.
6. See ibid., 2:195–201.
7. See esp. Homans, 153ff.
8. See ibid., 156–61.
9. See Cooper, 18–20. As Glennis Stephenson has observed, "The predominantly male critics who controlled the literary journals and magazines during the early nineteenth century had the power to define the nature of women's poetry; more importantly, they had the power to define the woman herself: the 'poetess' was overtly assigned a number of the characteristics that more usually remained within the subtext of nineteenth-century constructions of 'woman.' To be a literary success she had to establish an audience: to establish an audience she had to win the approval of the critics." As a result, she had to write according to a socially prescribed literary ideology or convince her "readers that [she was] doing so by presenting [herself] in the marginalized and strictly defined role of 'poetess' " (1–2).
10. See Cooper, 18–20; and Mermin, 31–32, 74–75, 106–8. For the best discussion to date of the social construction of Landon's poetry and her persona see Stephenson.
11. See, e.g., Browning and Browning, 9:164–65.
12. See Mermin, 162–74; and Cooper, 126–44.

IV. Matthew Arnold's Gipsies

1. The dates of composition for these poems are provided in Arnold, *Poems*.
2. A superficial explanation of Arnold's prolonged attachment to gipsy motifs in his poetry is provided by Behlmer: "Precisely because the Gypsies stood apart from the mainstream of urban-industrial life, they held a special fascination for the critics of that life" (232).
3. François Meltzer has usefully summarized the originally Hegelian self-other, master-slave dialectic: "For Hegel, the master-slave relationship is born of the confrontation between two consciousnesses, each seeking to be recognized as primary by the other. Obviously, one will win and one will lose. The winner will become the master of the loser. The master is the one who will be recognized, and the slave will be the unrecognized Other whose sole purpose is to feed and generally sustain the master. Ultimately, in Hegel, the roles will subtly reverse themselves: the slave, because he is working, is a maker and a producer of goods who has a purpose. The master, because

his victory allows for it, basks in inactivity; his only purpose is to consume the goods provided by the slave. . . . Thus the master is useless and must depend upon the slave for his existence. The slave, on the other hand, is only apparently suppressed: in fact, he is more independent and freer than the passive master" (157–58). In Arnold, as I shall show, the concept can be seen to apply not primarily to material relationships among classes and subclasses in society but rather to ideological relationships.

4. The most extensive discussion of Wordsworth's poem in its historical and biographical contexts appears in Simpson, 22–55.

5. See, e.g., *The Prelude*, bk. 8, ll. 676–81.

6. See Mayall (245–56) for a useful bibliography of nineteenth- and twentieth-century literature on the gipsies in England.

7. In 1857 Borrow published the work that made him famous for later generations, *The Romany Rye*. For a brief summary of pre-Victorian literary treatments of gipsydom see Simpson, 43–46.

8. "'[*The Book of Spain*] is a most remarkable book,' exclaimed the *Examiner*. 'Apart from its adventurous interest, its literary merit is extraordinary. Never was a book more legibly impressed with the unmistakable mark of genius.' The *Athenaeum*: 'There is no taking leave of a book like this.' The *Dublin University Magazine*: 'We have had nothing like these books before . . . *The Zincali* was the prize book of last season, and *The Bible in Spain* is likely to be the favorite of the present one'" (Collie, 177).

9. See ibid., 210.

10. See, e.g., ibid., 46ff. Dwight Culler also suggests the influence of Borrow upon Arnold, especially in "The Scholar-Gipsy" (193). Allott cites "The Wandering Mesmerist" as the original title for "The Scholar-Gipsy" on Arnold's list of poems for his 1852 volume (Arnold, *Poems*, 356).

11. For the full text from Glanvill see Tinker and Lowry, 205–6.

12. See McCord, 244–49; and Taylor, 24–70.

13. Despite a number of recent critics who disparage or deny Arnold's power, Jonathan Arac, like Edward Said, convincingly affirms it: "I . . . emphasize not Arnold's weakness but his power, both in those prophetic moments and in the present, for I find that the debate between 'Wittgenstein' and 'Nietzsche' in current criticism is also the struggle for control over one element in the Arnoldian apparatus." Further, in his own day Arnold, "associated . . . with the power of the growing educational bureaucracy, the traditional university, and the new world of publishing, . . . could feel confident that culture was a power. . . . It is an agency of Enlightenment, like so many of the characteristic modes of power in its time and ours, and like the panoptic eye of Bentham, its vision is productive. Culture produces both the synoptically seen 'tradition' and what Irving Babbitt called the 'all-seeing, all-hearing gentleman' who is the subject of that tradition—that is, empowered to a certain vision by means of a certain blindness" (Arac, 117, 132).

V. Christina Rossetti

1. Letter of 5 September 1894, quoted in Sandars, 267. The original of this letter is in the Spenser Collection, University of Kansas Library, Lawrence.

2. An archdeacon, quoted in Vicinus, 74.

3. The sequence of Rossetti's prose religious works is as follows: *Annus Domini: A Prayer for Each Day of the Year, Founded on a Text of Holy Scripture* (1874); *Seek and Find: A Double Series of Short Studies of the Benedicite* (1879); *Called to be Saints: The Minor Festivals Devotionally Studied* (1881); *Letter and Spirit: Notes on the Commandments* (1883); *Time Flies: A Reading Diary* (1885); *The Face of the Deep: A Devotional Commentary on the Apocalypse* (1892). For general discussions of these works see Stanwood, 231–47; and Bell, 285–318.

4. See Newton, 169; and Weathers, 81–89.

5. In an undated, unpublished letter to her close friend Caroline Gemmer, Rossetti responds to a suggestion that she herself might have joined a sisterhood: "So you think I once trembled on 'the Convent Threshold'—Not seriously ever, tho' I went thro' a sort of romantic impression on the subject like many young people. No, I feel no drawing in that direction: really, of the two, I might perhaps have less unadaptedness in some ways to the hermit life. But I suppose the niche really suited to me is the humble family nook I occupy; nor am I hankering after a loftier. Nor, I think I may truly say, did I ever wish to devote myself at any period of my prolonged life. It was my dear sister who had the pious, devotional, absorbed temperament: not I. How enviable she seems now" (private collection of Louise and Frederick Maser; quoted by permission).

6. Significantly, Rossetti always refers only to mothers when discussing "filial" relations. She was extraordinarily close to her own mother and dedicated two of her books of religious commentary to her.

7. For an extended discussion of Rossetti's love poems see Harrison, *Rossetti*, 89–186.

8. See, e.g., not only "Goblin Market" but also "The Convent Threshold," "No, Thank You, John," "Wife to Husband," "Twice," "An Apple-Gathering," "Grown and Flown," and "Love Lies Bleeding."

9. See "Goblin Market," in which the fathers of the apparently female children of the sisters Laura and Lizzie are, at the end of the poem, conspicuously absent; "Noble Sisters," in which a Lizzie figure tries but seems unable to prevent her sister from pursuing a misguided love; "The Lowest Room," in which one aspiring sister hopes by being "last" in this life to become "first" in the next; "Maiden-Song" and "Songs in a Cornfield," in which, as Weathers has noted (87–88), sisters "sing" each other home, attaining a kind of spiritual harmony and unity despite the physical separation their respective marriages require; and of course "A Triad," in which a kind of sisterhood in unfulfillment is realized.

10. Christina Rossetti's letters, published and unpublished, partially confirm her brother's view of his sister's reading, though he by no means understood the influence of the Romantic poets upon her. It is, however, also clear from her letters that she was a frequent reader at the British Museum, though she seldom discloses the works she studied there (see Rossetti, *Letters*).

11. For the best recent commentary on Rossetti's attempts to subvert Victorian materialist and capitalist values see McGann, "Introduction."

12. I am indebted throughout this section to Cantalupo.

13. For a thorough commentary on the Tractarian grounds of Rossetti's aesthetic values see Harrison, *Rossetti*, 64–88; Cantalupo; and Schofield.

14. Cantalupo discusses Rossetti's poetic appropriations of Tractarian theology.

15. For discussions of Rossetti's revisionist reworkings of Romantic precursors in "The

Thread of Life" see Cantalupo, 288–93; and on those in *An Old-World Thicket* see Harrison, *Rossetti*, 46–51, and Cantalupo, 293–99.

16. The most extensive commentary to date on Keats's influence on Rossetti appears in Fass.

17. See Harrison, *Rossetti*, 89–141.

18. See, e.g., Chapman, 170–97; G. B. Tennyson, 197–203; McGann, "Introduction"; and Schofield.

Bibliography

Altick, Richard. *The English Common Reader: A Social History of the Mass Reading Public, 1800–1900*. Chicago: Univ. of Chicago Press, 1957.

Arac, Jonathan. *Critical Geneaologies: Historical Situations for Postmodern Literary Studies*. New York: Columbia Univ. Press, 1989.

Armstrong, Isobel. *Victorian Poetry: Poetry, Poetics and Politics*. London: Routledge, 1993.

———. *Victorian Scrutinies*. London: 1972.

Arnold, Matthew. *Arnold: The Complete Poems*. Ed. Kenneth Allott. London, 1965. 2d ed. Ed. Miriam Allott. London, 1979.

———. *The Complete Prose Works of Matthew Arnold*. Ed. R. H. Super. 11 vols. Ann Arbor: Univ. of Michigan Press, 1960–77.

———. *The Letters of Matthew Arnold*. Ed. Cecil Y. Lang. Vol. 1, *1829–1859*. Charlottesville: Univ. Press of Virginia, 1997.

———. *Matthew Arnold*. Ed. Miriam Allott and R. H. Super. Oxford: Oxford Univ. Press, 1986.

———. *Selected Letters of Matthew Arnold*. Ed. Clinton Machann and Forest D. Burt. Ann Arbor: Univ. of Michigan Press, 1993.

Battiscombe, Georgina. *Christina Rossetti: A Divided Life*. New York: Holt, Rinehart & Winston, 1981.

Baum, Paull F. *Tennyson Sixty Years After*. Chapel Hill: Univ. of North Carolina Press, 1948.

Behlmer, George K. "The Gypsy Problem in Victorian England." *Victorian Studies* 28 (winter 1985): 231–54.

Bell, Mackenzie. *Christina Rossetti: A Biographical and Critical Study*. London: Thomas Burleigh, 1898.

Benjamin, Walter. *The Origin of German Tragic Drama*. Trans. John Osborne. London: New Left Books, 1977.

Bethune, George. *The British Female Poets: With Biographical and Critical Notices*. Philadelphia: Lindsay & Blakiston, 1848.

Blake, William. *The Poetry and Prose of William Blake*. Ed. David V. Erdman. Garden City NY: Doubleday, 1970.

Bloom, Harold. *The Western Canon*. New York: Harcourt Brace, 1994.

Borrow, George. *The Zincali*. London: John Murray, 1841.

Bowker, R. R. "London as a Literary Center." *Harper's New Monthly Magazine* 76 (1888): 815–44.

Bowra, C. M. *The Romantic Imagination*. Cambridge: Harvard Univ. Press, 1949.

Brenkman, John. *Culture and Domination*. Ithaca: Cornell Univ. Press, 1987.

Browning, Elizabeth Barrett. *The Complete Works of Elizabeth Barrett Browning*. Ed. Charlotte Porter and Helen A. Clarke. 6 vols. New York: Thomas Y. Crowell, 1900.

————. *The Letters of Elizabeth Barrett Browning to Mary Russell Mitford, 1836–1854*. Ed. Meredith B. Raymond and Mary Rose Sullivan. 3 vols. Winfield KS: Wedgestone Press, 1983.

Browning, Elizabeth Barrett, and Robert Browning. *The Brownings' Correspondence*. Ed. Philip Kelley and Ronald Hudson. 14 vols. Winfield KS: Wedgestone Press, 1983–97.

Buchanan, Robert. "The Fleshly School of Poetry." *Contemporary Review* 18 (Oct. 1871): 334–50.

Burstyn, Joan N. *Victorian Education and the Ideal of Womanhood*. New Brunswick: Rutgers Univ. Press, 1984.

Cantalupo, Catherine. "Christina Rossetti: The Devotional Poet and the Rejection of Romantic Nature." In *The Achievement of Christina Rossetti*, ed. David Kent, 274–300. Ithaca: Cornell Univ. Press, 1988.

Carlyle, Thomas. *On Heroes, Hero-Worship and the Heroic in History*. Vol. 5 of *The Works of Thomas Carlyle*. 30 vols. London: Chapman & Hall, 1904.

Chandler, James K. *Wordsworth's Second Nature: A Study of the Poetry and the Politics*. Chicago: Univ. of Chicago Press, 1984.

Chapman, Raymond. *Faith and Revolt: Studies in the Literary Influence of the Oxford Movement*. London: Weidenfeld & Nicolson, 1970.

"Christina Rossetti." *The Dial* 18 (16 Jan. 1895): 37–39.

"Christina Rossetti's Poems." *Catholic World* 24 (Oct. 1876): 129.

Coleridge, Samuel Taylor. *Biographia Literaria: or Biographical Sketches of My Literary Life and Opinions*. Ed. James Engell and W. Jackson Bate. Princeton: Princeton Univ. Press, 1983.

————. *Coleridge: Poetical Works*. Ed. Ernest Hartley Coleridge. London: Oxford Univ. Press, 1967.

Collie, Michael. *George Borrow, Eccentric*. Cambridge: Cambridge Univ. Press, 1982.

Connor, Steven. *Theory and Cultural Value*. Oxford: Basil Blackwell, 1992.

Cooper, Helen. *Elizabeth Barrett Browning, Woman and Artist*. Chapel Hill: Univ. of North Carolina Press, 1988.

Culler, A. Dwight. *Imaginative Reason: The Poetry of Matthew Arnold*. New Haven: Yale Univ. Press, 1966.

David, Deirdre. *Intellectual Women and Victorian Patriarchy: Harriet Martineau, Elizabeth Barrett Browning, George Eliot*. Ithaca: Cornell Univ. Press, 1987.

Doughty, Oswald. *A Victorian Romantic: Dante Gabriel Rossetti*. London: Oxford Univ. Press, 1949.

Eagleton, Terry. *Ideology*. London: Verso, 1991.

————. *The Ideology of the Aesthetic*. Oxford: Basil Blackwell, 1990.

Ellis, Sarah Stickney. *The Women of England*. London, 1844.

Evans, B. Ifor. "Sources for Christina Rossetti's 'Goblin Market.'" *Modern Language Review* 28 (1933): 156–65.

Fass, Barbara. "Christina Rossetti and St. Agnes' Eve." *Victorian Poetry* 14 (1976): 33–46.

Ford, Ford Madox. *The Critical Attitude*. London: Duckworth, 1911.

Foucault, Michel. *The Archaeology of Knowledge and the Discourse on Language*. Trans. A. M. Sheridan Smith. New York: Pantheon, 1972.

Girouard, Mark. *The Return to Camelot: Chivalry and the English Gentleman*. New Haven: Yale Univ. Press, 1981.

Gladstone, William Ewart. "England's Mission." In *Nineteenth-Century Opinion: An Anthology of Extracts from the First Fifty Volumes of* The Nineteenth Century, ed. Michael Goodwin, 268–72. Harmondsworth: Penguin, 1951.

Gosse, Edmund. "Christina Rossetti." *Century Magazine* 46 (June 1893): 211–17.

Gramsci, Antonio. *Selections from the Prison Notebooks.* London: Lawrence & Wishart, 1971.

Greenblatt, Stephen. "Culture." In *Critical Terms for Literary Study*, ed. Frank Lentricchia and Thomas McLaughlin, 225–32. Chicago: Univ. of Chicago Press, 1990.

———. *Renaissance Self-Fashioning: From More to Shakespeare.* Chicago: Univ. of Chicago Press, 1980.

Gunn, Giles. *The Culture of Criticism and the Criticism of Culture.* Oxford: Oxford Univ. Press, 1987.

Hagen, June Steffensen. *Tennyson and His Publishers.* University Park: Pennsylvania State Univ. Press, 1979.

Harris, Wendell. "The Continuously Creative Function of Arnoldian Criticism." *Victorian Poetry* 26 (1988): 117–33.

Harrison, Antony. *Christina Rossetti in Context.* Chapel Hill: Univ. of North Carolina Press, 1988.

———. *Swinburne's Medievalism: A Study in Victorian Love Poetry.* Baton Rouge: Louisiana State Univ. Press, 1988.

———. *Victorian Poets and Romantic Poems: Intertextuality and Ideology.* Charlottesville: Univ. Press of Virginia, 1990.

Helsinger, Elizabeth K., Robin Lauterbach Sheets, and William Veeder, eds. *The Woman Question: Society and Literature in Britain and America, 1837–1883.* 3 vols. Chicago: Univ. of Chicago Press, 1983.

Herbert, Christopher. *Culture and Anomie: Ethnographic Imagination in the Nineteenth Century.* Chicago: Univ. of Chicago Press, 1991.

Homans, Margaret. *Bearing the Word: Language and Female Experience in Nineteenth-Century Women's Writing.* Chicago: Univ. of Chicago Press, 1986.

Honan, Park. *Matthew Arnold: A Life.* New York: McGraw Hill, 1981.

Hyder, Clyde K., ed. *Swinburne: The Critical Heritage.* New York: Barnes & Noble, 1970.

Jauss, Hans Robert. *Toward an Aesthetic of Reception.* Minneapolis: Univ. of Minnesota Press, 1982.

Jump, John D., ed. *Tennyson: The Critical Heritage.* London: Routledge & Kegan Paul, 1967.

Kavanaugh, James H. "Ideology." In Lentricchia and McLaughlin, 306–20. *See* Greenblatt, "Culture."

Keats, John. *The Poems of John Keats.* Ed. Miriam Allott. London: Longman, 1970.

Kiernan, Victor. "Tennyson, King Arthur, and Imperialism." In *Culture, Ideology and Politics: Essays for Eric Hobsbawm*, ed. Raphael Samuel and Gareth Stedman Jones, 128–48. London: Routledge & Kegan Paul, 1982.

Landow, George P. *Victorian Types, Victorian Shadows: Biblical Typology in Victorian Literature, Art and Thought.* London: Routledge & Kegan Paul, 1980.

Lang, Cecil Y., ed. *The Pre-Raphaelites and Their Circle.* Chicago: Univ. of Chicago Press, 1975.

"The Late Miss Rossetti." *Times* (London), 7 Jan. 1895, 7, col. 4.

Le Gallienne, Richard. "*Poems* by Christina Rossetti." *Academy* 39 (1891): 130–31.

Levinson, Marjorie. "Back to the Future: Wordsworth's New Historicism." *South Atlantic Quarterly* 88 (summer 1989): 633–59.

———. *Wordsworth's Great Period Poems: Four Essays*. Cambridge: Cambridge Univ. Press, 1986.

Lindsay, Jack. *William Morris: His Life and Work*. London: Constable, 1975.

Liu, Alan. *Wordsworth: The Sense of History*. Stanford: Stanford Univ. Press, 1989.

Lootens, Tricia. *Lost Saints: Silence, Gender, and Victorian Literary Canonization*. Charlottesville: Univ. Press of Virginia, 1996.

Louis, Margot. *Swinburne and His Gods: The Roots and Growth of an Agnostic Poetry*. Montreal: McGill–Queen's Univ. Press, 1990.

Lourie, Margaret. "Below the Thunders of the Upper Deep: Tennyson as Romantic Revisionist." *Studies in Romanticism* 18 (1979): 3–28.

Macmillan, Alexander. *Letters of Alexander Macmillan*. Ed. George Macmillan. Glasgow: privately printed, 1908.

Mannheim, Karl. *Ideology and Utopia*. New York: Harvest, 1964.

Marcuse, Herbert. *Counterrevolution and Revolt*. Boston: Beacon, 1972.

Marsh, Jan. *Christina Rossetti: A Literary Biography*. London: Jonathan Cape, 1994.

Mayall, David. *Gypsy-Travellers in Nineteenth-Century Society*. Cambridge: Cambridge Univ. Press, 1988.

McCord, Norman. *British History, 1815–1906*. Oxford: Oxford Univ. Press, 1991.

McGann, Jerome J. *The Beauty of Inflections*. Oxford: Oxford Univ. Press, 1985.

———. Introduction to Kent, *Achievement*, 1–19. *See* Cantalupo.

———. *The Romantic Ideology: A Critical Investigation*. Chicago: Univ. of Chicago Press, 1983.

———. *Swinburne: An Experiment in Criticism*. Chicago: Univ. of Chicago Press, 1972.

McGuire, Ian. "Epistemology and Empire in *Idylls of the King*." *Victorian Poetry* 30 (1992): 387–400.

McSweeney, Kerry. *Tennyson and Swinburne as Romantic Naturalists*. Toronto: Univ. of Toronto Press, 1981.

Meltzer, François. "Unconscious." In Lentricchia and McLaughlin, 147–62. *See* Greenblatt, "Culture."

Mermin, Dorothy. *Elizabeth Barrett Browning: The Origins of a New Poetry*. Chicago: Univ. of Chicago Press, 1989.

Meynell, Alice. "Christina Rossetti." *New Review* 12 (Feb. 1895): 201–6.

Mill, John Stuart. *Autobiography and Other Writings*. Ed. Jack Stillinger. Boston: Houghton Mifflin, 1969.

Miller, J. Hillis. "The Two Allegories." In *Allegory, Myth, and Symbol*, ed. Morton W. Bloomfield, 355–70. Cambridge: Harvard Univ. Press, 1981.

More, Paul Elmer. "Christina Rossetti." *Atlantic Monthly* 94 (Dec. 1904): 815–21.

Morgan, Thaïs. "Victorian Sage Discourse and the Feminine: An Introduction." In *Victorian Sages and Cultural Discourse: Renegotiating Gender and Power*, ed. Thaïs E. Morgan, 1–18. New Brunswick: Rutgers Univ. Press, 1990.

Morris, William. *The Collected Letters of William Morris*. Ed. Norman Kelvin. Vol. 1. Princeton: Princeton Univ. Press, 1984.

Newton, Judith Lowder. *Women, Power, and Subversion: Social Strategies in British Fiction, 1778–1860*. London: Methuen, 1981.

Norton, Caroline. "'The Angel in the House,' and 'The Goblin Market.'" *Macmillan's Magazine* 8 (1863): 398–404.

Packer, Lona Mosk. *Christina Rossetti.* Berkeley: Univ. of California Press, 1963.

———. "The Protestant Existentialism of Christina Rossetti." *Notes and Queries* 204 (1959): 213–15.

Pater, Walter. *Appreciations, with an Essay on Style.* London: Macmillan, 1890.

———. "Poems by William Morris." In *Pre-Raphaelitism: A Collection of Critical Essays,* ed. James Sambrook, 105–17. Chicago: Univ. of Chicago Press, 1974.

Purvis, Trevor, and Alan Hunt. "Discourse, ideology, discourse, ideology, discourse, ideology . . ." *British Journal of Sociology* 44 (Sept. 1993): 473–500.

Reed, John Shelton. "'A Female Movement': The Feminization of Nineteenth-Century Anglo-Catholicism." *Anglican and Episcopal History* 57 (1988): 199–238.

Review of *Christina Rossetti,* by Mackenzie Bell. *Nation* 66 (7 Apr. 1898): 272–73.

Review of Dante Rossetti's *Poems,* 1870. *Spectator,* 11 June 1870, 724.

Ricks, Christopher. "Tennyson Inheriting the Earth." In *Studies in Tennyson,* ed. Hallam Tennyson, 66–104. London: Macmillan, 1981.

Riede, David G. *Matthew Arnold and the Betrayal of Language.* Charlottesville: Univ. Press of Virginia, 1988.

———. "Recent Studies in the Nineteenth Century." *Studies in English Literature* 28 (autumn 1988): 713–56.

———. *Swinburne: A Study in Romantic Mythmaking.* Charlottesville: Univ. Press of Virginia, 1978.

Rosenberg, John D. *The Fall of Camelot.* Cambridge: Harvard Univ. Press, 1973.

Rossetti, Christina. *The Face of the Deep: A Devotional Commentary on the Apocalypse.* London: Society for Promoting Christian Knowledge, 1892.

———. *Letter and Spirit: Notes on the Commandments.* London: Society for Promoting Christian Knowledge, 1883.

———. *Seek and Find: A Double Series of Short Studies of the Benedicite.* London: Society for Promoting Christian Knowledge, 1879.

———. *Time Flies: A Reading Diary.* London: Society for Promoting Christian Knowledge, 1885.

———. *The Complete Poems of Christina Rossetti.* Ed. R. W. Crump. 3 vols. Baton Rouge: Louisiana State Univ. Press, 1979–90.

———. *The Letters of Christina Rossetti.* Ed. Antony H. Harrison. Vol. 1, *1843–1873.* Charlottesville: Univ. Press of Virginia, 1997.

———. *The Poetical Works of Christina Georgina Rossetti.* Ed. William Michael Rossetti. London: Macmillan, 1904.

Rossetti, Dante Gabriel Rossetti. *Letters of Dante Gabriel Rossetti.* Ed. Oswald Doughty and John Robert Wahl. Oxford: Clarendon, 1965.

Said, Edward. *The World, the Text, and the Critic.* Cambridge: Harvard Univ. Press, 1983.

Sandars, Mary. *The Life of Christina Rossetti.* London: Hutchinson, 1930.

Schofield, Linda. "Being and Understanding: Devotional Poetry of Christina Rossetti and the Tractarians." In Kent, *Achievement,* 301–21. *See* Cantalupo.

Sharp, William. "The Rossettis." *Fortnightly Review* 45 (1 Mar. 1886): 414–29.

Shaw, W. D. *The Lucid Veil.* Madison: Univ. of Wisconsin Press, 1987.

———. *Victorians and Mystery: Crises of Representation.* Ithaca: Cornell Univ. Press, 1990.

Shires, Linda. "Reading Tennyson's Gender Politics." In Morgan, *Victorian Sages*, 46–65. *See* Morgan.

Showalter, Elaine. *A Literature of Their Own: British Women Novelists from Brontë to Lessing.* Princeton: Princeton Univ. Press, 1977.

Simpson, David. *Wordsworth's Historical Imagination: The Poetry of Displacement.* New York: 1987.

Sinfield, Alan. *Alfred Tennyson.* Oxford: Basil Blackwell, 1986.

———. "Tennyson and the Cultural Politics of Prophecy." *ELH* 57 (1990): 175–95.

Stanwood, P. G. "Christina Rossetti's Devotional Prose." In Kent, *Achievement*, 231–49. *See* Cantalupo.

Stein, Richard L. *Victoria's Year: English Literature and Culture, 1837–38.* Oxford: Oxford Univ. Press, 1987.

Stephenson, Glennis. "Laetitia Landon and the Victorian Improvisatrice: The Construction of LEL." *Victorian Poetry* 30 (1992): 1–17.

Storey, John. "Matthew Arnold: The Politics of an Organic Intellectual." *Literature and History* 11 (1985): 217–28.

Sussman, Herbert L. *Fact into Figure: Typology in Carlyle, Ruskin, and the Pre-Raphaelite Brotherhood.* Columbus: Ohio State Univ. Press, 1979.

Swinburne, Algernon Charles. *New Writings by Swinburne.* Ed. Cecil Y. Lang. Syracuse: Syracuse Univ. Press, 1964.

———. *The Poems of Algernon Charles Swinburne.* 6 vols. London: Chatto & Windus, 1904.

Symonds, John Addington. "Notes on Mr. D. G. Rossetti's New Poems." *Macmillan's Magazine* 45 (Feb. 1882): 318–28.

Taylor, A. J. P. *The Struggle for Mastery in Europe, 1848–1918.* Oxford: Oxford Univ. Press, 1954.

Tennyson, Alfred Lord. *The Letters of Alfred Lord Tennyson.* Ed. Cecil Y. Lang and Edgar F. Shannon Jr. 3 vols. Cambridge: Harvard Univ. Press, 1981–90.

———. *The Poems of Tennyson.* Ed. Christopher Ricks. 2d ed. 3 vols. Berkeley: Univ. of California Press, 1987.

Tennyson, Charles. "Tennyson as Poet Laureate." In *Tennyson*, ed. D. J. Palmer, 203–25. Columbus: Ohio State Univ. Press, 1975.

Tennyson, G. B. *Victorian Devotional Poetry: The Tractarian Mode.* Cambridge: Harvard Univ. Press, 1981.

Tennyson, Hallam. *Alfred Lord Tennyson: A Memoir by His Son.* 2 vols. London: Macmillan, 1897.

Tinker, C. B., and H. F. Lowry. *The Poetry of Matthew Arnold: A Commentary.* London: Oxford Univ. Press, 1940.

Tomlinson, John. *Cultural Imperialism.* Baltimore: Johns Hopkins Univ. Press, 1991.

Tucker, Herbert F. *Tennyson and the Doom of Romanticism.* Cambridge: Harvard Univ. Press, 1988.

Vicinus, Martha. *Independent Women: Work and Community for Single Women, 1850–1920.* Chicago: Univ. of Chicago Press, 1985.

Weathers, Winston. "Christina Rossetti: The Sisterhood of Self." *Victorian Poetry* 3 (1965): 81–89.

Williams, Raymond. *Culture and Society.* London: Chatto & Windus, 1958.

———. *Marxism and Literature.* Oxford: Oxford Univ. Press, 1977.

Williamsson, Marilyn. Introduction to *The Female Poets of Great Britain*, by Frederick Rowton. London: 1853. Reprint. Detroit: Gale Research, 1981.

Wordsworth, William. *Poems, in Two Volumes, and Other Poems, 1800–1807*. Ed. Jared Curtis. Ithaca: Cornell Univ. Press, 1983.

———. *William Wordsworth*. Ed. Stephen Gill. Oxford: Oxford Univ. Press, 1984.

Yeats, William Butler. *Essays and Introductions*. New York: Macmillan, 1961.

Young, G. M. "The Age of Tennyson." *Proceedings of the British Academy* 25 (1939). Reprinted in *Critical Essays on the Poetry of Tennyson*, ed. John Killham, 25–40. New York: Barnes & Noble, 1960.

Index

Academy, 48
aestheticism. *See* ideology
alba (aubade), 39
Albert, Prince, 20, 46
Alighieri, Dante, 36; *Vita Nuova,* 36
allegory, 55–64, 65, 66, 127, 142, 170 n.5; indeterminate, 8, 57–63
All Saints' Sisterhood, 136
Althusser, Louis, 3; concept of interpellation, 5
Anglican sisterhoods, 136–42, 173 n.5
Anglo-Catholicism. *See* High-Anglicanism
Argyl, Duke of, 68
Armstrong, Isobel, 49, 52–53, 169 n.2, 170 n.13
Arnold, Matthew, 19, 27, 28, 29, 34, 42, 43, 102–24, 125, 126, 127, 165, 166–67, 171, 172; Chief Inspector of schools, 34, 103; Civil List pension, 34, 103; as cultural sage, 120–24, 165; estranged from society, 104, 117, 121, 123, 125; and industrial capitalism, 119; Newdigate prize winner, 114; Oxford years, 103, 114; professor of poetry at Oxford, 34, 103, 105
Works: "Cromwell," 114; *Culture and Anarchy,* 105, 119; *Dover Beach,* 27, 32–33; *Empedocles on Etna,* 119; "The Forsaken Merman," 114; *A French Eton,* 119–20; "The Function of Criticism at the Present Time," 118, 122; *Poems of Wordsworth,* 106; "Preface" to *Poems* (1853), 118–19, 166–67; "Resignation," 103, 108–11, 121; "The Scholar-Gipsy," 30, 103, 111–24; "Thyrsis," 103, 122, 123; "To a Gipsy Child by the Sea-Shore," 103, 105–8, 114, 121; *Tristram and Iseult,* 19, 27, 29–33
Arnold, Thomas, 113

Arthur, mythical king of England. *See* medievalism; Tennyson, Alfred Lord, "Morte D'Arthur" and *Idylls of the King*
Athenæum, 83, 88, 98, 99, 172 n.8
Atlas, 101
Augustine, Saint, 146
Austria, 28, 34, 117
Aytoun, William Edmonstoune, 145

Bacon, Francis, 52
Bagehot, Walter, 68
Bahktin, Mikhail, 3, 53, 54
Bailey, Philip James, 10
ballad, 37, 40, 41, 77
Barrett, Elizabeth, 43, 46, 71–101, 141, 165, 170 n.3; ambition, 71–74, 82, 86, 99–100; originality, 77–79, 82, 85; poetic ideals, 3, 72–76, 78, 80–83, 85, 86, 98; political interests, 81–85, 101; religious values, 77–78, 85, 87–95; and suffering, 87, 90–91; as a woman poet, 72, 76, 80–81, 83–85, 87–98, 100; and Queen Victoria, 81, 83–87, 88, 89
Works: Aurora Leigh, 101; "Comfort," 100; "Cowper's Grave," 85, 88, 92; "The Cry of the Children," 82; *A Drama of Exile,* 92, 94; *A Drama of Exile and Other Poems,* 73, 80, 87, 95; *An Essay on Mind,* 71, 74, 75, 81; "Felicia Hemans," 85, 87, 88, 96–98; "Isobel's Child," 80; *Poems,* 1844, 71, 72; 73–74, 78, 79, 80–81, 82, 87, 100–101; "The Poet's Vow," 76–78, 85, 87, 88, 95; *Prometheus,* 71; "The Runaway Slave at Pilgrim's Point," 82; "The Seraphim," 87, 90–91; *The Seraphim and Other Poems,* 71–101; "Sonnets from the Portuguese," 141; "The Soul's Traveling," 88, 91–92; "The

Barrett, Elizabeth (*continued*)
 Student," 73–74; "Victoria's Tears,"
 81, 83, 85, 87; "The Virgin Mary to
 the Child Jesus," 88, 91, 92–95; "The
 Young Queen," 81, 83–85
Bell, Mackenzie, 127, 150
Bell and Daldy, publishers, 23
Benjamin, Walter, 8, 56, 58, 64
Bentham, Jeremy, 15
Besant, Walter, 84
Blackwoods Magazine, 73, 99, 100, 145,
 173 n.10
Blake, William, 145, 146, 147, 148–52.
 Works: "A Cradle Song," 148; "The
 Lamb," 150; "The Lily," 151; "The
 Little Black Boy," 151; "My Pretty
 Rose Tree," 151; "The Shepherd,"
 151; "The Sick Rose," 151; *Songs of
 Innocence,* 149–52
Bloom, Harold, *The Western Canon,*
 165–68
Bodichon, Barbara, 79
Borrow, George, 114–15, 116, 172 n.7,
 n.10. *Works: The Bible of Spain,* 114;
 Lavengro, 114; *The Zincali; or, An Ac-
 count of the Gipsies of Spain,* 114–15,
 172 n.8
Bowra, Maurice, 146
Boyd, Hugh Stuart, 71, 75
Brenkman, John, 6
Brown, Ford Madox, 38, 126
Browning, Elizabeth Barrett. *See* Barrett,
 Elizabeth
Browning, Robert, 19, 101, 114, 126
Buchanan, Robert, "The Fleshly School
 of Poetry," 38
Bulwer-Lytton, Lord Edward, 114
Burstyn, Joan, 129
Byron, George Gordon, Lord, 10, 32,
 33, 69, 76, 77, 78, 102–4, 124; *Man-
 fred,* 65

Camelot, 20, 21, 58, 62
capitalism, 6, 52, 104, 110, 119, 128,
 130, 145, 162
Carlyle, Thomas, 26, 49, 53, 57, 58, 111,
 114, 127; *Past and Present,* 32, 58
Chandler, Alice, 18, 169
Chapman, Raymond, 18, 135, 174
Chartist movement, 27, 82, 149
Chernevix, Richard, 40
chivalry, 18, 24, 25, 26, 48, 58

Christian values, 4, 21, 26, 27, 32, 35,
 36, 39, 43, 52, 53, 58, 62, 65, 74, 75,
 92, 93, 126, 127, 129, 131, 134, 136,
 145, 146, 152, 157, 160
Church of England Magazine, 113
class (social), 6. *See also* middle class
Clough, Arthur Hugh, 29, 111, 119, 120
Coleridge, Samuel Taylor, 14, 75, 76,
 145, 146, 147, 150, 152–55, 158;
 natural supernaturalism, 153, 154.
 Works: Biographia Literaria, 76, 154;
 Dejection: An Ode, 154–55; "Kubla
 Khan," 152; *The Rime of the Ancient
 Mariner,* 152, 154
Collinson, James, 149
Connor, Steven, 7
Contemporary Review, 38
Cooper, Helen, 95, 171 n.9, n.10, n.12
Cott, Nancy, 135
County Constabulary Act (1856), 113
courtly love, 18, 34, 35, 36, 37
Crabbe, Rev. James, 113; *A Condensed
 History of the Gipsies,* 113
Crimean War, 117
culture, 3, 6–8. *See also under* power

Darwin, Charles, 7
Derby, Edward Stanley, 14th Earl of, 82
Dial, 127
Dickens, Charles, 10; *Nicholas Nickleby,*
 10
Digby, Kenelm, 19
discourse, 3–17, 36, 43, 46, 48, 49, 71,
 72, 81, 83, 85, 86, 98, 101, 105, 115,
 122, 165; of capitalism, 125; of gender
 relations, 131, 133; imperialist, 65,
 112; of literary criticism, 167; of medievalism, 17–43; of motherhood, 54,
 72, 79, 84, 92–95; of mourning, 98;
 of nature, 155, 157, 158; of the Other,
 101–24; perfectibilian, 65; poetic, 49,
 76, 80, 96, 98; political, 28, 29, 30, 46,
 47, 49, 50, 68, 82, 83, 104, 117, 120;
 religious, 47, 51, 74, 79, 88, 89, 90–
 95, 125–44; of romantic love,
 34, 43, 54, 125, 127, 142, 160; of Romanticism, 146, 155, 157, 158, 163;
 sage, 51, 53–55, 56, 58, 67, 127, 144
discursive formations, 3–4, 6, 7, 10, 12,
 16, 17, 19, 33, 34, 43, 49, 55, 58, 93,
 103, 128, 133, 135
discursive practice, 5

Dodsworth, Rev. William, 135–36
Doughty, Oswald, 38
dramatic monologue, 8, 23, 26, 32–33, 39
Dublin University Magazine, 114, 172 n.8

Eagleton, Terry, 2, 9, 17, 39
Eastern question, 28
Edinburgh Review, 135
Edward, Prince of Wales, 66
Eglinton Tournament, 18
elegy, 88, 92, 105. *See also* pastoral elegy
Eliot, George (pseud. Marianne Evans), 53; *The Spanish Gipsy,* 114
Ellis, Frederick Startridge, 38
Ellis, Sarah Stickney, 89
Ellis and White, publishers, 23
English Review, 72
Erinna, 126
Evans, B. Ifor, 152
Eve, 129, 142

Factory Act (1833), 82
First World War, 18
Ford, Ford Madox, 126
Foucault, 3, 4, 166; *The Archaeology of Knowledge,* 17, 19, 43
France, 28, 34, 102, 117
Fraser's Magazine, 113

Garibaldi, Giuseppe, 28
Gaskell, Elizabeth, 74
Gauwaine, 23
Genette, Gerard, 43
Germ, 35
Germany, 28
gipsies, 7, 102–24, 171 n.2, 172 n.6, n.7. *See also* Arnold, Matthew
Girouard, Mark, 18, 20, 69, 169
Gladstone, William, 45, 51, 66, 68. *Also see under* Tennyson, Alfred Lord
Glanville, Joseph, *The Vanity of Dogmatizing,* 104, 114–15, 117, 121, 124
Gosse, Edmund, 48, 126
gothic, 18, 76, 77
Gramsci, Antonio, 3, 5, 6
Greenblatt, Stephen, 8
Grey, Lord, 112
Guenevere. *See* Morris, William
Guenivere. *See* Tennyson, Alfred Lord
Gunn, Giles, 7

Hagen, June Steffensen, 9
Hall, Stuart, 5
Hardy, Thomas, 27
Harper's Magazine, 127
Harris, Wendell, 121–23
Harrison, Antony, 1, 169 n.6, n.7, 173 n.7, n.11, 174 n.12
Hegel, Friedrich, 49, 171 n.3
Hemans, Felicia, 86, 87, 88, 96–98; "The Grave of a Poetess," 97
Herbert, Christopher, 7
High-Anglicanism, 125–44, 147; as a discursive formation, 128
Highgate Penitentiary for Fallen Women (St. Mary Magdalen's), 134, 136, 138
Hilary, Saint, 140–41
Hill, Herbert, 28
Homer, 69, 87, 146; *The Iliad,* 166
Honan, Park, 103, 114, 124
Hopkins, Gerard Manley, 126
Hotten, John Camden, 42
Howitt, William, *The Rural Life of England,* 113
Hungary, 28
Hunt, Alan, 2, 3, 5–6
Hurd, Richard, 19

ideological effects of poems, 4, 12, 13, 19, 23, 24, 27, 28, 35, 37, 45, 53, 68, 72, 82, 85, 95, 100, 103, 105, 122, 125, 128, 158
ideology, 22, 32, 33, 36, 43, 49, 54, 58, 63, 68, 70, 78, 79, 81, 87, 101, 103, 118, 123, 124, 134, 145, 146, 167, 170, 171; aesthetic, 36, 85, 153; amatory, 32, 34, 42, 43, 85, 86, 129, 142, 144, 146, 158–64; definition of, 3–5; domestic, 83, 84, 85, 86, 93, 128, 129, 130, 133, 136, 139, 142–43, 144; emergent, 23, 43, 79, 95; imperialist, 58, 65, 67, 170 n.10; patriarchal, 26, 139, 141, 144; religious, 42, 52, 88, 144, 148, 152
imperialism, 22, 58, 112, 170
industrialism, 6
intertextuality, 7, 16, 43, 97, 103, 104, 105, 106, 110, 121, 148, 158
Italy, 28, 34, 117, 149

Jauss, Hans Robert, 42, 70, 86, 87, 100
Johnson, Brimley, 48
Johnson, Lionel, 126

Kavanaugh, James, 4

Keats, John, 14, 115, 116, 117, 145, 146, 147, 157, 158–64. *Works: La Belle Dame Sans Merci,* 159–160; *Endymion,* 1, 159, 160; *The Eve of St. Agnes,* 158–59, 160; *Isabella; or the Pot of Basil,* 159; *Lamia,* 159, 160; "Ode on a Grecian Urn," 159; "Ode on Melancholy," 161; "Ode to a Nightingale," 161; "To Autumn," 162–63

Keble, John, 56, 153, 154; *The Christian Year,* 146

Kempis, Thomas á, 146

Kristeva, Julia, 43

Lady of the Lake, 22

LaGalliene, Richard, 126

Lancelot, 24–26, 69

Landels, William, *Women's Sphere and Work,* 89

Landon, Letitia, 85, 87, 88, 96–98

Lansdowne, Lord, 28

League, 101

Levinson, Marjorie, 122, 169 n.3

Lootens, Tricia, 72, 126

Louis Napoleon, 28

love, 22, 24, 25, 27, 29–34, 39–43, 72, 77, 79, 85, 93, 131, 137, 140–43, 145, 146, 147, 155. *See also* discourse, of romantic love; ideology, amatory; sexual passion

Macmillan, Alexander, 11–13, 15

Macmillan's Magazine, 11

Mannheim, Karl, 5

Marcus Antoninus, 73

Martin, Juila, 91, 98

Martineau, Harriet, 78–79, 81, 84, 101

McGann, Jerome, 49, 70, 169 n.3, n.5, n.8, 173 n.13, 174 n.20; *The Romantic Ideology,* 14–15

medievalism, 58, 69, 169

medievalist discourse, 5, 7, 18–43, 54, 58

Medusa, 128, 129

Mellyagraunce, 23

Merivale, Charles, 93

Mermin, Dorothy, 72, 86, 95, 97

Metropolitan Magazine, 99

Metternich, Prince Klemens Wenzel Nepomuk Lothar von, 28, 34

Meyers, Frederick, 55, 68

middle class (Victorian), 2, 87, 89, 93,
101, 102, 103, 112, 113, 119–20, 122, 123, 140, 158, 165

Mill, James, 15

Mill, John Stuart, *Autobiography,* 11, 13–16, 100

Miller, J. Hillis, 59, 64

Milton, John, 81, 88, 95, 99, 115, 146; *Lycidas,* 97; *On the Morning of Christ's Nativity,* 93–94

Mitchell, Jerome, 18

Mitford, Mary Russell, 72–73, 80, 82, 83, 89, 96

Moldavia, 28

monarchy, 21, 83, 84. *See also* Victoria, Queen of England

Monthly Magazine, 97

Monthly Review, 88

Morris, Kevin, 18

Morris, William, 8, 19, 27, 28, 43, 169; "The Defence of Guenevere," 23–26, 30; *The Defence of Guenevere and Other Poems,* 23

Moxon, Edward, 44

Moxon & Co., 19, 42

Mudie's Library, 42

Murray, John, 114

Naples, King of, 34

Nation, 127

Neale, J. M., 40

Newman, Cardinal John Henry, 135, 146, 154

New Poor Law Amendment Act, 82

New Review, 48

Newton, Judith Lowder, 130, 134, 173 n.4

Nightingale, Florence, 79, 139

Norton, Caroline, 152

Open Court, 48

Oresteia, 166

Oxford Movement, 88, 135, 136, 138, 139, 146, 152–58, 164

Packer, Lona Mosk, 135, 136, 150, 152, 153, 159

Pall Mall Gazette, 48

Paris. *See* France

pastoral elegy, 97, 98, 103

Pater, Walter, 36, 37, 56, 167–68

perfectibilism, 20, 32, 62, 65

Petrarchism, 36

Plato, 146
poetry (as a mode of cultural discourse) 8, 10. *See also* power, of poetry
Poland, 28
power, 2, 9, 22; cultural, 19, 38, 43, 44, 46, 52, 54, 55, 68, 72, 100, 105, 117–24, 165, 167; of poetry, 15, 70, 71, 73, 77, 78, 79, 85, 87, 90, 94, 95, 99, 101, 121, 134, 146, 165
Pre-Raphaelite Brotherhood, 35, 36, 146, 149, 159
Prussia, 117
Purvis, Trevor, 2, 3, 5–6
Pusey, Edward, 135, 136

reception of literary works, 9, 16. *See also individual authors*
Reed, John Shelton, 139, 140
Reform Bill: first, 15, 50, 82; third, 51
religion, 21, 72, 74, 79, 89, 90, 93, 136, 140, 154. *See also* discourse, religious; High-Anglicanism
revolution (political), 28–30, 34, 50, 117, 148–49, 169. *See also* France
Ricks, Christopher, 49
Riede, David, 115, 117, 118
Robert, Samuel, *The Gipsies; their Origins, Continuance, and Destination,* 113
Romance of the Rose, 36
Romantic poets, 145–64. *See also under individual writers*
Rossetti, Christina, 7, 15, 19, 27, 43, 125–64, 165; as antimaterialist, 134, 145, 164, 173 n.13; as antivivisectionist, 153; on "the feminine lot," 131–33; feminism, 125–44; and High Anglican religion, 125–44, 146, 147, 152–58, 164; and Highgate Penitentiary, 134, 136, 138; on love, 127, 131, 137, 140–42, 145, 146, 147, 155, 158–64; on marriage, 127, 136, 140–44; on motherhood, 142–44, 173 n.6; on nature, 145–47, 154–58; renunciation of "the world," 125–44; and the Romantic poets, 145–64; as sage and prophet, 126, 127, 144, 147, 164; and suffragism, 142–43
Works: "An Apple-Gathering," 134, 138, 173 n.8; "At Last," 160; "Autumn," 163; "A Better Resurrection," 137–38; "Brother Bruin," 153; *Called to be Saints,* 133; "Cobwebs," 152;

"Consider the Lilies of the Field, 154; "The Convent Threshold," 134, 136, 138, 152, 173 n.5; "Dream-Love," 142; *The Face of the Deep,* 133–34, 141–42, 144; "From House to Home," 152; "Goblin Market," 11–13, 58, 133, 134, 136, 138, 142, 158–60, 162, 173 n.8; *Goblin Market and Other Poems,* 152; "The Heart Knoweth Its Own Bitterness," 162; *Later Life,* 147; *Letter and Spirit,* 141; "The Lowest Room," 133, 173 n.9; "Maude Clare," 133; "On Keats," 159, 162; "Monna Innominata," 133, 140, 141, 155, 161; *An Old-World Thicket,* 155, 174 n.17; "Paradise," 157–58; "The Prince's Progress," 133, 134, 142; "Rejoice with Me, 150–51; *Seek and Find,* 125, 131, 154; *Sing-Song,* 150–51, 153; "Sleep at Sea," 153; "Sleep, sleep, happy child," 148–49; "Sweet Death," 163–64; "The Thread of Life," 155–56, 174 n.17; "Three Nuns," 136, 161; "Three Stages," 155, 156; *Time Flies,* 130–31, 133, 138, 141, 149; "A Triad," 133, 136–37, 173 n.9; "Two Parted," 161–62; "The World," 128–29, 130, 147, 163
Rossetti, Dante Gabriel, 5, 12, 19, 27, 28, 34, 35, 36–39, 42, 43, 126, 127, 165; "The Blessed Damozel," 19, 27, 34–36; and parody, 35; *Poems, 1870,* 8–9, 19, 34, 36, 37, 38
Rossetti, Gabriele, 34
Rossetti, Maria Francesca, 136
Rossetti, William Michael, 135, 150
Rowton, Frederick, 81
Ruskin, John, 53, 56, 127; "The Nature of Gothic," 32
Russia, 28, 117

Said, Edward, 120, 172 n.12
Sappho, 126
Sardinia, 28
Satan, 129, 130–31, 144
Saturday Review, 26
Saussure, Ferdinand de, 3
Scott, Sir Walter, 19
Scottish Review, 10
Select Committee on Police (1852–53), 113

sexual passion, 24, 25, 30, 39, 40, 43, 138, 147, 163. *See also* love

Shakespeare, William, 52, 146, 166

Sharp, William, 127

Sharpe's London Magazine, 113

Shaw, W. D., 56, 57, 170 n.4

Shelley, Percy Bysshe, 10, 57, 69, 78; *Adonais,* 97; "The Masque of Anarchy," 47; "Ode to the West Wind," 47; *Prometheus Unbound,* 65

Shields, Frederick, 126

Showalter, Elaine, 134–35

Sicily, 28

Sinfield, Alan, 49, 52–53, 64–65, 67, 170 n.6

Smith, Alexander, *A Life-Drama,* 9

Smith, R. J., 18

Society for Promoting Christian Knowledge, 136

Southey, Robert, 74

Spasmodic poets, 166

Spectator, 37

Spedding, James, 46

Spenser, Edmund, *The Faerie Queene,* 56, 59

Stanley, Lord. *See* Derby, Edward Stanley

Storey, John, 119

Stowe, Harriet Beecher, *Uncle Tom's Cabin,* 10

Strachey, Lytton, 84

"structures of feeling," 2, 13, 55, 79

subjectivity (social), 2, 3, 5, 9

suffragist movement, 143–44

Sunbeam, 99

Swinburne, Algernon Charles, 5, 19, 27, 40, 42, 43, 114, 126, 165, 169. *Works:* "The Ballad of François Villon," 40; "Dolores," 40; essay on François Villon, 40–42; "Hymn to Proserpine," 39; "In the Orchard," 39–41; "Laus Veneris," 39; "The Leper," 39; *Poems and Ballads, First Series,* 38, 39, 42; *The Tale of Balen,* 40; *Tristram of Lyonesse,* 40; "The Triumph of Time," 39; "Villonaries," 41

Symonds, John Addington, 36, 37

Symons, Arthur, 126

Tablet, 26

Tennyson, Alfred Lord, 7, 9, 27, 32, 43, 44–70, 72, 78, 82, 99, 126, 127, 165; and William Gladstone, 45, 51, 66, 68; politics, 49–53; and Queen Victoria, 45, 46–48, 49, 65–67. *See also* discourse, sage

Works: "Balin and Balan," 65–66; "Captain Guide," 51; "The Charge of the Light Brigade," 50; "The Coming of Arthur," 59–62; "Compromise," 51; *Enoch Arden,* 9–10, 67; "Freedom of Old," 57–58; "Guinevere," 20, 21, 59; "The Holy Grail," 62–63, 146; *Idylls of the King,* 8, 9, 18–23, 24, 26, 31, 46, 48, 49, 56–70, 146; *In Memoriam,* 49; "The Lady of Shalott," 19, 57; "Locksley Hall," 49, 50; "Locksley Hall Sixty Years After," 50; "Mariana," 65; *Maud,* 49, 50, 65, 67, 70, 170 n.13; "Merlin and Vivien," 58–59, 63, 65; "Morte D'Arthur," 19, 22, 23, 24, 28; "Oenone," 65; "The Palace of Art," 57, 76, 77; *Poems,* 7th ed., 47; "The Poet's Mind," 57; "Politics," 51, 58; *The Princess,* 49; "The Queen of the Isles," 46–47, 53; "To The Queen," 46, 65, 67; "Vastness," 50

Tennyson, Sir Charles, 45, 46

Tennyson, George, 135, 146, 153–54

Tennyson, Hallam, *Alfred Lord Tennyson: A Memoir by His Son,* 52

Thiele, J. M., *Danske Folkesagen,* 114

Thun, 28, 29

Ticknor and Fields, 69

Times, 46, 84, 112

Tractarianism. *See* Oxford Movement

Trench, R. W., 40

Trollope, Frances, *The Vicar of Wrexhill,* 91

Tucker, Herbert, 22, 23, 169, 170

Turkey, 117

typology, 56, 59, 147

utilitarianism, 13, 15; attacks upon poetry, 9

Vicinus, Martha, 138, 139

Victoria, Queen of England, 45, 46, 47, 66, 83–85, 86, 88

Victorian poetry, market for, 9

Virgin Mary, 39, 88, 91, 92–95

Volosinov, V. N., 3

Wallachia, 28
Warren, Herbert, 69
Watts-Dunton, Theodore, 126
Webster, Augusta, 142–43
West, Rev. J., *A Plea for the Education of the Children of the Gipsies,* 113
Westminster Review, 46, 84
Wilde, Oscar, 126
Williams, Raymond, 2, 3, 5, 7, 13, 78; *Culture and Society,* 6; *Marxism and Literature,* 79, 169 n.2
Wilson, John, 99
Woolf, Virginia, 126
Wordsworth, William, 10, 14, 30, 32, 47, 69, 75, 76, 77, 78, 80, 83, 88, 99, 104, 108, 115, 122, 145, 146, 147, 152, 154–158, 169. *Works:* "Gipsies," 104, 107–10, 172; *Lyrical Ballads,* 14; "Ode: Intimations of Immortality Recollected from Early Childhood," 14–15, 30, 47, 94, 104–6, 155–56; "Preface" to *Lyrical Ballads,* 76, 107, 108; *The Prelude,* 65; "Prospectus" to *The Recluse,* 47, 157, 164; "Strange fits of passion I have known," 30; "Tintern Abbey," 108–9, 169 n.3

Yeats, William Butler, "The Happiest of Poets," 27–28

Victorian Literature and Culture Series

DANIEL ALBRIGHT
Tennyson: The Muses' Tug-o-War

DAVID G. RIEDE
Matthew Arnold and the Betrayal of Language

ANTHONY WINNER
Culture and Irony: Studies in Joseph Conrad's Major Novels

JAMES RICHARDSON
Vanishing Lives: Style in Tennyson, D. G. Rossetti, Swinburne, and Yeats

JEROME J. MCGANN, EDITOR
Victorian Connections

ANTONY H. HARRISON
Victorian Poets and Romantic Poems: Intertextuality and Ideology

E. WARWICK SLINN
The Discourse of Self in Victorian Poetry

LINDA K. HUGHES AND MICHAEL LUND
The Victorian Serial

ANNA LEONOWENS
The Romance of the Harem
Edited by Susan Morgan

ALAN FISCHLER
Modified Rapture: Comedy in W. S. Gilbert's Savoy Operas

EMILY SHORE
Journal of Emily Shore
Edited by Barbara Timm Gates

RICHARD MAXWELL
The Mysteries of Paris and London

FELICIA BONAPARTE
The Gypsy-Bachelor of Manchester: The Life of Mrs. Gaskell's Demon

PETER L. SHILLINGSBURG
Pegasus in Harness: Victorian Publishing and W. M. Thackeray

ANGELA LEIGHTON
Victorian Women Poets: Writing against the Heart

ALLAN C. DOOLEY
> *Author and Printer in Victorian England*

SIMON GATRELL
> *Thomas Hardy and the Proper Study of Mankind*

JEFFREY SKOBLOW
> *Paradise Dislocated: Morris, Politics, Art*

MATTHEW ROWLINSON
> *Tennyson's Fixations: Psychoanalysis and the Topics of the Early Poetry*

BEVERLY SEATON
> *The Language of Flowers: A History*

BARRY MILLIGAN
> *Pleasures and Pains: Opium and the Orient in Nineteenth-Century British Culture*

GINGER S. FROST
> *Promises Broken: Courtship, Class, and Gender in Victorian England*

LINDA DOWLING
> *The Vulgarization of Art: The Victorians and Aesthetic Democracy*

TRICIA LOOTENS
> *Lost Saints: Silence, Gender, and Victorian Literary Canonization*

MATTHEW ARNOLD
> *The Letters of Matthew Arnold*, vols. 1–2
> Edited by Cecil Y. Lang

EDWARD FITZGERALD
> *Edward FitzGerald*, Rubáiyát of Omar Khayyám: *A Critical Edition*
> Edited by Christopher Decker

CHRISTINA ROSSETTI
> *The Letters of Christina Rossetti*, vol. 1
> Edited by Antony H. Harrison

BARBARA LEAH HARMON
> *The Feminine Political Novel in Victorian England*

JOHN RUSKIN
> *The Genius of John Ruskin: Selections from His Writings*
> Edited by John D. Rosenberg

ANTONY H. HARRISON
> *Victorian Poets and the Politics of Culture: Discourse and Ideology*

JUDITH STODDART
> *Ruskin's Culture Wars:* Fors Calvigera *and the Crisis of Victorian Liberalism*